Equestrian vaulting

Equestrian vaulting

A handbook for vaulters and vaulting trainers

Jutta Wiemers

J. A. ALLEN: LONDON

British Library Cataloguing-in-Publication Data
A Catalogue record for this book is available from
the British Library

ISBN 0.85131.595.X

Published in Great Britain in 1994 by
J. A. Allen & Company Limited
1, Lower Grosvenor Place
Buckingham Palace Road
London, SW1W OEL

Typeset in Hong Kong by Setrite Typesetters Ltd
Printed in Hong Kong by Dah Hua Printing Press
Co. Ltd

Edited by Susan Beer
Designed by Nancy Lawrence

To Hanna, my staunchest little vaulter; Susan Ferguson, who lets us use her horse, Sky; and Kern Bawtinheimer, who built our wonderful stationary horse, Hippos

Contents

Foreword

The ancient sport of vaulting, which was already timetabled twice weekly in the eighteenth century for the young J.W. von Goethe, is now enjoying increasing popularity across America. As with any other sport, its survival depends on regular training and coaches who are able to pass on their expertise. This direct handing down of experience and knowledge is essential for the propagation of any kind of sport, but in countries with a large geographical structure such as North America, the vast distances to be travelled can present a great obstacle to this type of development. There is therefore a real need for an instructive modern handbook to enable the individual to begin learning this fine sport.

Jutta Wiemers' book has managed to fill this gap admirably. Her inclusion of really instructive illustrations deserves particular mention. Also, from the point of view of a member of the FEI Subcommittee for Vaulting, it is especially pleasing to discover that Ms Wiemers includes the concept of the 'Basic Score' – first published in January 1991 by Mrs Müller-Kaler at the International Judging Seminar in Würzburg – as well as my own 'Analysis of the Scissors', published in August 1991 at a seminar in Vancouver. Both the basic score and the definition of the scissors will become components of the new FEI regulations and will become effective in January 1993.

It only remains for us to wish this handbook much success and widespread publication!

Dr Gernot Spitzer

Preface

This book was primarily written for vaulters and prospective vaulting trainers in countries where there is still an information gap about this sport, and to alleviate the lack of literature about vaulting in the English language. It is not necessarily meant for use in Central Europe, where vaulting has been established for half a century and most trainers are ex-competitors and fine vaulters themselves. In these countries, where vaulters have achieved world level performance, ample material, literature (especially in German), and vaulting experience are accessible to anyone, vaulting workshops are scheduled frequently, and travel distance to the next one is usually short.

In Canada we are just beginning to get this sport, still virtually unknown even to most members of the equestrian community, off the ground. There are hardly any vaulters, let alone ex-competitors, and therefore many beginners will have to be trained by people who, although enthusiastic and knowledgeable in other equestrian disciplines, have to learn vaulting out of the book. The same applies to remote areas all over North America: distances on this continent are great and clinics not easily accessible. Young people are getting interested in this sport in countries as far away as Russia and Brazil and, by offering the necessary basic information in the English language, we hope this book might help anyone who needs to start out without personal instruction.

The many illustrations will clarify questions of detail, from how to take the grips, to various stages in complicated moves. I have even tried to show in the drawings how certain motions should coincide with certain phases in the canter stride, to gain

greatest momentum from the horse's movement. It is my hope that these pictures will really help new vaulters to find out which (and why) techniques are correct.

But this book also aims to help prospective trainers to look in the right direction and aim for adequate goals. To facilitate recognition of the most common faults, all the things that in the course of training you *will* see, but should not, are illustrated as well. You should be able to train the children in *safety* and professionally, so they receive the correct ground work, regardless of whether they plan to vault on a purely recreational basis or aim for competition later on.

I have myself been involved in vaulting for thirty years and competed in Germany as a youngster. The performance level has greatly improved since then. Competition and judging rules have changed and, as the sport moves rapidly to ever more interesting and difficult exercises, we have continually to educate ourselves – and our vaulting children have some quick learning to do! The trainers and the parents need to be the first to show the necessary commitment and dedication to make this possible. It is the aim of this book to help in this endeavour.

As I present the material of this book to you, I am assuming that you have seen some vaulting and that you possess the Vaulting Rule Book, either an English translation from the German Manual or the International Rulebook for Vaulting, which you can order from the FEI at 1005 Lausanne, Avenue Mon Repos 24, Switzerland (Federation Equestre Internationale, Fax: 0041 21 312 8077). In this book the rules and drawings will not be reproduced, but enlarged upon and explained as a supplement to the above mentioned books.

Introduction

Vaulting can be defined as 'gymnastics on a cantering horse'. It is a marvellous sport, and it is no wonder that its popularity is growing rapidly. In a way, it has existed as long as men and horses have been partners, and we can trace the roots of this sport back to the Bronze age through cave drawings showing representations of artistic riding. Gymnastics on horseback have been used as training tools for refining equestrian skills from the Roman times up to the 1920s, when, for a brief time, vaulting was an Olympic Sport and performed under the title of 'Artistic Riding' by soldiers. When the horse lost its importance for the military, the interest in vaulting also decreased, and for a long time it was regarded as a children's pastime practised while they were waiting to grow big enough for 'serious' riding.

The first rules for vaulting competition were worked out in Germany in 1958 and subsequently other countries became interested and involved. The first international meetings took place in 1978 and the first International Rules for Vaulting came out in 1983. Only since then has the sport been recognized by the Federation Equestre Internationale (FEI). The first World Championships were held in Switzerland in 1986; in 1984 vaulting was a Demonstration Sport at the Summer Olympics in Los Angeles. This means that vaulting is now an internationally accepted equestrian discipline in its own right, which opened the horizon for such events as European and World Championships. Up to eighteen nations are presently taking part in international competitions and astonishing feats are being performed in individual (male and female) competitions, *pas-de-deux* routines (two vaulters performing as a pair) and team performances.

There are different rules for these three categories, one being the age limitation imposed internationally. Individual or *pas-de-deux* competitive vaulters must be at least sixteen years old to compete, whereas a vaulter competing in a team must cease to perform in a team, when s/he reaches the age of eighteen. (This does not apply to shows!)

There are hopes that vaulting will become an Olympic Discipline again in the not too distant future. European vaulters are presently at the front, especially in team competition, but the United States already have a generation of very good vaulters, and we in Canada have some fast catching up to do, if we don't want to miss the...horse!

Apart from the attraction of competition, I believe that vaulting addresses and promotes the best qualities in people, more so than many other sports. There is room for all sizes, all ages in this sport! Many children start as early as three years old – and quite a few parents have become active leisure vaulters as a result!

The love of animals exists in most children, and the love and companionship with a horse is indeed experienced in all equestrian disciplines. But what makes vaulting special is that the contact is so much more immediate (no saddle), and the child can concentrate so exclusively on the feeling, the experience of the motion. There is no fear of the horse running off with the little rider, as it is restrained by the lunger. The child constantly picks up the movement of the horse in his own limbs, and a successful vaulter becomes *one* with those canter strides. And since as a vaulter you don't dominate the animal, you so very much more clearly depend on its goodwill and love. This brings about true cooperation between horse and vaulter, if trained correctly. Once a vaulting horse has understood his job, he can cooperate in a very active way: he will sense before a fall occurs and try his very best never to step onto a child. Also, horses will show real compassion for a poor beginner...often more than the child shows to the horse – and this is just part of the valuable learning experience!

Another most important thing to learn from vaulting is cooperation with your team mates — and more than that: *real* team spirit. I have experienced team spirit in many ways as a youth, on volley ball teams, school teams and so on, but never as intensely as in vaulting. The difference is simple: not only do the judges in a competition count all team members' scores together, so the vaulter knows he would let everybody down by performing badly, but also all team mates constantly hold and help, physically carry and lift each other in their double or triple exercises. This promotes a very special experience of working together, a necessary trust and dependence, and feeling of responsibility for each other.

Coaching vaulting offers a variety of challenges to the interested adult. Many different considerations go into a vaulting show or a good team kur. Apart from the necessary knowledge of equestrian matters as well as gymnastic and acrobatic components, it challenges the trainer's ability to choreograph the beauty and flow of activity, as well as the children's capability of bringing it off: they learn accuracy, elegance and sense of perfection, exactitude in timing, feeling for music and consideration for the performance of the others. The sport highlights strength (in many of the 'male' exercises) and dance-like qualities, therefore offering varied attractions for both male and female vaulters — as well as the aspect of pair performance, as displayed in the *pas-de-deux* kurs.

One great attraction of vaulting lies in the 'glamour' of shows, and the more frequently shows are scheduled, the better for the enthusiasm of the children. Learning to 'show' without 'showing off' is an important part of the training. To drill the vaulters not only for perfect appearance as a team, but also to drill perfect manners into the team is part of the trainer's job...and not an easy one!

Vaulting as an introduction to equestrian sports

Vaulting is a wonderful introduction for a child to the horse. There are generally between eight and ten children to a vaulting class, so the sport is much cheaper than riding lessons. Small children quickly lose their fear of the horse, as suitable vaulting horses are patient and of subdued temperament. They do not gallop at full speed, they can't run away because they are on a lunge, they don't stop suddenly and they generally like children. By continually jumping up and down children lose their initial fear of the height. They develop good balance and they learn to fall and roll safely. They become close friends with the horse and develop team spirit among themselves, especially as they get into team kur exercises and physically start to support and depend on each other.

Vaulting in its own right

Vaulting is, however, much more than just a preparation for other equestrian disciplines. If you are planning to train a children's 'playgroup on horseback' (which would be age three at the earliest up to age six), this book will help you in some points, but it will not primarily be directed at you. Ideally, the toddlers' playgroup should develop into your 'juniors' team' (age six and on), and from there you will eventually recruit the best vaulters for your 'show team'. Many sections in this book will be directed at training 'competitors', whether this may mean for local stable competitions or later hopefully our 'National Championships'!

Guidelines for vaulting should be international

For all of these cases the guidelines will be the same: international rules have been formed over half a century and improved and revised by very experienced vaulters, coaches and judges. They have the goal of achieving good sportsmanship, fairness and above all correct technique, which means *safety* for your children and a good reputation for the sport as a whole. This is why we will follow them. Also if learned and adhered to right from the start, they will eventually facilitate the transition to international competitions. (American vaulters for example make up their own rules. If you plan to compete there, you will have to enquire beforehand. The rules will not be covered in this book.)

1 *Vaulting — how to start*

So you are interested in vaulting and want to start a group in your stables.

What do you need?
What must your horse be like?
How much do you need to know about vaulting?
How do you and the children have to be insured?

What kind of horse do you need?

Before we look at your future vaulting horse, let me stress that any horse will only be as good as your treatment of him. As many vaulters come from a non-riding background, and the ability to ride is indeed not a prerequisite for vaulting, it can not be overemphasized how important proper care of your horse is in this sport.

Vaulting is an equestrian sport, and this presupposes a certain knowledge of the needs and behaviour of your animal partner. If you don't have this knowledge you *must* acquire it! Don't be shy to ask other riders around your stable — every true horse-man will respect you for your questions rather than let you blunder through inexperience and make the horse suffer as a consequence.

We will assume that you have the use of a suitable horse (mare or gelding, although called 'he' in this book), because if the horse is not suitable — don't vault. Suitability depends partly on what you are proposing to do with him, but the most important characteristics of a vaulting horse are:

- He should have been ridden before, have basic training in dressage, and be able to sustain a regular gait, especially in canter.

- He should be fully grown, strong and healthy.

- He must be good tempered and not resent vaulting! Not every horse is willing to bear the weight shifts that are a vaulting horse's fate. Some horses will play along for a while and then start showing their displeasure. A horse that bucks, sidekicks, rears, or bites will never be a vaulting horse you want to entrust your youngsters to.

- He must be able to canter, trot and walk evenly on the lunge, with the necessary ability to bend on the circle. Egg shapes instead of a circle, and speeding up or stopping make good vaulting nearly impossible.

- He should be able to canter evenly, rhythmically, energetically, and step under, using his hindquarters efficiently. He should eventually be able to canter for up to fifteen minutes without difficulty, and this while carrying the weight of approximately 160 kg, which he has to counter-balance!

- He must also be willing to do so! A placid, but really lazy horse can make vaulting rather painful, as he will perform without energy and will have to be urged on all the time, which makes for very uneven motion!

- A broad and flat croup and a fairly long back that moves gently (rather than in the staccato canter some horses show) are a vaulter's dream, but are not absolutely necessary. The horse must however be fairly insensitive to pressure in the kidney and flank areas.

- His size only matters when you get into competitions with older teenagers. For junior groups a pony or small horse's size of about fourteen to fifteen hands is quite fine. If a few of your team 'undermen' are sixteen to eighteen years old, it gets too heavy for a pony, looks out of proportion and does not give the vaulters enough room on the horse's back for their triple exercises.

- If you start with a pony that does not canter, you are limiting your children's future abilities unnecessarily and the ambitious vaulters will lose their interest.

What kind of equipment do you need?

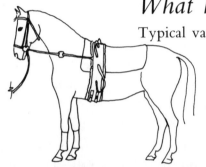

Fully tacked-up vaulting horse

Typical vaulting equipment consists of:

>   a snaffle bridle
>   the surcingle
>   an optional vaulting pad (soft pliable material extending not more than 70 cm behind and 10 to 15 cm in front of the surcingle. Width from side to side not over 90 cm)
>   a lunge line (approx. 8 m long)
>   side reins (with rubber rings)
>   optional bandages
>   a long lunging whip (3 to 3.50 m long, as light as possible, with crack long enough to reach the hock of the horse)

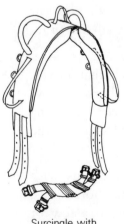

Surcingle with detachable girth

The surcingle will be your main acquisition, and unfortunately, these things are expensive! Most good surcingles are presently imported from Europe, as hardly anybody in North America makes them. You should only use one which is reinforced on the inside by a steel rim and has high padding right and left of the withers. The rim of the surcingle may never touch the withers! Soft surcingles are fine for therapeutic vaulting, but for real vaulting, where pulls occur on the surcingle in all directions, they are very uncomfortable for the horse and cause sore spots.

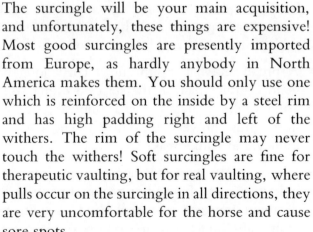

Snaffle bridle

What do the vaulting children need?

The vaulters should be dressed in comfortable clothes, similar to those they would wear for a sport session in school. The material should be stretchable (cotton or lycra trousers, no tight jeans) and both trousers and T-shirts or sweat shirts should not be too wide and baggy, so the trainer can recognize incorrect body posture. The vaulter needs gym shoes, with a flexible, non-slip rubber sole. Any shoes which are so solid that the child cannot stretch his toes are unsuitable.

For continuous winter training you might suggest a larger pair of shoes to fit two pairs of socks. Leg warmers like the dancers use are excellent for keeping the joints warm. During waiting periods in the cold times of the year make sure the vaulters keep moving, and use jackets as soon as they are off the horse.

Some things have *no* place in the vaulter's outfit: jewellery should not be permitted, no necklaces, bracelets and long ear-rings! Even big watches can make the grips during team exercises rather difficult, and torn earlobes are no fun at all, when a 'flyer' gets tangled up in earrings during a high exercise. As a trainer you don't want to have to deal with injuries like that.

If there are several female teenage vaulters on your team, you may have a discussion about beautiful long fingernails as well... You can't force them to cut them off, but mention it to the parents and point out who will get blamed in case of injury! I have seen nasty rips in fellow vaulters' faces caused by such displays of vanity.

Another thing you will not permit is gum-chewing during training — unless you are *really* up-to-date on your first-aid choking procedures! Anything which might get stuck in a throat during a fall should be forbidden.

What do you need to know to start out?

For 'training' your toddler group you don't need in-depth knowledge about vaulting. But you need to know enough to start them out with correct instructions and to instil the little ones with confidence − read about how to start them in the chapters about compulsories. You will need your legs more than anything else, because you will walk along, lift them up, steady them, and guide them down. To children aged three, four and five you cannot really *explain* a complicated exercise like the scissors: they will not understand, and if you talk too much (except for words of praise, which will always go down well) they simply get bored, because their attention span is still so short. Of course there *is* danger in just letting them have fun and do whatever they have seen, because without properly understanding the safety rules, the exercise may result in a fall. Here the greatest danger is not that the children will really hurt themselves, because they are so flexible, but they will lose their enjoyment and your club will lose its good reputation. So unless you have a lunger and can devote all of your attention to the toddler on the horse, I do not recommend taking on children so young. 'Training' is not the same as 'playing' and you know who will get blamed for the falls!

● The trainer should have some knowledge of horses, the more the better. How else will you recognize suitability, and how else teach your vaulters what they *have* to know about their horse?

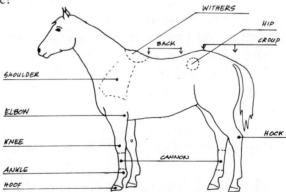

● The trainer should know how to lunge, even if s/he does not have to do it her/himself during training. How else will you

recognize mistakes in the lunging which can become dangerous to the vaulters and also spoil your horse for this sport?

- The trainer should know some basics about coaching —
obviously!

- The trainer needs to have completed a first-aid course and
should take refresher courses every few years.

- A feeling for choreography is helpful when you start com-
posing your shows or help your vaulters to prepare for
competitions.

- Basic knowledge about gymnastics (and spotting) is essential.

- When you train for competitions you must be acquainted
with the rules by which your children's performance will be
judged.

- And last but not least you must know about the vaulting
itself:
    correct preparation for vaulting
    correct technique (mechanics)
    essence, form and scope of exercises
    degrees of difficulty
    consideration of the horse (within exercises) etc.
- Ideally you should know enough to 'phase' your corrections
during training to the applicable experience and ability of each
vaulter.

The vaulting trainer's insurance

Vaulting is a sport performed without a hard hat (unlike other
equestrian activities) and sooner or later the question of the
trainer's insurance will come up. You can find out more about
this through your provincial associations (either your Vaulting
Association, if in existence, or other horsemen's associations, as
applicable. See Appendix A for some tips on insurance).

Your best insurance however is your good training, which

means that you will never be proven negligent. Always ensure that safety rules are followed, train your team with discipline, show and instil respect and confidence and gauge your vaulters' ability correctly, so you know when to urge them on and when to put on the brakes. No matter what your position in the club or stable is, you must make sure you have the right to exclude any member from your team if your safety rules are not followed. Surprisingly often it is a parent who demands that his or her children be 'now put into better exercises' (which means more flashy, more daring): 'surely they are ready for it'. It must always be the trainer's decision whether a child is ready for the next level of difficulty; and showing off must never influence this decision.

Accidents involve either self-inflicted injuries or are caused by other people — or a combination of both. In vaulting they could also be caused by the behaviour of the horse, which in turn is dependent on the environment. You should not agree to train with a horse you deem unsafe — even if that means no vaulting at all. Nothing is worth having a child permanently handicapped after an accident! You must ensure the training or performing space is safe (removal of jumps, avoidance of sudden loud noises etc., correct kind of surface for the horse) and you need and should insist on the necessary cooperation of the people around you (no riders around the circle where you train).

Give your vaulters a proper warm-up, take care of minor injuries quickly and let them heal properly, and check equipment (of horse and children) on a regular basis. Check the correct fit of the surcingle personally before beginning your training session! Everything else involves anticipation of problems — lots more about that throughout this book — and therefore easy prevention.

As long as safe procedures are followed, the sport of vaulting has a very good health record! Skiing is much more dangerous, and in all the years of my vaulting past I have never suffered from more than bruises, and neither have my teams.

2 Most important team member: the horse

Your vaulting team, and club, such as it may be, will consist of the following partners:

the vaulting horse
the vaulting children
the lunger
the trainer
the vaulters' parents, whose support you need

When vaulting, the horse is your most essential partner — no horse, no vaults! It is never too early for the vaulters to understand this! So there must be interaction in the consideration between the humans and the animal.

Refer to the next chapter if you have to train an inexperienced horse for vaulting. It makes sense that it takes quite a while for a horse to understand *what* those people are doing up there! With *good* training it takes approximately one to two years to get the horse to be as balanced, understanding, calm and reliable as you wish him to be. So have patience.

Please don't choose a twenty-five year-old horse for competitive vaulting, because he is 'patient and good natured'. A vaulting horse must be strong and healthy, and should be able to get through a vaulting session without working up a profuse sweat. In competitive vaulting and in most shows, a horse must be able to canter for about fifteen minutes. This corresponds to a distance of approximately 7 km! Never forget that a vaulting horse carries double or triple load (up to 160 kg) *and* endures weight shifts which are making the canter harder work than in riding, because he has to counterbalance all the time.

For national competitions a horse must be at least five, international, six years old. Don't use a horse which is not fully
grown. Above all, train him with patience: it always pays off!

Don't use your horse for vaulting only. Give him plenty
of other exercise, because vaulting is a very one-sided stress for
the horse. The horse should frequently be lunged on both leads
(without vaulter), should have basic training in dressage
(including cavaletti work) and be ridden often in the countryside, if
at all possible. This will greatly improve strength and stamina.
(You can find more information on how to train your horse in
the Rule Book for Vaulting.)

Vaulting children should be introduced to the horse in two
ways: first of all the horse will be their friend. This means that
the trainer will try to eliminate the fears that might exist in a
beginner's little heart: that horse is *so* big seen from down there!
But at the same time even a five-year-old *must* understand that s/
he can not expect that horse to be a friend if it is not treated as
one. And they must understand that a horse is intellectually
inferior to them (although that is sometimes hard to see!) and
therefore they have the *obligation* to care for it. If a child is too
good to dirty his/her hands for the horse, that child does not
deserve to vault. Make this quite clear to the parents, before a
new vaulter enters your team.

Being that horse's friend should not manifest itself only in
stuffing his mouth full of sugar cubes. On the contrary: in my
opinion it is much more important to brush him, speak to him,
find the spots where he loves to be scratched. The grooming
aspect cannot be overemphasized! Treats, however, should mainly
be given when earned.

Every child must take part in the grooming, taking turns and
doing this job in twos or threes together. If some of your five-
year-olds are afraid to clean out the horse's hooves, don't let
them skip it. Also don't stand aside and force them to do it,
although they are afraid. Do it *with* them, help their hands,
explain how to stand and keep their faces away from a potential

kick, and *explain* why it is important to take such good care of those feet. If the horse pulls away his leg, *explain* why he did that at this moment. If you don't, a frightened child will always assume the horse wants to kick him — and never trust that beast. Demonstrate the correct position to kneel in, when bandaging the horse's legs. Even if the horse loves the children, he can still get spooked by something and kick. Don't allow the children under the horse's belly. It is not necessary to show off the trust like this. Always emphasize safety.

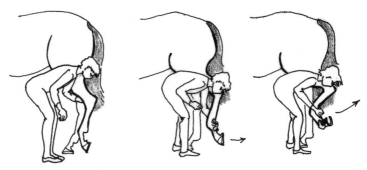

Correct way to pick up a hind foot

Make sure (and check before each vaulting session) that the equipment is correctly in place and fastened. Let the children check each time under your eyes that the buckles of the surcingle will not rub behind the legs. Consideration of that horse must become a natural impulse with your vaulters, no matter how young they are. If there are sore spots, show the children how to take care of them and make *them* do it. They will be proud of their knowledge and proud of being so important to such a big animal.

If a vaulting horse does not show it recognizes the vaulters after half a year, your team is doing something wrong. The children must understand that if they 'don't have time' to brush the horse before vaulting and cool him out and brush again after, they should take to bike racing instead. A bicycle can be parked, and rust removed after time of disuse. A horse is not a machine.

The grooming before and after are *part* of the vaulting lesson, just as the warm-up for the children is. Tell the parents to allow at least two and a half hours for the whole session, including the care of the horse and warm-up gymnastic for the children.

The children should get an understanding of the horse's way of thinking and learn to understand his body language. This is especially important for children who do not ride at the same time. What does it mean, when the horse starts swishing his tail like that? (Point out the reason for his nervousness or anger.) Why does he throw its head around today? (flies?) Why did he buck? (You stepped down hard right into his kidneys, it hurts!) Children are egotistic beings, and often too spoiled to be able to think of someone else's troubles — with the horse they have to learn just this!

Don't *ever* allow a child to take out his anger or frustration about a badly executed exercise on the horse. Explain how confused that horse must be for getting punished (kicked, yelled at) for something he did not do. (Children *do* understand that sentiment!) Make them leave the training session until they have cooled down; if angry, they will only make the horse nervous. Always make the vaulters say 'sorry' to the horse and pat him, after coming down hard on his back or stepping into the kidneys. This will heighten their awareness of the horse's feelings and make consideration of the horse an integral part of your training sessions.

3 *How to train your vaulting horse*

Criteria for a good vaulting horse

Don't start training a horse which is not suitable. The criteria for a good vaulting horse are outlined below.

- Make sure you train a horse which you are able to keep for a while. Training this horse will require a good deal of effort, time and patience, so make sure the owner does not sell him as soon as he is trained! It will take approximately half a year before you can truly start to 'vault' on a new horse, and it is really discouraging to a team never to be able to show their best abilities, because they keep having to start out on a new, untrained horse.

- Make sure your horse is not a pensioner! 'Good temperament' should not mean that your horse is too tired to protest. You want active cooperation from your horse, as vaulting is a strenuous job, and your horse should be young (but fully grown) and strong.

- The horse must have a suitable temperament; don't train a very nervous, excitable horse. He must like children, be reasonably calm even under noisy conditions (music, clapping at horse shows and in unknown environments) and generally have a friendly disposition.

- Choose the correct size and strength for the age of vaulters. If you plan to train teams with several teenagers (fifteen years and up), don't start on a small pony.

- Your horse must be *long* enough in the back to accommodate three almost grown-up bodies. He must have a relatively insensitive back to accept the feet and knees of the vaulters all along his back, be *strong* enough to support their weight, have a *chest wide* enough for large lungs and heart to be able to do the job (up to 15 min. canter under three vaulters!), have *legs strong* and healthy enough to support him in this, a *neck long & strong* enough for the exercises in front of the surcingle, *hooves* hard and large enough for the weight and work, and a *croup* flat enough securely to accommodate a standing vaulter.

- The horse should have suitable capability of balance and collection. Some horses have, although their bodies look ideal for vaulting, great difficulty in ever learning a collected canter. Many heavy horses, for example, as wide as they are, can only canter at a fast pace, which can make them highly unsuitable for vaulting.

How to start training the inexperienced horse

We will not assume here that you attempt to train a horse which is not saddle broken. Your horse must have been ridden and must have learned to sustain all the basic gaits, walk, trot and canter, in an even and balanced manner. We assume he is used to being lunged. (See chapter 7 about correct lunging.) So there are three basic things left that the horse must learn on top of what he knows already:

that vaulters come running towards him and this does not mean a threat or demand to stop

that vaulters will mount while the horse keeps running and then shift their weight in curious ways — and this does not mean a fall (and therefore does not mean the horse has to stop)

that more than one person will be on his back at one time

On top of that he will learn:

that he must stay on the prescribed circle without falling in or
  pulling out
that he may never speed up or slow down, but keep an even
  pace
that he must react to voice aids promptly and accurately
to recognize a fall and help protect the children by never
  stepping on them

First teach your horse that you wish him to continue walking on
his circle at an even pace, when someone approaches him. He
will stop − expecting you to mount or give him a treat! If he
stops, take him by the side reins and make him walk on. When
he does it correctly, pat him and praise him. If he is very shy of
vaulters approaching him, let them approach only half way
along the lunge at first and then retreat back to the centre. Once
the horse is used to this procedure (an activity around him to
which he is expected *not* to react!) in walk, do it at trot. Let your
vaulter run along, praising and patting the horse. Always make
sure that the vaulter approaches the correct way along the lunge
line, so the horse can plainly see what will happen.

Practise approaches along the lunge line until the horse continues his path with an even gait

When you let your first vaulter mount, let someone give him
a leg-up so the weight shifts are minimized. The vaulter then
may start to accustom the horse to weight shifts by passing a leg
over the front gently, back and forth, and with pauses of balanced
seat in between. Lots of praising for the horse, if he tolerates this

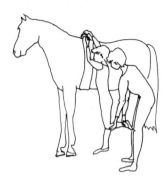
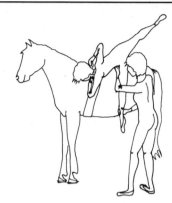

Give a 'leg-up' to minimize weight shifts

Practise simple leg swings

without stopping! Remember that he is trying to be nice by stopping, when he feels you falling — because that is what these strange weight shifts will mean to him in the beginning. Get him used to dismounts (via leg over the front), so he gets used to moving on while vaulters slide on and off his back. Don't let him stop! Now you progress into the other exercises: the mill, some kneeling. If possible, you should always use your best vaulters for training a new horse, as they are most balanced and least disturbing to him.

Once you feel that the horse relaxes and accepts these exercises, you can move into trot. Use patience and try to think like your horse: he will probably not refuse because he is unwilling, but because he is truly confused about what is going on his back. Remember how a trained horse in dressage is taught to react to the slightest weight shifts of the rider, and to recognize them as aids, that is as commands that mean something which is expected of him. Our vaulting horse presumably learned some dressage to be able to sustain even paces, collect himself and react to aids via reins and bridle. Now you want him *not* to react to weight shifts any more — naturally he is confused! Explain to him patiently what you want of him — repetition of course is the answer to this. Don't get frustrated, because it takes so long — the more thoroughly and lovingly you teach him now, the better your vaulting horse will be in the future.

Try to keep in mind what the horse can and cannot see about the things you are doing on his back. Swinging legs are confusing, because the horse catches the feet whizzing by just out of the corner of his eye. Things that can't be clearly seen often seem threatening. Since the horse is an animal which seeks safety by running away, he may therefore spook and charge. Approaching towards the hindquarters of the horse (instead of along the lunge), and falls and high dismounts to the rear fall into the category of exercises which will make the inexperienced horse spook, and should therefore be put off until he is well used to other vaulting activities. Don't punish the horse for spooking if you scared him — reassure him instead and repeat the situation in a milder form until he understands that such events can be considered 'normal' in vaulting.

It goes without saying that roll dismounts and all exercises which involve landing next to the hindquarters or behind the horse must be avoided until you can be reasonably sure that this horse will never intentionally kick out after the vaulters. Let the vaulters move, press, touch the horse's whole body, always accompanied by pats and good words. Teach him gently that you intend not only to occupy the part of his back where the saddle used to be, but his neck and croup as well, and even his sides, when you go into a cossack hang!

We use him from croup to neck

Let vaulters mount in trot. Repeat all the exercises you have done in walk. Check if the horse seems comfortable with this. Move on to canter, but leave out all exercises that comprise big swings (like the scissors and the flank) to the very last. When you get your horse used to those, let them be done only by vaulters who are experienced enough to come down very gently ('like on a raw egg'). Always keep in mind that there is not much you can do, once your horse gets 'his back up' against vaulting and decides to become 'unsuitable'! You *must* train him in such a way that he comes out of every vaulting session with the feeling: this was not too bad and worth it for the praise and treats...

Get him used to weight on the croup

You will progress into double and triple exercises basically along the same lines, as you will have trained your vaulters: from low and safe to higher and more precarious. *Never* built up higher exercises until you can be sure of the horse's tolerance of this! If your horse reacts adversely to some positions (like standing on the croup), repeat it again and again with safe vaulters (who know how to jump off) and give lots of praise when the horse tolerates it.

Give your horse a good variety of activities. Don't use him exclusively for vaulting, just because he did you the favour of becoming patient and tolerant. Remember how one-sided and demanding vaulting is, and that a horse detests boredom just like you. The best activities are the ones emphasizing balance and action of the hindquarters (such as cavaletti work and basic dressage), and working up stamina (rides in the countryside).

Switch leads frequently while training an inexperienced horse. All the running to and from the horse can be done on whatever side, and in my opinion it does not hurt the vaulters either to experience some variety! Mounts on the 'wrong' side (that is the right lead) will prepare them for outside mounts done on the left lead later. Make sure you let the 'new' vaulting horse stretch in between the short working periods! Take the side reins off frequently, so your horse does not fall into the mistake of cramping up his back, which will result in back pain and make him unwilling to work for you. Unless you have significant problems restraining your horse on the lunge in the beginning, always do the warm-up without side reins at all: you want the horse relaxed and in full use of his back musculature.

When you can see that the horse's attention is not with you any more, introduce something new to capture his attention again: often a change in direction will do the trick. And don't overestimate your horse's attention span either. For a young horse half an hour is plenty; he won't learn more after that. It is better to train a young horse more frequently, but in shorter exercise periods, than to try to grind him down into obedience by getting him tired. An unwilling horse is not a good vaulting horse.

4   *Vaulting equipment*

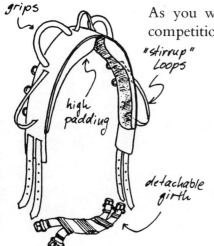

grips

"stirrup" Loops

high padding

detachable girth

Surcingle

Slanted grips for handstand

As you will later have to adhere to the international rules in competition, get used to the correct equipment right away. The surcingle should be of the type which has an embedded steel structure and is highly padded at the withers for the comfort of the horse. There are basically two types: on one the grips are slanted to the front, on the other they are upright. Some vaulters prefer the slanted type for handstands, so they can slip their arms through and grip at the buckle for the side reins. I personally have my reservations about that, as should the horse stop dead and the vaulter fall over the neck, he would certainly break his lower arm this way. It is perhaps time for some completely new design, with a lighter fibreglass frame, made for different horse sizes, and more innovative grips, which might be used in two directions, to give more stability in handstand exercises.

If you are planning to use a pony and a bigger horse for your beginner and advanced teams, order a surcingle which has a detachable girth at the bottom, so you can fit two different sizes! The surcingles now available (and you might have to order them from Europe) only come in one size, and if they are too big for your pony, you can't pad — this will never be safe enough for your vaulters, as the surcingle will certainly turn when pulled on.

The cover is leather, and must be cleaned with saddle soap and taken good care of with leather oil, otherwise this expensive piece of equipment will soon become brittle and unsafe to use. Some surcingles have a white plastic coating — this must rather be cleaned with some cleaning substance as used for car seats.

The surcingle should be under-padded for the whole length when on the horse. It is possible to buy ready-made vaulting 'fuzzies' like this, but they fuzz out rather soon in the wash, and a piece of foam, covered with some home-made sleeve, does exactly the same trick. There are no rules for how high the padding under the surcingle should be — so be nice to your horse!

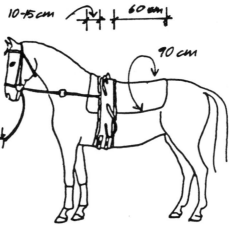

The use of a blanket under the surcingle is optional, but a nice thick pad is definitely easier on your horse's back! The blanket should not project more than 70 cm (2 feet) behind the surcingle and 10 to 15 cm in the front (4 to 6 inches). From side to side it measures not over 90 cm (3 feet). According to international rules it should not be more than 2 cm thick (just over half an inch) and of a non-rigid material, but this applies to competition only. It prevents it from becoming a stiff board to which the vaulter may hang on, evading difficulty in the exercises. In training you may use thicker material to protect your horse, but take care that your vaulters don't lose the feeling of being close to the horse's back.

The fit of the surcingle must be as shown in the illustration.

Do not tighten it at the very beginning of the session, and before you have warmed up the horse! Just tighten it enough so it stays in its place, then do it again before the vaulters start to train. Loosen the surcingle (as well as taking the side reins off) during work pauses.

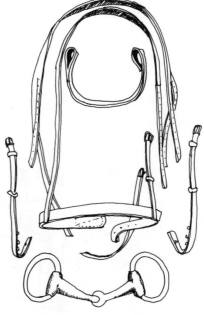

Snaffle bridle

The bridle should be a snaffle bridle, and any horse book will tell you how to take care of that, so it need not be repeated here. Cavessons and rubber bit-guards are permitted. The bridle will be fitted to the horse in the same way as for riding: one hand should fit under the throat lash, two fingers under the nose band, and the cheek pieces should pull the bit up just high enough so the corners of the horse's mouth barely 'smile'. The bit should be long enough, so it protrudes just 0.5 cm on either side of the mouth when held so the joint is straight. A narrow bit will pinch the horse's mouth, whereas a wide one will allow the horse to stick his tongue over it. If it is much too big, it might 'saw' back and forth in the horse's mouth and cause soreness.

Only side reins of the type shown in the illustration are permitted, with a rubber ring inserted for some give. Please refer to chapter 7 for alternate ways to rein your horse in training, as this type of side rein, as prescribed for competitions, has some serious drawbacks.

Your lunge line should be at least 7 m long, so only one loop remains in your hand when the horse moves on the correct circle of 6.5 metres. It can be any type, but should remain untwisted during use for correct contact with the horse's mouth. See chapter 7 for the different permissible ways to fit the lunge. You must avoid at all costs pulling the bit sideways out of the horse's mouth: if he pulls strongly, use cavessons, different side reins and fit the lunge over the head.

The lunge whip must be long enough so you can reach the horse's hock with the end of the crack. Travelling with those long whips can present a problem! But now there are nice new types on the market, which are constructed of very light-weight material like fishing rods, and which can be taken apart into two or three pieces for travel. There is also the telescope type which, however, is expensive, much heavier and quite brittle.

Bandages for the horse are optional.

Always check with your vaulters, that the buckles behind the front legs are well covered by some padding, because otherwise your horse will immediately become sore. Vaulting is not comparable to sitting in a saddle; the surcingle must be tighter than the girth in riding, as the pulling action on the grips is substantial, especially with beginners. The same applies for generous padding under the part which lies over the withers. If the padding slips during training, stop and refit the surcingle with care.

5 *The vaulting child*

Some children come to you experienced in horse matters, some as novices. Some come courageous, some overconfident, some shy and some afraid. Try to find out initially *why* the children are brought to you. Asking the right questions at the beginning saves you a lot of trouble later and spares them disappointment.

> Is it their own burning wish to vault?
> Have they seen vaulting before?
> Did they get pushed into it?
> Do they ride?
> Do they have background in gymnastics?
> Have they ever seriously trained for anything?
> Do they like horses? Animals in general?
> Are they afraid of height, of a fall? (You can't vault without ever falling!)

If the children brought to you are overweight, don't ride and show that they are afraid of horses — be careful! They just might take *your* smile out of the training sessions...

Before accepting a child for training, I would always approach the horse with him/her and see how s/he reacts. Observe how the child reacts to you as well — a child who can not be separated from his mother for two seconds is too young to train! (You will always have the mother in the ring with you — we'll get to that topic later.) Ask the child to do a somersault for you on the ground, make him hop up onto the dummy horse (or lift him up) and observe how he reacts to the 'challenge'.

In chapter 8 we ask: what are you training for? Obviously your expectation of the children will vary with the type of performance you are training for. But no matter for what reasons the children joined your club, the talented ones will always want to push on after their first successes. So you will end up by dividing the committed ones from the ones who just want to play — that way all can have fun.

Trainers come with very different talents and interests. But no trainer has the time and energy to do everything: train children for serious vaulting competition *and* run a daycare *and* correct all the psychological problems a child might bring from home *and* educate the parent at the same time. Children who seriously want to train, or show, or compete, must know who has the authority around the horse. The trainer must be trusted and listened to. Children who really make your job as a vaulting trainer too difficult must learn that they risk being excluded.

Tell them early in the game what you expect from them: show them the difference in commitment when they move from one group to the next level (for instance from playgroup to juniors, or from there to show team), and don't let them get the idea that they will be 'promoted' just because they get older. The right performance, attendance and attitude (towards the sport and the team) must be there too! All of this will improve through correct training.

I cannot give you a recipe for instilling psychological trust and friendship in your vaulters. Children are very different; some will take to you and some might not. In general I think children recognize honesty, and if they realize that in your training you don't show personal favouritism and administer positive criticism to help them improve, and praise only when it is deserved, they will respect you. The physical trust is easy to achieve: run along and hold them. Prepare them for exercises by training on the ground and on the dummy horse until they trust your judgement that they can indeed perform this exercise. Never force children into something they are not ready for (fear causes accidents), but rather grip them by their pride if they shirk without reason.

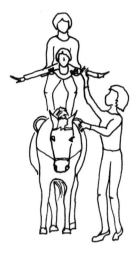

Don't overestimate their understanding! Some vaulters can be very agile and courageous, but truly do not understand the risks of a fall or the limit of their strength or ability. Young vaulters have to try out and experience — they have little use for words — older ones can get the finer points through explanation. Adjust your training to the different age levels and performing groups, otherwise some will drop out frustrated (because they don't follow) or bored. Also group your children according to their ambition if you can, and challenge the ones who want to get ahead.

The things I personally do not accept are:

- 'I can't do it!': The children are not in training to be able to do it, but to *learn* to do it. Tell them to say instead: 'I find this difficult to do', which is true and always acceptable. Children have very different thresholds of frustration, and I don't think you necessarily have to take a psychology class to get to the bottom of it. Just deal with it. Ask them if their sentence is really meant to tell you: 'I'm not willing to try', or 'I'm scared.' If they are scared, again: run along and hold them. When beginners start standing in canter, I first sit on the neck, holding them, later I run a lot... But it is important to let them try, and they will want you to take that hand away before you know it (and before you should!) Move exercises from walk to trot to canter, but if they can do an exercise well in walk, still run along in canter... Always be there when they want you there, offer to run, but tell them you resent running unnecessarily. If they are not willing to try, pass over it, they may have a bad day or be tired. But if this occurs frequently, they should not vault, or drop back into the play-group so as not to hold up the others.

- 'But it hurts...': Sure, sometimes they get a bruise when vaulting. But no sport is learned without bruises. Some children have the attitude that it is their job to show *you* how

Some will eternally
wait for a push...

hard vaulting is. Some people will hang on the side of the surcingle and eternally wait for that push. I would tell them that *I know* how hard it is and never promised it to be easy. I've done it for years. And personally I don't push children any more after I know that they can, and have seen them, mount by themselves. Some children still get their shoes tied by their mother at age twelve...that might be the problem you're dealing with. Tell them you're not their servant, and that their attitude is a misunderstanding of your position.

Other children are trying to tell you by this behaviour that they don't want to vault at all — find out who pushes them into it...and let them quit. If their heart is not in it, they will have accidents, and you know who will get blamed... In team exercises children sometimes use this excuse to tell you that they do not want to perform with a certain partner. Again, the reason can be dislike (in which case: rewrite your kur!) or distrust. Distrust usually has valid reasons: make them talk about it, and concentrate practice in the areas of concern. Dislike can sometimes be mended, especially when the older of the two (often we are talking about an 'underman' and a younger 'flyer') is mature enough to help in this process. Reasons can be physical (like bad breath or clammy hands), or psychological. If you can't find out what it is, separate the children. Cooperation is a must in team exercises, and sometimes it does wonders for them to understand that they are not irreplaceable, and that in case of dislike, someone else will take over their exercise.

Make it work!

- Abusing team partners: when a double or triple exercise does not work, all partners can get very frustrated. But they have to understand that blaming each other will not make the performance better, and that the goal is to make it work, not to fight. It is the trainer's job to find out exactly *why* the exercise does not work and correct the mistakes which make it fail. If the vaulters have constructive criticism (often they detect the faults themselves) they can help each other by making suggestions. They have to learn that the exercise with *all* partners will only get praise, look good or achieve good marks in a competition, if *all* partners in it do their best. Vaulting is an excellent tool for learning real cooperation and team work! Never support them in laying blame!

- Taking their frustration out on the horse: As mentioned before, this is in my opinion a reason for sending the children out of the ring, until they have cooled down sufficiently to distinguish who of the two, the horse or the child, should show more brains and understanding. *Never* let them get away with making the horse suffer. If the horse needs to be yelled at, this is the lunger's job, not the vaulters'.

Normally, children within a vaulting team form close friendships and show excellent abilities in cooperation. It is a joy to see team spirit grow, and trust develop between them. Working on a problem together and physically supporting each other, and then 'shining' together when show time comes around, forges them into an entity. In competitions (although they must learn always to show an attitude of good sportsmanship to the competitors) one can then really observe how they 'stick up' for each other, and how protective and proud they can be!

Treat your vaulters with respect, and if they show intelligence and willingness, give them credit for their social abilities as well. They should all have to take on certain responsibilities early, such as learning the sequence of a show, taking care of the horse and cleaning the equipment. The older ones can take over 'baby-sitting' jobs within the team, supervising a little one in the stable and during shows. They also do much of the explaining and can take quite a load off the trainer's shoulders. They can prepare the horse (plaiting etc.) before a show, get him wrapped for travelling, and assemble the equipment necessary for the event. When you have a good team together (and that takes a year to grow) everyone is proud and supportive of everyone else.

Although the older vaulters in your club might train as individual competitors or *pas-de-deux* partners, the team aspect should never be neglected, as it is in my opinion the *best* part of this sport. Eventually most children will quit vaulting, very few go on to World Championship level or become professionals. But the experience of real team spirit will have done something very valuable to their heads, and will hopefully be transferable to other situations later in life!

Trainers have very varied opinions about the right age to start vaulting. I believe that the trainer, through his interest, patience and general ability to deal with children, will determine to a great degree at which age his vaulters can start to learn something useful. Attention span in young children is of course a factor, as well as the size. Naturally a child is limited in his vaulting, if he can't reach even the inside grip of the surcingle. But size and mental capacity can not necessarily be tied to age: I have trained some five-year-olds, who were incredibly focussed! It is indeed true that groups with very young children should have smaller numbers, so the children do not get bored and scatter in all directions... For playgroups it is very important that the trainer have at least one helper to oversee and supervise.

6   *The vaulter's parents*

Parents, as every child can tell you, can be a great interference — but are also your greatest support! Parents can be involved in many ways, from promoting the sport in general, to helping with the organization of events (especially stable competitions), and they will likely have to take on duties such as costume making. It is important that the parents see this sport as beneficial to the mental and physical health and development of their children, so the improvements in these directions should be pointed out to them when warranted. The parents of the more ambitious children can also be a valuable direct help in the training if they are willing to learn the rules and regulations of this sport. A great number of the vaulting parents of my teams have regularly attended my workshops on judging and instructing vaulting, and several are now certified judges and deeply involved in the promotion of our sport.

Parents of beginning vaulters must learn what to expect from the sport as well as from the coach. There must be a basic trust between the parents and the trainer. I advise parents to watch a training session before letting their children try with me. They may have watched the performance of your show team, but not know how you start out the beginners. They may not like your training style: they may think that you push the young vaulters too fast into certain exercises — while you think that this is necessary to keep the interest going. They may think that you are too slow in your training, that the children should learn certain things faster — when you are making sure that they are really secure in what they are doing, before moving onto the next level. Some may tell you that their children 'are just not used to discipline yet'. Ask them if they mean they should not *have* to submit to discipline. If so, they cannot train with me. I am responsible for their safety during vaulting and I cannot ensure safety without discipline. Or does it mean they have simply so far not encountered any in their lives, because the parents are too soft? It's never too late to start, but beware: do those parents plan to interfere and teach you how you ought to coach vaulters — something they usually know nothing about?

The trainer and the parents must work together. This means that it is clearly established who has authority where. Parents should not be in the ring while training is going on (except for picture taking sessions and so on with permission of the trainer) and should not counteract the trainer's discipline and authority. (If they feel you're negligent in your care, they should talk to you privately, not in front of the children.) When they undermine your authority in the ring, they undermine the safety of their own children.

Normally all this is no problem. But what happens when the child has his first fall? You have pointed out before that falls *will* happen. A fall does not mean an accident (in the training section of this book we will elaborate on the difference and discuss how to prepare for falls). A fall simply means losing your balance and experiencing an involuntary dismount. The toddler in diapers does it on the ground, the beginning vaulter does it on or off a horse. But parents can make it *seem* like an accident, if they storm into the ring, start shouting and shedding tears. First falls can very easily be misinterpreted.

The likelihood that the child is hurt, especially when falling from an exercise in walk, is very minor. Children are flexible and the ground is soft (if you are training on grass, more precautions must be taken). But the child does experience a little shock: it is a strange feeling to fall from that height and it looks scary, *if* the more experienced trainer and the more experienced parents (who *must* know, because they are older) react scared!

In case of a fall, parents should stay out of the ring until called in. The trainer should collect the child, check for injury (you have absorbed your First Aid Course) and reassure him or her. He will cry his tears, you will dry them away, and praise the vaulter for his good example to the team, if they dry up fast. Take the child in your arms — hugging is so reassuring — then stop talking about it and start explaining *why* the fall happened: whether the horse tripped, or whether it was the vaulter's fault and how to avoid it next time. If the child is scared after that, let him have a rest. Don't let mother drag him home, if nothing is wrong. Let him sit in the ring and watch the rest of the session, he may join in again by himself. The attention of the team will do the best job of healing and rebuilding confidence. They will all tell him how it was when they fell for the first time — and so the new child will learn that a fall is part of the game and nothing to be made a drama of.

In case of injury you of course involve the parents immediately, but keeping a handle on panic. Show reassurance in your bearing and keep your calm. If the parent is too shaken, offer somebody or yourself to drive them to the doctor. The trainer should preferably stay with the team, and discuss the incident with them. They have witnessed it, it scared them too, and they have to get it out of their system by talking about it. Don't down-play it, but don't let them dramatize it either. Finish the session by asking them all to do some familiar exercise in walk. Don't let them run off without taking proper care of the horse. Everything should stay as normal as always, and things will fall into perspective. (Check Appendix A on Insurance questions on how and when to give first aid.)

Some children are so used to getting away with drama that they will stage quite a show for your benefit. If kicking and screaming starts — let the parents have the child and get him off the premises (always assuming you *did* make sure that nothing was wrong and it *is* a temper tantrum). Don't let him upset the whole team! Observe that child in the next session, if he ever comes back (those children usually don't...) and talk to the parents about this unacceptable behaviour. If the parents don't agree to staying out of the ring, question their trust in you. Either they *do* trust you, or they should not entrust their child to you — they have to make up their mind.

When the parents pick up their child after the training (if they have not watched the session), mention the fall to them. They should always hear these things from you, so they get the story straight, but also because some children will not admit to having twisted their foot slightly for instance, and parents should be able to follow up at home. If ever the parents get the feeling that you are trying to 'keep the danger from them', they will lose trust in you and you will lose your most valuable support.

Some parents want to make sure that their child is closest and dearest to your heart — show them right from the start that you are impartial. Don't go for politicking; the children will detect it immediately! Children don't get 'better' exercises in a show, because the parents are nice enough to support the club generously. Children don't get extra attention, because they have a history of a weakness or sickness or other. (Of course you take into account if a child has a health problem — but you don't favour them for it!) If a child is so sick that he *does* need special care, that child's place is not on a vaulting team. It is too risky. If a child is so spoiled or shy that she needs special care — you are not running a day-care, and the shyness will most likely be taken care of by the other children.

In case of misbehaviour or disruption of the team, keep your freedom to expel that child from the team temporarily or remove him from the show team into the junior one. Prepare the way for this in a way so you don't lose the parents' support, explain that you are doing it for the sake of safety in the sport. Surely nobody can argue with that.

7 *Lunging and the lunger*

Horses are worked on a lunge for various reasons: to learn certain things before being ridden, to learn or re-learn things while being ridden, to be exercised in 'horse gymnastics', to relax from being ridden — or to be vaulted on. Even if you have learned how to lunge a horse, you have to realize that lunging for vaulting is different in its requirements from lunging a horse as a training preparation for riding. In this chapter we assume the lunger to be a person with expertise, so we only have to point out the particularities applicable to vaulting.

Good lunging is an art in itself. It does not mean hanging on to a horse on a rope, so he does not run away! It is a way of controlling the horse *and* giving aids and commands to him, to ensure that the horse properly uses himself, stays attentive and understands and supports the activity carried out — on his back in the case of vaulting. Horses can be lunged with one or two lunge lines, and you may have seen films of the amazing feats the Lipizzaner horses perform on a lunge in the Vienna Royal Academy of Riding — exercises as difficult as piaffes and caprioles!

It is very important to remember that a horse expresses his state of mind in the way he uses his body, and that he can only use his body in an optimal way if he feels at ease in his mind. So wrong lunging can do great damage to your horse. For example, if a horse gets excited or frightened, he will swing up neck, head and tail steeply and cramp up his back muscles — the psychological tension leads to physical tension, which in turn will lead to pain in his back, especially when carrying three persons in canter!

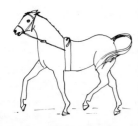

Therefore it must always be wrong to try and force obedience by letting a horse run on the lunge until exhausted, or indeed train him in any way which challenges the horse's resistance and unwillingness to work. Tolerance and harmony with the horse is what the lunger must strive for, and this book can of course only touch the tip of the iceberg in terms of what a good lunger should know. There is ample literature available to study it in more depth.

A bad lunger, especially with a young horse, can do as much damage to him as a bad rider on his back. The basis of good lunge training consists in trust, attentiveness, willingness to work and a quiet relaxed atmosphere. If the lunge line is hanging in the sand, the lunger pulls back his arm to avoid stepping on it or guides it over his head to avoid turning in the circle, the horse can clearly not be on the aids.

First the equipment must be in order and fitted correctly: side reins must neither be too long (then they are useless) nor too short (this ruins the horse's ability to use good strides). They should be fitted so the horse's head is positioned just in front of the vertical, and if necessary for the bending of the horse on the circle line, the inner side rein will be shortened by one hole.

Side reins   too short   correct   too long

For vaulting competitions, only side reins fastened from the bit to the surcingle as shown in the illustration are permissible. However these are by many people not considered the best solution for training. The apparent softness of the rubber rings inserted in these side reins is deceptive. The horse is really very fixed in his head's position in between them and pulls himself in his mouth when he moves his head up or down. So he will try to avoid this 'punishment' and keep his head rather rigid, which again leads to cramped back musculature. If he tries to relax his neck and stretch downward, he has to do that in a backwards motion (to avoid pulling on the bit), which in turn hinders the shoulders and front legs from stepping out to the front as desired. But as you are trying to encourage your horse with the whip to use his hind legs to 'step under' as much as possible, his back results in a restrained, stressed position, and cannot swing with the motion as it should. Especially for young horses it is essential that they be able to stretch their neck downwards and to the front, as only like this can he develop his back musculature correctly.

Any kind of running, looped reins, where the horse can stretch downward and forward is preferable, and should at least be used when the horse is worked on the lunge without vaulters. The worst mistake in lunging is to induce the horse to 'refuse' his back — that is carry his head high and make a hollow back. Particularly in vaulting, where we rely so heavily on industrious 'stepping under' of the hind legs, and need strong back muscles for the load of two to three vaulters, correct training to develop this muscle strength and correct body posture in the horse is essential.

Effect of the chambon

For training a horse on the lunge we therefore recommend lunging with a chambon. As you can see in the illustrations, the basic idea behind this method is this: if the horse assumes the wrong body posture, that is, high head and hollow back, he punishes himself in the mouth and also feels a more or less strong pressure directly behind his ears. As soon as he starts to move his neck and head downward—forward, the connecting rein (which passes from the bottom of the surcingle in between

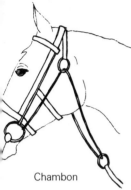

Chambon

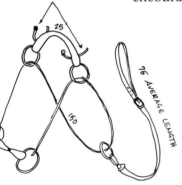

Chambon: how
to attach it

For performance
a level neck

the front legs to the head) becomes looser, and pressure on the head as well as in the mouth vanishes — the horse rewards himself for doing the right thing. Furthermore, most horses have the tendency to look down (which is positive for this stretching motion) when a strap comes up to the bridle from the belly, whereas sidereins flapping at the side of their head irritate them and lead to head-shaking and further tendencies to try and escape upwards. Working with a chambon leads to the desired posture by the horse correcting himself. The lunger may then concentrate on keeping him moving forward in an industrious gait with clean rhythm between the guiding hand and the encouraging whip.

Later in vaulting performances we are not keen on the horse stretching down so steeply, as we need the support of a level neck for many exercises. But remember that your horse will become unsuitable if he takes to refusing his back, as this leads to pain and therefore unwillingness to cooperate. By trying to 'duck away from under the pain' a horse can also become so disjointed that the hind legs literally don't know any more what the front ones are doing, because the connecting back is missing. This way it is impossible to achieve a good canter with clean rhythm and a strong, freely swinging back, which is essential for vaulting, and your horse would be unhealthy and unhappy.

In vaulting we only use one lunge line, fitted into the inside ring of the bridle or passed through the inside

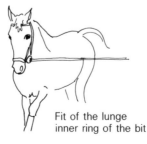

Fit of the lunge
inner ring of the bit

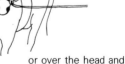

or over the head and
into outer ring of bit

ring of the bit. Another way to affix the lunge, which is mentioned in almost all lunging literature, is to pass it through the inner ring over the head of the horse into the outer ring. An aid given over this kind of connection can be extremely harsh and *it is not recommended in the hands of an inexperienced lunger*! (Keep in mind that the horse has a very vulnerable spot at the poll; hence we protect him there when travelling). It is generally applied for truly spoiled horses where strong corrections are warranted, and the lunger can actually throw a horse down to the ground with a strong pull when the lunge is passed over the head like this! When used by the knowledgeable lunger this *can* enhance the effectiveness of the aid, as the pull of the lunge also presses on the top of the horse's head in the right direction for downward extension. It is *not* recommended for young horses, as a strong divergence from the circle line will have a powerful leverage effect of the lunge, through which the rings of the bit are pulled up. This might result in the horse's resistance and a 'hard mouth'. The lunge line should be about 7 metres long, so that if your horse goes on the prescribed circle of 6.5 metres, you will end up with one or two loops of lunge left in your hand.

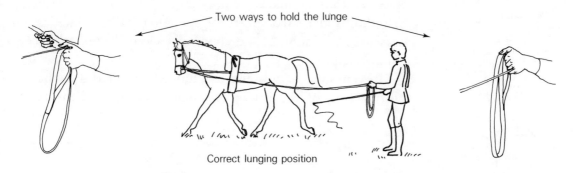

— Two ways to hold the lunge —

Correct lunging position

A horse not yet introduced to lunging will have to be led out onto the circle by a helper, and if you do this calmly, the horse will almost always understand this lesson within the first ten minutes. Later, you let the horse move away from you, egging him on gently with the whip from behind and lengthening the lunge loop by loop until the horse has reached the desired circle diameter. Train your horse right from the start always to use the whole length of line given to him and to hold soft contact with the guiding hand. Be as gentle as possible with your aids to the bit to keep your horse 'soft' in the mouth and to not contradict the lesson, which the horse is teaching himself over the aid of the chambon. Do not ever let your horse come in toward you: anticipate this and be ready to point the whip to his head to prevent him, or lightly throw the lunge in a wave-like motion toward him. Also, always make him halt on the track of this circle, when the lesson is finished. Never give him his reward when he comes into the centre for it!

Keep the horse out with voice and whip

If you are training a young horse, which has the tendency to pull on the lunge, try to use a lunging cavesson (which must be correctly fitted) and get this bad habit out of him by giving him a good yank on the nose, before you use a lunge hooked into the ring of the bridle. A good vaulting horse must be able and willing to react to very slight aids on the lunge (no yanking is advisable when you have three vaulters in a high exercise!) and this cannot be achieved, if wrong lunge training has made him hard in the mouth.

If your inexperienced horse constantly pulls to the outside, start lunging him in one corner of the ring, or put visual barriers around. Don't shorten the inner side rein too much! The horse must not be bent in his neck more than the curve of the circle. If he pulls in combination with running away, it might mean that he is afraid of the whip: regain his confidence by calming him with your voice, with half-halts and patience. If he starts to canter on the wrong lead or disunited, he is still tense (not properly warmed up) or simply so young that he still has problems sorting out his legs. If he constantly falls into canter on the wrong lead, lunge him in a corner and step towards the wall, when giving the command to canter. This will make him lean toward the middle, and he will use the correct legs! Check the adjustment of the side reins (and don't forget to re-adjust, when switching sides).

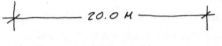

Take care to explain to your club that the lunger must be experienced, as he carries part of the responsibility for the success of the exercises performed, and consistent. The vaulting horse should be trained to the voice, as the aids on the lunge should be minimal and the whip only *shown* to the horse, but never 'used'. Therefore the vocal commands used should always be the same. Rather than using words to give those commands it is advisable to use sounds, such as clicking the tongue, because during a vaulting lesson a lot of talking is going on anyway, and it takes a smart horse to figure out which words are meant for him. Later, in competition, 'word' commands are frowned upon anyhow. Try not to use the whip for punishment with a vaulting horse! If he learns to fear it, he will eye it nervously all through the performance and charge off every time you move it. And that means every time you have to let a vaulter through the 'gate'! If he has had bad experiences like that, make sure you always keep the whip pointed to the ground when letting vaulters through.

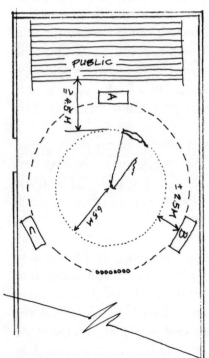

The circle must be regular, which can only be achieved if the lunger does not walk around and follow the horse. (Remember that in competitions the lunger also gets marked as part of the team.) The lunger's left arm (because you are vaulting on the left lead), which holds the end of the lunge in neat folds, should hang relaxed at his side, with the lower arm forming a right angle to the upper. The right hand holds the whip, which should point at the horse's hindquarters. With most horses you have to take care to open the 'gate' for the vaulter slowly, by lifting your elbow but pointing the whip to the ground, so the horse does not mistake your movement as a command directed toward him.

The vaulter then approaches the horse, after passing under the lunger's 'gate', along the lunge. The correct way to approach will be described under the basic exercises. The way to and from the horse, back to the group, must always be as shown in the illustration below.

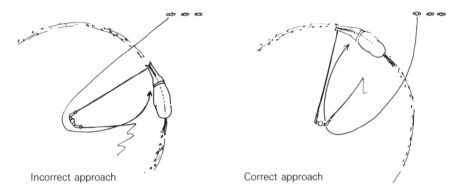

Incorrect approach   Correct approach

Never allow a child to run in front of the lunge, and also don't let them approach the horse via hindquarters. Don't let them wave their arms as they run — not only do they have to learn how to behave correctly, you also have to make it clear to your horse what to expect. If the children and the lunger behave in a very consistent manner, the horse will pick up what is expected of him all the faster. *And* he will learn to react to *unexpected* situations — namely falls of the children. A good vaulting horse learns to help avoid accidents, but in order to do so, he must be able to recognize that what *is* happening *is* an unusual situation.

As mentioned before, the correct circle for vaulting has a 6.5 m radius. If your stable has jumps positioned in the ring permanently, as is the case in many hunter–jumper stables, it will be quite hard for you to fit in the correct size of your circle. Of course the horse will get used to the distance to the lunger, and if you train on a circle which is too small, it will later be hard to force him out to the correct path in competitions. Try to explain to the stable management, how important it is to use the correct length of lunge and that around this 13 m circle you need an additional 2 m space as safety area for falls. Centrifugal force is not to be trifled with when you jump off at canter and you don't want your vaulters to smack into walls or jumps if they come off a bit out of control!

The lunger should turn on the same spot in the centre of that circle. If the horse 'falls in', he waves the whip in front of his face and uses his voice to direct him back to where he belongs. Pulling the left arm back or retreating, when the lunge goes slack, is a mistake. The horse draws conclusions out of the lunger's behaviour! He might just think it is his job to drive you around the ring in ever such neat spirals... When he pulls, it is not the lunger's job to follow; don't 'herd' him around the show ring! In a freshly raked ring there should ideally be only one track with the lunger's footprint in the centre. (In competitions this centre may be marked for the lunger and he must stand on the mark.)

For effective training of your vaulters, it is always preferable to have a lunger who is *not* the trainer at the same time, although I realize that often vaulting still plays such a minor role among the equestrian disciplines that the owners of the stables, or the club, don't deem this extra employee necessary. As I pointed out before, the trainer should be able to instil confidence in the young vaulters by walking along and supporting them. As soon as that is not necessary any more, the children will get into more difficult and complex exercises, because they want to do doubles and triples. The compulsory exercises alone lose their attraction very soon (for little children the basic exercises do not yet take on the importance that they later have for competitors) and many of the single kur exercises which exist are still too hard for them, whereas doubles are fun (you work with a friend) and seem flashy. However, in their first experiences as doubles, they will need your support again. Later they get into triples and ever greater height, and into somersaults, saltos and so on, and again you will support them.

The lunger warms up your horse on the right lead, then switches to the left lead for vaulting. A vaulting horse should never be allowed to run out of control, not even in the warm-up period. The horse must get a chance to loosen up, before the vaulting session begins, and for this you should set aside about ten to fifteen minutes. The horse will go in a strong and attentive walk as well as trot, at first without the side reins fastened. The lunger checks for soundness and whether the horse's back begins to swing, as he loosens up. At the end let him canter a few rounds, still with loose side reins. The lunger sets the pace, which will be regular and collected at all times. While the whip drives the horse forward, frequent soft half-halts stimulate him to seek contact with side reins and the lunge.

Correct lunging should achieve that the horse willingly seeks this contact and then moves diligently, in a relaxed and rhythmically even way. He will need this attentiveness and uncramped attitude and posture to counter-balance the difficult double and triple exercises. Apart from good balance, the following are the goal of correct lunging:

- *Rhythm*: Walk is a four-beat stride. When the horse moves in an awake and active way, the hind feet should step over the track of the front hooves. Trot is a two-beat stride: outside

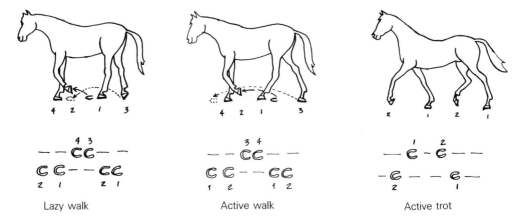

Lazy walk   Active walk   Active trot

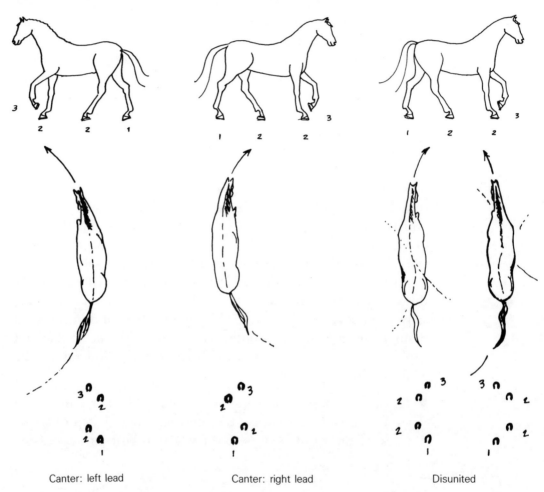

Canter: left lead   Canter: right lead   Disunited

front and inside hind leg (and vice versa) are moving in a parallel and simultaneous motion and the horse's back swings up and down evenly. Canter is a three-beat rhythm, and it should be a clean three-beat! Many vaulting horses show some kind of 'tranter', where the front feet canter, while the rear trots. This is often a sign of an aching back! Canter is the only stride with a 'lead', i.e. the inner front leg must reach forward further than the outside one. If this is not the case, the horse is 'on the wrong lead' and can't balance himself around the corner — let alone with several vaulters on his back. He may actually fall over. By 'disunited' canter we mean that the front feet are on a different lead from the hindquarters, obviously an unbalanced motion, which results in a wiggly line of the horse's spine. This is bad for the horse and difficult for the vaulters — if a horse becomes disunited, the lunger must immediately bring him back to trot and start the canter anew.

- *Relaxed motion*: By this we mean that the horse has a loosely swinging back, with nicely carried tail and neck extending forward—downward. Real balance and getting to be one with the horse can only be achieved by the vaulter if the horse has reached this degree of looseness.

- *Contact*: By this we mean that there is a constant and even connection between lunger and the horse's mouth, via the side reins and the lunge.

- *Animation*: We want to see energetic, but smooth movement in the horse, while keeping the even rhythm. Only then can a vaulter make the best use of the momentum of the canter stride.

- *Alignment*: The horse must be bent on the line of the circle, so his hind feet step into the tracks of the front ones. If the horse throws his hind feet further out, beyond the circle track of the front, it becomes very difficult for the vaulter to keep his balance and align his gravity point with the one of the horse.

- *Collection*: The opposite of a horse 'falling apart'. It means that the hind feet step under, reaching for the front, so that the horse thus carries most of his weight (because he jumps under his own gravity point) on the hindquarters. Especially when carrying up to three vaulters on his back, this is very important to relieve his front legs, where he will otherwise soon show fatigue. Collection is achieved through urging the horse on to animated strides with the whip, while restraining him with soft half-halts over the lunge. To know which aid is necessary at which moment, the lunger must constantly observe the horse's stride.

A good lunger, especially if you don't own the dream vaulting horse, must therefore be able to concentrate on the pace all the time. Often he will constantly have to correct the horse, to keep it from speeding up or slowing down or falling into trot...all of these things can really kill a vaulting exercise! The more difficult the exercises become, the more the lunger has to be there for lunging alone. I realize that many people disagree with me in this, but I also think it is the reason why vaulting progress takes so much longer in some clubs: divided engagement of the trainer can necessarily not show the same results.

A lunger for a vaulting team, especially as you get into higher exercises in canter, must be experienced and reliable. S/he must concentrate on the horse's gait instead of enjoying the vaulters' performance! But s/he must be aware of *what* is going on up there at any given moment to be a help in difficult exercises or in case of falls.

Lunging aids must be very gentle here

Dealing with a horse on the lunge when three children are moving around on top is more refined than the lunging most people seem to consider adequate for training young horses. Most of the aids must be softer, transitions gentler. Train your horse to the voice as much as you can. Make everyone use the same commands. Beating a vaulting horse with the whip is totally out of the question and will cause problems for a long time to come, as mentioned before. Even touching the legs with the whip should be avoided (and is unnecessary, if the voice-training is done consistently!) If it is at all necessary it should be done during the moments when the vaulters are not in precarious positions (like standing) or in the process of building up or dismantling high exercises. Such transition periods often harbour more potential danger than a fully built-up exercise (which in itself is quite a stable configuration, although high). If your lunger chooses to use the whip at the wrong moment, this can mean an accident to your team. If your lunger does not pay enough attention and can't anticipate what the horse will do next (within reason!) s/he should not lunge for vaulting sessions.

A good lunger must be able to react fast and in the correct way to falls: if a child ends up under the horse after sliding off — does your lunger know how to make the horse avoid stepping on him or her? Can s/he prepare the horse during training for such eventualities by teaching him to recognize falls? A horse which is kept attentive during the whole vaulting session (even in walk) will cooperate much better than a beast which is just taught to endure.

An expert, helpful and attentive lunger is a very valuable team member! If you have one, you are lucky. The trainer as well as the vaulting children should understand the importance of this and show their appreciation accordingly!

8 You — the trainer

People will expect all sorts of things from you — and if you disappoint them in their expectations, they will get the impression that you are not the 'right kind' of trainer. Clarify your role right in the beginning.

What does your stable management expect from you?
What does the vaulting club expect?
What do the parents expect to be your job?
What do the children expect from their trainer?

Your first and foremost job should be to teach vaulters correct and safe technique of the sport of vaulting. To further the children's mental and physical development...to ensure they have fun...to be a moral example...can you feel how the ground is getting slippery? Have you given up smoking yet?

Being the trainer of a team also means that you will be at least marginally involved in a thousand other issues:

The booking of shows
The writing and constant revising of shows
Procuring and taping suitable music for the shows
Assembling information for your older vaulters who might
    want to compete elsewhere
Arranging the transport, assuring stabling, lodging for vaulters
Attendance lists, vaulting bills, club memberships
Updating insurance status (you want to be sure your vaulters
    are properly insured *before* an accident occurs!)
Design of uniforms, ordering of new ones for new members
Ordering of new equipment or taking care of repairs

Photo sessions and newspaper articles, general promotion

Fund-raising events for team activities

Vaulting newsletters for the club

Calling parents' meetings, advising changes in training or show times etc.

Representing the club within the provincial or national association

Arranging fun events (BBQ etc.) for the team

Arranging stable competitions

and this is not the end of the list! You can see how much time will be left over for training if you are expected to fulfil all of the above duties!

It is *not* the trainer's job to keep all of these things going. Call a parent meeting as soon as your club comes to life or at the point when you are taking over from the previous trainer. Then establish clearly which jobs you are willing to take on, and where you will only have time to help coordinate.

Don't underestimate the time it will take you to write your team kur exercises and to tape the music for your shows! With twenty years of experience it takes me approximately two hours to write a good and fair team kur (equal turns for vaulters with equal performance level), and up to six hours to find, choose, fit and tape suitable music, depending on the record library at hand! (I take pride in the fact that our shows are never the same, and never use the same music.)

The role of the coach

Get clear in your mind why you want to coach vaulters and how deeply you want to be involved.

- Are you a riding teacher and this is one more discipline you wish to be knowledgeable in? Are you an ex-vaulter yourself? On which level did you perform? Do you want to get the vaulters of your town into the picture? (task approach)

- Do you want to be a winning coach at competitions? Do you want to be 'the BOSS'? Do you want to be the guidance and idol of your youngsters? (self approach)

- Do you want to help the sport? The community? Do you want to morally influence children through this sport? Do you like kids and want to give them a good time? Do you want to affect their minds through the learning of team spirit, discipline, responsibility? (social approach)

I think all of the above reasons are valid, if handed down in an acceptable way. But you should state to your team with which goals in mind you are taking over, to avoid later disappointments. I am personally not interested in running playgroups (so I don't take on three and four-year-olds), but interested in good and ever-improving performance (so my club attracts ambitious vaulters). I am not interested in instilling in my vaulters the greed to win at competitions and am very strict on good sportmanship (although they win their fair part, when they give their best). I want my children to have a good time — but not at the expense of my weary nerves after a full day at work...

When I read books on what kind of human being I should be to make a good coach, I feel I should grow wings like an angel... No, I can't always be polite, cool, positive, supportive and enthusiastic! I yell at them when they do dangerous things, although I have explained just *that* again for the hundredth time a minute before. And there are days when it is too cold and I am too tired at night to be encouraging for anyone... But on the whole it is easy to produce all these wonderful virtues, when your team is *with you*, when you see that they are trying hard and showing progress.

Be qualified

- educate yourself on vaulting matters: take time to study the books and the videos available

- try to arrange clinics with knowledgeable coaches if possible when you feel the need for the 'next step up'

- plan your training from easy to complex (know the difference!)

- if you don't know how to do an exercise, don't pretend. Make it a goal to find out in a safe way together with your vaulters. If you are not an ex-vaulter — how should you know? (read this book again...)

- take the time to learn the rules and regulations, so you can train and answer questions competently

Be positive

- set realistic goals for your vaulters — especially for beginners! (It is safe to say that *no* beginner can do the scissors correctly — they'll feel better, when they know that off hand!)

- praise the effort, as well as results

- give encouraging feedback, take things step by step

- be attentive enough *always* to note improvements and mention them immediately. Ask if the vaulter can feel the difference, if s/he understood what s/he had done more correctly this time and why it worked out better

- note and mention desirable behaviour around the horse, the team etc., the voluntary responsibility taken on, the hand lent without being asked to

Correction to mistakes

- use careful and intelligent observation (if you have not *seen* where the mistake lies, how can you correct it?)

- give clear and specific information in corrective statements

- give corrective instruction in a simple and positive way to minor mistakes

- adjust your explanations to the age level and mental development of the vaulter

- give encouragement immediately and take the time to explain how to do better next time

- if you shouted: it should be warranted by the occasion. Explain the dangers and the possible consequences of dangerous habits, the seriousness of mistakes. Explain why you must *insist* on your instructions being followed

- if you demonstrate: don't use that situation to show off!

- otherwise: use your sense of humour! be reassuring

How to gain respect

- set an example and *earn* that respect!

- don't take your eyes off the vaulter on the horse. They are training with you to get your input − you must watch!

- be honest: a praise must mean the performance or the effort was good, or it becomes meaningless

- give your vaulters credit for brains, if they have any! don't preach to them, explain things briefly, but in a way they can understand (depending on age level)

- If you demonstrate: show courage, before you demand it!

- show that you are a competent and willing teacher

- be fair and considerate − don't favour anybody

- don't pretend to know what you don't know: always diffuse awkward situations by using your sense of humour

- never pressure children into something they are afraid of doing. Never ridicule their fright. There is *always* a better way to get them where you want them! Don't force them to *say* that they are afraid: observe it and overcome it by helping. A frightened vaulter causes accidents

- let them play trainer from time to time — to get to know the frustrations and the responses that might trigger! (to better understand your not-so-positive reactions sometimes...)

Deal with parental pressure

- try to communicate with the youngsters directly

- communicate with the parents aside

- if you feel pressure from home: emphasize safety and fun!

Be a good listener

- make your communication (verbal and non-verbal) meaningful

- ask for opinions, share concerns, get suggestions, show genuine interest and acceptance of their feelings, paraphrase and ask them for clarification if you don't understand what they mean. Don't forget: *they* know what it feels like to be way up there and not to trust the grip of your undermen... you may have never experienced it or long forgotten! Their comments are valid and necessary to good training; it's not a thing you should just do to make them feel better!

Maintain discipline

- establish clearly what is expected

- explain clearly *why*! (safety, impression of the team, your aching throat if you have to shout too much)

- establish clearly how lack of discipline will be dealt with

- establish a balance between freedom and structure

- emphasize the *team* aspect and responsibility

Deal with violations

- allow them to explain, and listen to, their side of the story

- if punishment is necessary, use the *restriction* in involvement of something which is desirable. Explain the dangers, and why it would be stupid on your part to take on unnecessary risks for their fun. (Most North American children *do* understand the concept of getting sued!)

- don't lecture or embarrass a single child, or if lecturing is necessary, do it aside

- be consistent and impartial in the enforcement of your rules

In competitions

- set the example for the behaviour during the event:
    don't show nervousness, spread reassurance: 'you're well prepared, now just do your best, don't worry about the others or winning', 'get into the event, enjoy the excitement and adrenaline, but take care you don't lose that honest smile!'
    emphasize that participation is more important than winning
    be the first 'good loser' and the most gracious good winner
    express your training philosophy by showing it honestly: what is your response to a poor performance in competition?
    live good sportsmanship in front of them
    don't let them brag or verbally abuse other teams!

show them the politeness you expect them to show towards competitors and officials!

- teach them acceptance of rules and rulings in good grace... even if they sometimes seem unfair. 'Learn from the experience and the marks. Learn what the judges want to see, let's discuss their comments', etc.

- show them that *you* are able to accept their mistakes (even if it damaged the team) if they were not intentional (which they almost never are!)

9 *Planning training sessions*

Basic knowledge of sport psychology can make your training so much more enjoyable and the results better and faster. Since vaulting is a sport where a lack of self confidence contributes to potential danger, it is important to arrange your training so this courage and confidence can grow in a realistic and natural manner.

Objectives to be endorsed by trainer and vaulter

- To develop sport skills, improve health and fitness, emphasize the general obligation an athlete has toward his body: this means healthy food, no smoking, no drugs of course! But it also means improving your vaulting by exercising in other sports as well: swimming, jogging, jazz dancing — it all ties in with a good vaulting performance.

- To have fun, form friendships: the social aspect is the easiest one to achieve, as vaulting parties and sleep–overs, picnics and travel together are rarely turned down! Arrange carpooling in a way so the children don't always get pulled out of the stables straight after the practice session — if the stable management will allow them to hang around for a while. Looking for lost horseshoes in the paddocks together can be quite as 'bonding' for the team mates as the practice itself, and often they need something other than vaulting to decrease tensions which may have come up during training.

- To acquire the interest and desire to stay active, and participate in something meaningful: nothing is worse for a teenager than just hanging around at the Seven Eleven with nothing to do! With shows and competitions scheduled during the season the desire to show off and *be* somebody can be very positively fulfilled — there is no need to attract attention by getting into trouble. Active involvement in a sport is the best way to keep youngsters away from drugs, alcohol, smokes and undesirable characters, and the ambition to stay on the show team (which also depends on good behaviour around all others involved) will be an incentive to show at least minimum discipline...

- To find the sense of accomplishment through individual improvement: to recognize this you just have to look at how the kids arrange their trophies and ribbons! And this is an important reason why those should be handed out (preferably down to fifth or eight place). If not enough competitions can be scheduled in your area, due to lack of opportunity of finding anyone to compete against, create your own 'award system'. There always must be a goal to work toward. And this goal must be attainable by the individual vaulter.

- To gain personal satisfaction and well-being: part of that is the sense of accomplishment, but the other part is that with correct training the children will actually feel fitter, stronger and generally more energetic.

- To balance work and play: interject 'play sessions' even for the older vaulters, especially after they have trained hard for the show season or a competition. Let them choose what new things they would like to try out, even if you know that this will not work. Just make sure they don't attempt anything dangerous! But a play session, where every single exercise collapses, can be a lot of amusement. Don't take it out on the horse, however! Let the collapses happen on the barrel...

- To teach desirable values (cooperation, honesty etc.): always show your appreciation when good cooperation happens! Make it known that you notice: don't present the desirable behaviour as glowing examples of virtue to the others, who don't behave that way yet; keep it light. A remark like 'there she is again, just when I need her — how did you guess?' with a smile and a pat on the back will do the trick very nicely. Hopefully the others will notice as well and follow suit. If they choose not to notice, make it clear that it would be quite stupid of you to take the misbehaving ones onto your next fun trip — why invite more work and trouble than necessary? They don't want to volunteer their efforts — why should you?

- To teach personal adjustments: adaptability, sociability, team spirit, self esteem, self reliance, responsibility for others and an animal etc. Give them responsibilities early on; if not they will get the impression that there is a way to get around the jobs at hand. There isn't: if you are part of the team, it is equal rights and responsibilities for all. Some will be better with the horse, never forgetting that he might need water — even in the best moments of their personal glory after a show. Others will have the talent to keep track of your baby vaulters, who always run off at the most inopportune moment, because they have to go to the bathroom. Some are punctual and can be the 'time keeper' for the team; assemble them at the right time and right spot when needed. There is a place for everyone on a team to show their worth. The building of the team spirit cannot be overestimated; it is a most valuable learning experience. Make them observe the other teams and note good or undesirable behaviour (they have a much sharper eye for the competing team than for themselves...). This way they can learn how bad a bad loser looks — and how good a friendly helping hand from the 'enemy team'! And how wonderful it is to belong to a team which really sticks together.

- To give them the chance to develop respect (for each other, the horse, the trainer, the lunger, the promoters of an event etc.), as well as trust, confidence, and knowledge: give them opportunity to put themselves in the trainer's place sometimes, and explain the promoter's concerns around a show. Discuss the difficulties of the judges' job (and how judging errors might occur despite the best intentions, because fatigue sets in after a few hours) and let them judge some videos — that really drives the point home!

- To teach them to be a good sportsman, honest and fair, a gracious winner and a good loser. For this you as the trainer must be the first example!

Self image of the young vaulter

Self image is *learned*. It is moulded by the reaction of others and is a reflection of how the child thinks s/he is being perceived from the outside. It is susceptible to change (any vaulting team has teenagers in puberty!), but immensely important for team work and performance.

A positive self image must first be developed, before it can be emanated to the spectators. You want to teach your vaulters that reflecting the confidence, ease and charm of this sport is part of the achievement — as in any show sport!

We actually train for this kind of body language: when the little vaulters first mount onto the barrel horse (and later the horse) make them hold out their arms directly after the mount and shout out their name. They should announce themselves as if this was their presentation to the spectators 'here I am, and I'm worth looking at!' Because if they are not convinced of this, why should anyone want to look at them? It is in the beginning very difficult to make a timid little vaulter shout anything at all...but when they *do*, you will immediately see their posture change! You can't proudly shout out your name with a rounded back and a slumping head while contemplating your belly button...

Self image can be deceiving and wrong even when it is not negative. If you can, let the vaulters train in front of a mirror (maybe there is one installed in the riding ring, or you can put one up next to the barrel), and/or film them on video, if a camera is available. The kids enjoy this tremendously — and it *does* get the point across, when you stop the picture and they can *see* all the faults, which they never quite believed they *have*.

Self image affects motivation, learning ability and performance, the personal relationships the team makes with the coach and others, as well as personal and life satisfaction. The trainer influences it by his/her way of accepting the vaulter, as athlete and as person, and by his/her management style of the training and critiquing. If clarity, fairness, consistency and a supportive and caring atmosphere prevail, you will hopefully see trust, a sense of responsibility and respect in return. It is mostly true that you will get the results you expect!

Don't overemphasize winning

One of the nice things about vaulting is that it is in most clubs more a show sport than a competition issue at this point. Competition does something very valuable to the motivation of the vaulters: it really gets them going! But even small stable competitions, as long as other clubs are involved, will do for that purpose. When competition gets more serious (which we hope we will also achieve over the next few years) take care to avoid its negative aspects:

- loss of enjoyment: if goals are set too high and unattainable, the sport loses all the fun and becomes work only; the result is loss of confidence and self esteem

- restricted participation: the lesser skilled may be eliminated, although they may be valuable in terms of team cohesion, personal fun etc.

- undesirable behaviour may result from feeling overtaxed: cheating, blaming others, complaining etc. may be tried to compensate for perceived 'failure'

- poor performance may result from high anxiety level

- the total, personal and physical development of the athlete may be restricted

Plan your sessions

Your training sessions should not turn into a boring routine, although it is important to learn many things through repetition. Use variation in your approach.

Creative mixing: Overall goals (such as creating your own club, getting a show team together, planning competitions, creating team spirit, going on shows outside the home stable etc.) must be interrelated with specific goals. These must be realistic, achievable and measurable in their success. They can be goals for the day, non–skill related ('no negative words between the team members today') or for the foreseeable future and skill related ('in three weeks we'll all be able to do that in canter') and any combination of these.

- Give equal opportunities to all vaulters most times.

- Then give opportunity for individual activities: a vaulter wants to find out what s/he can do as a 'single star'.

- Then combine them with a partner: compose *pas-de-deux* routines, which they can perform with a close friend.

- Move to team: the cooperative approach. Make clear to them that success of an exercise depends on best performance of *all* involved. Point out that if the exercise fails, they must help each other more. Instil pride in the undermen that you trust them with the life of your flyer. Instil pride in your flyer by teaching him/her to make it easy for the undermen – the team will do the rest! Every underman loves a flyer who can sustain him/herself!

- Simulate competition: mark your vaulters, make them give scores to each other. Teach them the judging rules. Plan strategies of how to avoid deductions in a competition. Teach good tactical approaches to improve a performance.

- Simulate clinics: video your vaulters and discuss their exercises with them, while they watch themselves.

- Train for a show, involve them in the costume design.

- Train for 'impression of the group' with run-ins, bows and/ or more flashy displays and pyramids etc.

- After competitions and big shows: let them relax, order free play time. Ask them which new exercises they would like to try (this gives you an excellent insight into their ability to assess their own performance level). Put them up to new things you expect them to be able to take on.

- Let them play 'trainer'. Let them mark their team mates: this will give you an insight into their fairness, their knowledge, their perception, their personal dislikes and favourites. Let them judge you: you may learn something from their criticism and it could turn into a really funny session!

- Let them organize a 'parent vaulting night', complete with drawings for the invitation, the creation of funny medals to hand out (Fimo will do fine!), and their own 'evaluation rules'. We had hard hats, huge pillows, ropes and rope ladders for the protection of the vaulting parents — it was great fun, and the kids were very proud that none of the parents could do what they could do...

10   *Training — what does it mean?*

The essence of training in sports is the ability of the human body to adapt to new situations — by which we mean demands of a higher level. So, in order to train a vaulter adequately, you must determine each vaulter's stage of development and technical ability.

Training should be concentrated equally on different parts of the body, especially since in vaulting we are often concerned with the growing child. The strength and endurance of a growing child must be taken into account, and sustained overloading of the muscles or joints must be avoided at all costs.

The ways of training mentioned hereafter may seem very specific and superfluous, especially if you only train a little show team with no ambitions for competition. Indeed, this is how the champions train, except that I am simplifying it for this book, sparing you detailed training schedules. But the basic principles are the same — and your ambition and wish to learn will grow with the successes you achieve on the way!

In order to understand why a certain way of preparing and training is better than another, one must have a basic understanding of how the body works and which parts are most affected by the sport.

The joints

tendons are the muscle to bone connections
ligament is the bone to bone connection
cartilage is the 'padding' between the bones, the shock absorber

The joints should never have to take on the major stresses. The stress on the joints in high jump–off exercises (such as those the world champions perform) can be as high as five times the vaulter's body weight! Exercises in training should ensure that the muscles around and supporting the joints are built up and so strengthened that the stress on the joints is minimized.

The muscles

Muscles are organized in pairs and we use these pairs in two ways:

- preliminary movement, where one of the pairs is tensed while the other muscle relaxes (this is for example the *swing* before the push in the scissors, or the crouch before the salto off)

- and the 'payoff movement' (the jump or the height in the scissors we were aiming for), where the 'preliminary' partner relaxes

When we are *holding* a posture, both muscle partners are used at the same time, both contract to sustain the 'still movement'.

Basic understanding of energy and the body

Muscles are energy converters which transform chemical energy (food) into kinetic energy (movement). In sports we basically deal with three different kinds of energy, which are described by the following attributes: 'aerobic', if intake of oxygen is required to produce energy (anaerobic being the opposite); 'lactic', if the muscle produces lactic acid while active (alactic being the opposite).

start-up energy	*fast-twitch muscle energy*	*slow-twitch muscle energy*
	after 10 secs changes to	after 2 minutes changes to
basic prerequisite to any movement anaerobic alactic	high speed for short time needs carbohydrates & produces lactic acid anaerobic	lesser speed for longer time needs fats and carbohydrates produces carbon dioxide, aerobic, alactic

To guide and diagnose effective training you must understand how the muscles work, how to start, to increase and plan your overall training.

Muscles are only able to contract or to lengthen against loading. We call this concentric and eccentric movement. The energy needed for that comes from glucose (blood sugar), which splits into triphosphoric acid, for which process we need oxygen. Since in a healthy person there is always enough blood sugar present, the question is: is there enough oxygen for what we want the muscles to do? If there is *not* enough oxygen, lactic acid is formed. This we experienced as muscle soreness. One can have the level of lactic acid tested in a body, but for our purposes it is much easier to measure a different way (and I am simplifying the medical language on purpose!) You know that oxygen is transported from the lungs (where the fresh oxygen is taken into the blood stream) by the blood via the pumping of the heart. If the body realizes that for an activity there is not enough oxygen present, it tries to make up for the deficiency by making the heart pump faster. So if you measure the pulse (the heart rate), you are actually in a way measuring the oxygen deficiency in the muscles. And you are also measuring the training load on the body.

Endurance training load

Endurance training develops the muscles, but keeps them thin (the typical image of a marathon runner versus a weight lifter). Endurance is the most valuable attribute in a vaulter, because vaulting is not really a power sport.

Here you must ask yourself: what is the training load for, and when is it effective? Remember that we call training the adaptability of the human body to higher levels of performance. Therefore, if your heart rate (our way to measure if the body has enough oxygen or not) does not change, we are not trying to adapt the body to any higher level of performance — we are missing the point, there will be no change, no progress. We are, in fact, not training.

- It follows that training with a heart rate of below 120 beats per minute is not effective.

- Any training, which elevates the heart rate above 120 beats per minute must be sustained for at least ten minutes — otherwise the body will not understand (in laymen's language) that we request it to get used to this new condition and actually improve its oxygen household. This means that pauses can be included, which we call effective pauses, as long as the heart rate stays above 120. (Because this still indicates a lack of oxygen in the muscle cells.)

- 'Aerobic' means in other words that there exists an oxygen debt, and aerobic exercises try to get the body used to making better use of the oxygen available. The body will adapt with correct training — the heart rate will sink below 120, and you will have to increase the training load to again stay effective and incite the body to get used to the next higher level of performance, by starving it of oxygen again.

Plan your endurance training so the heart rate stays above 120 for at least ten minutes per group of muscles. Training with low resistance means that the athlete will work at a level of plus-minus thirty per cent of the maximum power, with pauses, during which the heart rate may however not decline to under 120 beats per minute.

Cardiovascular workout is excellent for endurance and fitness. As it takes at least ten to fifteen minutes to raise the heart beat for a sustained period, often the allotted training times in the stables do not allow for these kinds of activities within the training program, so try to influence your vaulters to engage in these laudable undertakings on the side.

Excellent endurance training is jogging, swimming, rope skipping and the like. Train at least three times per week.

Periodicy

By this word we mean that we always have to catch the right moment to build new training on top of the new efficiency, which we just reached. Recreation periods will be included (and are necessary), but they may not be long enough for the body to forget that we now request this new level to be the normal one. This time span should not be longer than twenty-four hours. With always new training on top of the new efficiency we reach a build-up in terms of training results.

Muscle power training

In muscle power training, (strength) we want to ensure that we do *not* run into oxygen starvation. Muscle power training thickens the muscles (which means, it creates more muscle cells) and therefore adds weight (like in body building), which for vaulters is not necessarily desirable. In power training the heart rate should therefore stay below 120 beats per minute, that is, the load will be higher, but the pauses much longer (to keep the heart rate down). This we call 'anaerobic training' (no lack of oxygen in the muscle cells).

Pyramid training

An example of power training is weight lifting: determine the maximum power at the time (for example fifty pounds), then increase this by fifty per cent. This is your goal. Now lift weights corresponding to eighty per cent of this goal four times, then eighty-five per cent three times, then ninety per cent of that twice to peak to the new maximum power (your goal). Then measure the heart rate: if it is above 120 beats, pause. Don't create a lack of oxygen! Do at least three sets per muscle.

Combination of both

It is *not effective* to combine power and endurance training in one session! (because in plain words then your body does not know what on earth it is supposed to get used to.) Rather counter-balance power training with endurance training (which will have a tendency to thin the muscle again).

In vaulting we do not only want thin bodies, but also stress the fact that optimum technique means that the vaulter will need a minimum of strength to perform the exercises, that is, achieve the optimum action efficiency. So train mainly for endurance: good vaulters should be able to perform all compulsory exercises five times in a row without pause, after which the pulse rate should decrease to normal within three minutes. (If this does not sound difficult to you, try it!) Endurance is needed in vaulting for being able to increase technique through repetition, whereas maximum power is not so important.

Muscle stiffness

Because of the make-up of the muscles — protein and water — they react to heat in a similar way to oil: cold temperatures make them stiff, warm ones fluid and easier to work. Hence the need for warm-up exercises before any training session. But anxiety or tension also influence the muscles' performance, as they hinder relaxation. So for best performance and safety we are striving for: a good warm-up, balanced muscle work, and a positive atmosphere. With adequate and well planned training muscle stiffness should not occur!

Stretching and warm-up sessions before vaulting

Other publications cover in depth how to stretch correctly to gain the necessary flexibility for good athletic performance. Increasing flexibility means being able to use a greater range of motion about a joint. It shall just be mentioned here that the prescribed warm-up *directly before* a vaulting session however should not be an endurance test, but consist of exercises to loosen and stretch the muscles. It should result in no more than a very light sweat on the forehead at the most. It is a wrong understanding of warm-up to exhaust the vaulters (especially the less fit beginners) by rigorous running and stretching for an hour before they get onto the horse. Developing the necessary stamina, flexibility and strength for vaulting competition is a daily routine, which must happen *in addition* and outside the vaulting sessions.

Let us assume you have determined the oxygen levels of your vaulters through a training test somewhat along the lines described above. You must now determine the training load of the vaulters according to their age and stage in development. Try to respect all conditions and cover all lack of endurance, power etc. In a team, for example, it should always be the weakest link who determines what we allow the vaulters to perform. So look at the underman's lifting power — see how much weight s/he can lift — *then* determine and check how long s/he can hold the flyer in such position. (Take into account, and re-check accordingly, that often flyers grow and get heavier at a faster rate than the lifting power of the underman increases.)

A good vaulter or vaulting team *must* be forced into training for endurance. Although you will encounter resistance (which is called laziness, and even vaulting trainers succumb to it sometimes...) nobody else can do this part of the home work for them. They can't expect you to turn them into good vaulters, if they don't take care of building up the necessary stamina.

Nutrition

It is no secret that a healthy diet greatly contributes to your fitness. So don't let your vaulters see you at the chocolate bar dispenser! There are plenty of books to give you plans for well balanced nutrition. Here is just an outline of how it works:

energy	is gained from fat and carbohydrates
muscle build	from proteins
replacement for sweat	take in water and minerals
body chemistry	to regulate body chemical reactions, the athlete needs vitamins

A summary of the basic training principles

For flexibility, endurance and strength, which are necessary for good vaulting, the basic principles of training are as follows.

- *Training must be continuous*: the essence of training is the ability of the human body to adapt to new situations. By these changes we mean an improvement in terms of our sport. However, our body is not only adapting to new situations as we create them by asking for higher efforts or longer performances, but it also adapts to the pauses which we include. Therefore training must be continuous if higher levels of performance are to be reached.

- *Training load must increase*: Say our goal is to achieve the ability to do one hundred sit-ups in a row. Of course one must start slowly, because this load can't be reached in the beginning (otherwise the goal is set too low), so we start with ten. It is of no use to then stick with ten per day, but obviously the load must be increased in increments eventually to reach one hundred. The load must increase continuously.

- *The training must be effective*: for effective training the load of the training must be fixed according to the abilities as well as the goal to be reached.

- *The training goal must be set with each vaulter individually and must be attainable for him or her*: if you set goals that under-challenge the vaulter's abilities, the training results in stalemate boredom. If you over-challenge, the vaulter can't experience any feeling of success and will stop training, discouraged.

- *Training must be periodized*: you need to set highlights and vary the training accents: one day you might emphasize strength of muscles, the next endurance, then flexibility etc.

- *Training must be planned correctly*: known medical facts must be taken into consideration, when planning how to train your vaulters:

  up to 6 years in age: this phase is called the 'imprinting phase', which means a sensitive phase for imprinting things into the child's memory. This is why vaulters should have contact with horses early (not just barrel training), in any form possible. It is a bit like the 'bonding' that people talk about between parents and child.

  7 to 12 years of age: here children have the best ability to learn technical things, so this is the age when you should include a lot of barrel training to explain and train the technical aspects of moves with them. It is not the age to train for optimal muscle strength, although strength can be increased significantly during this time. But building up strength now, means short-term success and a letdown later.

  12 to 16 years of age: here the body is able to bear biological loading of training: it is the time to increase muscle strength. Meanwhile, of course, good technique has to improve further. During this phase endurance is built up.

  from 17 years on: a good and effectively trained vaulter will reap his or her international successes...

11
Talent and technique

Vaulting is by definition the sport of 'doing gymnastic exercises on a cantering horse', so the principles of gymnastics apply, except that we don't use lifeless equipment, but a moving horse.

When we discuss the gymnastic principles involved, we should never forget that this type of gymnastics is performed on a moving, living partner. The best gymnast will only turn into a good vaulter if he is able to become *one* with the movement of the horse. A vaulter who is not capable of timing his own movements in perfect harmony with the canter stride will never achieve optimum performance. This is particularly obvious in all the exercises which need a swing to achieve good height above the horse. The vaulter can't time the swing according to what feels most comfortable to himself, but must do it exactly on the rhythm of the horse's movement.

Indication of up and down movement of croup, shoulder and neck during one canter stride

Indication of forward movement in one canter stride, approximately one length of the horse, depending on speed

Beat 1 of the 3-beat: outside hind foot pushes off

Beat 2 of the 3-beat: f 2 and 3 push off diagon

The horse's movement is twofold: he covers a certain amount of ground within one canter stride, and this forward movement and the resulting speed give the vaulter the momentum which he must use for good mounts and jumps. And also there is an up-and-down movement in the horse's swinging back and croup, which the vaulter uses as momentum for his swings while on the horse.

Talent for vaulting

A good potential vaulter needs certain attributes in terms of body build, understanding of techniques and sense of timing. This does not mean that a person *not* possessing all facets of his talent can't enjoy this sport tremendously. As mentioned before, we are not looking at vaulting only as competitive activity. But a vaulter with hopes for a competitive future must possess certain physical motor abilities, without which he cannot achieve the necessary skills.

- *The ability to straddle the legs*: by this we do not mean the physical skill of already being able to perform the splits down to the ground — a skill can be learned, if practised, if the ability to do such movements at all is there. Of course, all healthy children can learn the necessary skills well enough (if they do their homework) to make decent show team members, since for this full splits are not required. In a show team the trainer can use the vaulters in the areas where they perform best — but in competition, they must be able to perform all

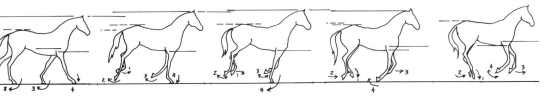

Beat 3 of the 3-beat: foot 4 pushes off

Flight phase: the 'jump' of the canter stride

skills to a good level. Serious competitors should be mobile enough in their hip joints to learn the complete splits. The diagrams show some general leg stretching exercises.

Insufficient flexibility   Sufficient   Good full splits   The 'grasshopper' stretching exercise

- *The ability to achieve shoulder extension*: a certain agility in the shoulder joints will give the vaulter greater freedom of movement, which is necessary for optimum execution and artistic expression in many exercises, like for example the bridge. An exercise to improve shoulder flexibility is passing a stick over your head, back and forth with extended arms, and grabbing it ever closer to the centre.

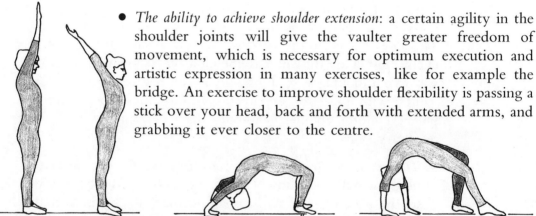

Insufficient   Excellent flexibility
shoulder
flexibility

Stiff shoulders

Great shoulder extension

- *Suppleness of the spine*: a flexible back is a prerequisite for certain freestyle exercises (often in conjunction with suppleness of the legs, as shown in the Bielman, flag etc.). Exercises to improve spine suppleness: bridges, pushing up from the floor lifting torso over the back, then relaxing while exhaling, and lifting back again, etc.

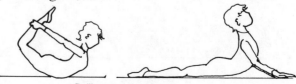

Lifting and bending   Pulling and pushing

- *Strength of muscles*: this can of course be built up with correct training and regular exercise in any healthy child. Back and stomach musculature are as important as leg muscles and arm strength. Exercises to improve muscle strength: push-ups and chin-ups, sit-ups, general floor exercises, lifting legs all positions.

- The other important part of talent is the capability of the vaulter of understanding and learning optimal technique. Most of this can be explained, but the last fine tuning has to be instinctively grasped by a good vaulter to achieve optimal performance with best timing.

Optimum technique

Technique in terms of bio-mechanics is the flow of movements with an optimal, that is, minimal, quantum of action. This means that the vaulter will perform an exercise in such way as to use the least energy, that is, just enough strength to produce the best performance, therefore achieving highest efficiency which is part of optimal technique. This can only be achieved if the vaulter has certain motor capabilities such as flexibility, endurance and strength. Keep in mind that vaulting is not a power sport: flexibility and endurance are more important than sheer muscle power.

- *Correct timing*: a good sense of timing is hard to teach to someone who does not possess it instinctively. As a trainer you should be able to detect if and when timing is the problem, and try to give useful directions to correct the mistake. For this you must be able to analyse when a push or jump-off etc. must occur, and if you are not a vaulter or gymnast yourself, this may be difficult.

    Many beginners have timing problems, not because they can't feel the movement of the canter stride, but simply because they do not yet possess the necessary body control and precision to perform moves fast enough to fit them onto said canter rhythm. Here it greatly helps to practise swings etc. on the barrel in varying speeds. Ask them to speed up the swinging exercises and so slowly get them to learn precision — which means enough body control to decide themselves how fast or slow they want to perform a move.

- *Correct body posture*: body posture has two components: the technically correct posture and aesthetical body posture or 'artistic expression'. It is clear that the artistic expression of body posture comes into play after the technically correct posture has been mastered, and must never work against the technically correct one.

  Technically correct body posture means the position of: holding the extremities (hands, arms, legs, feet), the head, and the torso in a certain position (the correct one depends on the exercise) and also correctly in relationship to the horse. It is this position which will allow the vaulter to achieve maximum effect with minimum effort, and correct body position applies to static and dynamic exercises equally. It also depends on correct body tension, which is discussed below.

Technically correct posture remains the same despite variation in expression

Expression in body posture means expression *while holding* a position: the extremities, head and torso should achieve an aesthetical show effect, without affecting the technically correct posture adversely. Artistic expression can be achieved without changing the technically correct posture, by varying the posture of arms, head, torso, toes and fingers. In the example shown the technical posture of the kneel remains unchanged, while posture above that line may vary. Optimum execution of an exercise means having achieved the *sum* of very good technical posture *and* very good aesthetical posture.

- *Correct holding*: part of holding himself correctly in an exercise presupposes that the vaulter is positioned in the right spot on the horse. Take an example of the flag: when the supporting leg is in the wrong spot on the horse's back, the vaulter will be off centre with his gravity point and needs significantly more strength (in the supporting arm) to maintain balance. (No optimum action quantum achieved, he is wasting energy to make up for a mistake.) The supporting points in any exercise (three in the flag: the arm, the knee and − all along the shin − the foot) must receive even weight distribution to result in best efficiency and balance. Refer to the chapters on the compulsory exercises for description of correct position on the horse.

    The other aspect of holding is how the vaulter holds his own body in regard to the relationship of different body parts to each other and to the gravity point. Let's take the simple example of the basic seat. As described under the compulsory exercises, the vaulter must achieve a straight up-and-down line, vertically from head to shoulder to hip to ankles and pointed toes, when seen sideways. The knees must be pushed down, that is, they must stay as close to that vertical line as possible, although they deviate from it a bit, because of the curvature of the horse's belly. And this is not only for aesthetic reasons, but rather because it is technically correct. Let's analyse what effects are to be seen, when deviating from the correct position.

    If the vaulter pulls up his knees, he must tilt his pelvis backward in order not to lose his balance on his seat. His hips

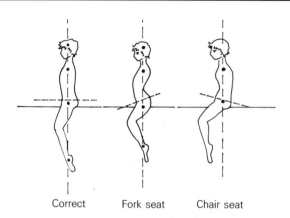

Correct   Fork seat   Chair seat

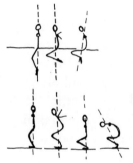

and pointed toes will leave the prescribed vertical line, and his arms will try to make up for the shift in gravity point by overstretching to the back, while his head tilts to the front. The loss of balance is obvious even in the stick–man drawing.

Another example is the stand: observe the summation of mistakes which occur when the vaulter tries to correct one evil with another. A tilted line in these drawings means loss of balance — or a fall.

● *Correct muscle tension*: part of correct holding is also correct muscle tension. The vaulter may hold his body neither limply, nor tensely or cramped up. All joints and muscles must be supple at all times to absorb the horse's motion softly and fluidly. Loss of balance always means that the vaulter will tense up in an effort to regain control. A good way to train for adequate body tension is to tip a vaulter back and forth between two supporting partners, while in the handstand. Make sure the whole body follows the tilting movement, not just the legs through curving the back! Explain to young vaulters that they must feel as if somebody pulled them up the ceiling by their toes, and the only joint moving in the exercise should be the wrists.

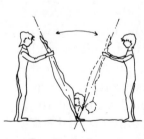

Exercise for improving body tension

Overextending muscles or joints by force has the same effect of tensing up: this is why flexibility plays such a major

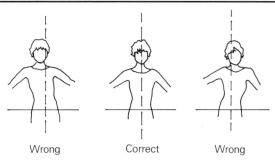

Wrong   Correct   Wrong

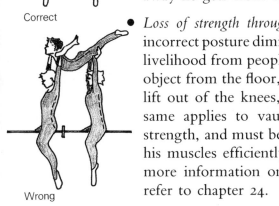

Correct

Wrong

role. To achieve with ease the holding of a difficult and extended posture without stiffening up with the effort, is what optimum body posture strives for. We have all experienced the effect it has on our neck and back muscles when we squeeze the telephone receiver under the same ear, or carry the heavy purse always on the same shoulder. We instinctively try to make up for the one-sided stress by tilting other body parts, in order to get the whole 'configuration' back into plumb! So if your sitting vaulter kinks in some way, as seen here from the front, he has to adjust it with another wrong kink somewhere else to regain balance. Thus mistakes multiply, the further he deviates from the correct posture, and therefore the more his muscles tense up with the effort − the further away he gets from optimal technique

• *Loss of strength through incorrect posture*: You also know that incorrect posture diminishes strength. Chiropractors make their livelihood from people disregarding that. When lifting a heavy object from the floor, you should keep your spine straight and lift out of the knees, that is, the back and leg muscles. The same applies to vaulting: a lifting underman needs all his strength, and must be able, through his correct posture, to use his muscles efficiently and minimize stress on the joints. For more information on correct training of team kur exercises refer to chapter 24.

12 *Preparation before vaulting*

Now that we know about all the participating members — the horse, the trainer, the lunger, the children, the parents — the stage is set to start the first session.

Skill analysis

There is a certain technical skill to all movements, and you have to analyse if your children are doing them correctly, even in the warm-up. To make a movement technically correct, the children must use *all* the joints and muscles involved in it (maximum effect through summation of forces), use them in the proper *sequence*, without *gaps or breaks* (continuity of joint forces) and with the proper *timing* between the components of the movement. Usually the joints with the larger muscles are used first, then the smaller ones, resulting in a fast and continuous flow of movement.

Tell the vaulters which joints and muscles must be used in each movement, teach and correct them 'whole — part — whole'. Explain what you expect from them in 'slow motion'. It is not obvious to all children that an efficient jump consists of a preparatory crouch (with arm swing) and then a take-off involving thigh muscles, knees, calf muscles, ankle, ball of the foot and toes, all in correct sequence. Many children have the tendency never to use the ball of their foot or their toes for jump-offs and landings (I call them 'flatfoot'), which is extremely hard on the joints. You should always stress that muscles must be built up, before one can put any stress on the joints, and that to save yourself from injury those muscles must be used correctly to relieve the joints.

Preparatory movement   Pay-off movement

Each training session will start with a warm-up for the children. This should never be omitted and is especially important in the winter time, when muscles are cold and limbs are stiff. If you train as we do — all year around in our mild coastal climate — the children have to understand how important it is to keep the muscles warm to prevent injuries in case of falls.

The complete warm-up routine before you actually start on the horse consists of four parts:

stretching exercises and breathing
vigorous exercises (calisthetics)
rolls and falls exercises
simulation (training on the stationary horse or barrel)

This warm-up will not replace general fitness training, which has to happen on the side — and should happen every day. No stiff body will learn the splits by doing a half-hour warm-up once a week, and no stamina will be built up this way either. Your more serious vaulters, who want to compete, must do their homework: stretching every day and jogging, cycling, swimming or rope skipping to build up endurance, push-ups and so on to increase strength.

The warm-up routine should be systematic (using the correct sequence mentioned above), but show some variety to prevent the children from getting bored (and always coming late to miss it). Make sure they use muscle control during those exercises.

Training flexibility should be a daily routine

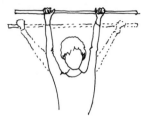

Increase shoulder extension: passing a stick over the head

Grabbing the hand behind the back and pulling

Allow for individual differences between the vaulters; not everyone was given the same talents. The aim is to stretch the muscles, heat the body and prepare the mind for the session to come and to build up strength, flexibility and endurance. Whatever part of this can't happen within your allotted training time should take place on the side (gymnastic and endurance training).

Stretching

Stretching is the beginning of the warm-up and we start with the upper body, bending sideways and stretching to reach the ceiling. Then progress to the leg muscles, bending to touch the toes. Warm up the ankles and knees by moving on the spot. Rotate the arms and improve shoulder flexibility. Proceed into some pre-split exercises, again stretching slowly (take care that the children always breathe correctly) and in a relaxed manner. Do head rolls slowly. Don't let the vaulters jerk their muscles, don't let them force anything to show off. All of this will seem silly to some − explain *why* it is important (especially to the boys, who will complain that they did not join the team to become ballet dancers…) − and do it to music if you can (whatever is 'cool' at the time!); it is more fun that way.

Bending torso   Stretching legs   Kicking and throwing legs

Vigorous exercises

From 'pre-warm' go into 'warm' with running on the spot. Observe if the children use their whole foot correctly: rolling off in the toes, the ball of the foot, the ankle and the knee. This is very important for soft landings after jumps from high positions! A wrong technique can be very hard on the joints. It is also crucial to achieve the best jump-off (and therefore height), as jumping power comes from the knee as well as the foot, if done correctly. Now let them throw their legs upwards, first with a loose kick in the air, then in a straight and pointed position. Make sure they breathe! A red face is a sign that the children forget to breathe, often because they concentrate so hard, which means in turn that they will get exhausted fast and are not relaxed as they should be.

You should basically go through a complete warm-up, touching every part of the body from head to neck, to shoulders, torso, hips, to legs and feet. If you teach your vaulters to take this part seriously, they will be able to do this warm-up by themselves after being shown a few times. If one of the parents does jazzercise, he or she might correct the children in the warm-up. Always make sure though that the vaulters do not arrive 'cold' and drop into the splits right away. Once a muscle gets pulled, your vaulter is off for several weeks and might not be fully 'usable' again for up to three months! Explain to them that this means letting the team down! Showing off is no part of the warm-up!

Keep in mind that the warm-up should not be used as the time for strenuous exercise to build up stamina. It makes no sense to let the vaulters run for half an hour, if this exhausts them to the point that they are then incapable of showing their best on the horse. The pre-vaulting warm-up should raise no more than a light sweat on the vaulter's forehead. The number of push-ups and chin-ups to build up strength, and the jogging to get heart and lungs into good condition, have to be done on a daily basis aside from your training.

Rolls and falls

If you have a mattress, get it out at this point. If not, try to get permission to use part of the ring (with soft ground) and spread carpet samples.

In the rolls and falls routine we try and get the 'protect your

Except for the hands, the shoulder should be the first part to touch the ground

head and roll into a small ball' instinct into the vaulters' system. Children who are able to learn early to do this *instinctively* will not get hurt in falls. Start with somersaults. Make sure they don't touch the ground with their heads — the exercise is to learn falling without *ever* hitting the ground with either neck or head! Check that their backs are properly rounded! Make them observe if they can *hear* the landing — if they do, it is too hard! Once they can do soft, comfortable and quick somersaults, let them do the same with a jump. Teach them to jump higher, coming down *gently* on their wrists (using *all* the muscles and joints involved in hands and arms!) and roll into a ball *before* touching the ground. Then do the same jumping *wide*. Put a rope onto the ground and increase the jump-off distance. (Please vary the distance of the rope for children of different size and ability! Never increase either height or distance for someone who still has hard and 'loud' landings!)

The long jump: the head may not touch the ground

The next step is to do somersaults without touching the ground with the hands. This sounds much more difficult than it actually is, so demonstrate it to them. Make them stoop in front of the mattress and bend their head to the side, hiding it in front of one shoulder (let them choose which side feels more comfortable to them. In this example let's say the left one). Make them pass the arm, of the *opposite* side of where the head lies (in my example

Somersault
without hands

the right one), in front of their stomach, protruding at the other
side (in my example the left side). Now tell them to imagine that
someone gives them a strong and sudden jerk on that hand —
which makes them fall and roll over their shoulder (the one
where the head does *not* lie, that is, in this example the right
one). Start with a small and low movement with a little hop.
Then increase the scope slowly, until your vaulters feel completely
comfortable in this exercise.

Another rolling exercise is developed out of the handstand.
Once your vaulters are balanced enough to hold a handstand for
one or two seconds, let them hold it until you clap your hand
and then contract very fast into a ball *before* touching the ground.
Spot them in the beginning; many a child will come down as
stiff as a plank! Lack of spatial orientation is a great factor in
potentially dangerous falls, and often children *think* they are
rounded, when indeed they are bent the opposite way! It is
important that the command to roll come unexpected, to train
the fast reaction you are aiming for. (I do the same in team kur
exercises: when I shout 'fall' they have to be able to simulate,
each person knowing exactly which way to go.)

The quick roll-off out
of the handstand

On the barrel

Now you will proceed to the stationary horse. I always start with some jumping exercises, where we emphasize the importance of using the foot as well as the knees for the jump–off, and the arm action and the timing, *when* the arms kick in. Exact technique of this will be described, when I explain the compulsories on the horse. Start by letting each child jump in front of the barrel, first with legs straight, then open, then both legs to the side, then either flanking over or squatting through. See illustrations for the sequence. If your barrel is approximately 4 feet (or 1.20 m) high, even your little 'flyers' (who will be approximately 1.25 to 1.30 m tall) can all easily squat *onto* it, if they are using the correct technique. Some can even flank over.

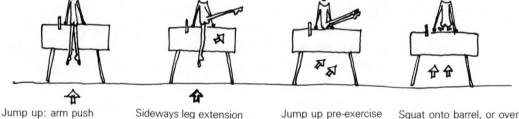

| Jump up: arm push | Sideways leg extension | Jump up pre-exercise for flank-over | Squat onto barrel, or over |

If you are lucky you possess a stationary horse, which resembles a horse somewhat in form . . . , and grips that are similar in shape and position to the ones of the real surcingle. You can also build a dummy horse, onto which you can strap your surcingle for practice. New vaulters should be able to learn the various grips and preliminary jump exercises, before they go onto the real horse to save 'horse-time'.

Apart from the energetic jump–off with both feet, the vaulter must learn also to use his arms correctly for a good mount. The aim is to fly up and land softly, with the vaulter's gravity point coming down directly over the gravity point of the horse, and in the right place behind the surcingle. The mount is described in

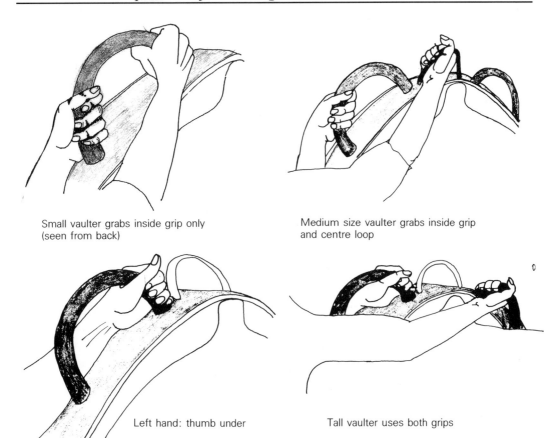

Small vaulter grabs inside grip only
(seen from back)

Medium size vaulter grabs inside grip
and centre loop

Left hand: thumb under

Tall vaulter uses both grips

detail under the compulsory exercises, but the way to grip the handles can greatly assist the vaulter in achieving a good mount.

See how the small vaulter in the illustration uses the elbow, and later the wrist, to push the upper body into the correct position. Please note that these drawings were done 'slow motion' and that the trick with the wrist should not be this visible! Taller vaulters grip both handles so they rely less on the wrist trick, because their outer arm can do more effective pulling. So the arms must do three things during the mount: the inner arm pushes, the outer arm pulls, and both arms give directional control, so the vaulter lands in the correct spot, right behind the surcingle.

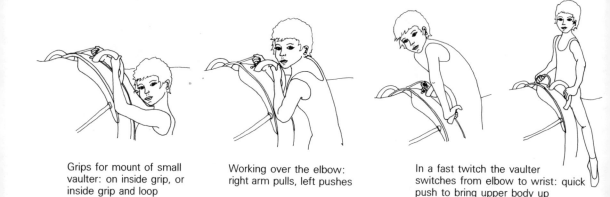

Grips for mount of small
vaulter: on inside grip, or
inside grip and loop

Working over the elbow:
right arm pulls, left pushes

In a fast twitch the vaulter
switches from elbow to wrist: quick
push to bring upper body up

Once on the horse, there are basically four ways of holding the grips, and no rules prescribing which ones the vaulter must use. Let your vaulter try out: depending on their strength they will choose what works best for them. Grip 1 is used for the seat and mill etc., grip 2 by many for scissors and flank. I usually advise the vaulters first to use the grips from below (palm up) for the swinging exercises, because it seems easier that way to most. Some vaulters grab the outside grip down low (as shown in 3) to flank off. Grip 4 is used on either side for various exercises, but mostly in the flank, or the backwards scissors (right palm up).

With beginners you will go through all the compulsory exercises on the barrel, where they have to work reasonably well,

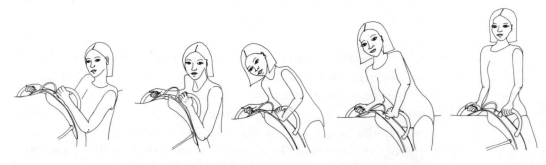

Work over your elbow and wrist: outer arm pulls, inner pushes

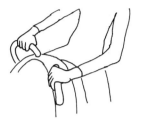
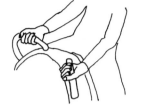

1 Gripping from the top   2 From the bottom   3 At bottom of outside grip   4 Any combination of 1 and 2

before being tried on the horse. See the chapter on compulsories for correct technique. With more advanced vaulters, you should always go through pre-flanking and pre-scissor exercises to warm up the arm muscles, regain the feel for the correct swing and prove control of those soft landings, without which these exercises should not be allowed on the live horse.

A very good exercise for swings on the barrel is the assisted swing into handstand with a partner. The vaulter goes into the swing as described under the vault-off, scissor and flank exercises, and a partner catches his up-swinging legs. He then pushes the partner into the handstand, who in turn needs strong armpush, good balance and good body tension to make it up there! The vaulter will learn from his nose-dives: more push-ups at home...

Typical 'nose plant'

Assisted swing to handstand

and how to find the balance point, where his gravity point is actually over his hands. Emphasize continued armpush, when coming down. This is how the vaulters learn soft landings. This is a very good exercise, which should work reasonably well on the barrel, before a beginning vaulter starts swinging on the horse.

When we get to the section on compulsory exercises I will explain in depth how to train for correct procedures. The basic skills in vaulting, namely balance, strong jump and soft landings can all be practised on the barrel to at least the extent that strong disturbance is spared to the horse, when you start trying it out 'for real'.

Arm control (crucial for soft landings on the horse and safety), spatial orientation, accurate timing, and correct technique for carrying of partners (see chapter on team kur exercises), should all be practised and explained on the stationary horse to a great extent, to save training time on the horse later.

The coordination of several vaulters and their individual timing as partners within a group exercise, and their communication with each other *while* in the exercise, is a crucial part of the barrel training. Coordination in case of a fall should be practised on the barrel for each high exercise. See chapter 23 on team kur exercises and 'bailing out'. Set different scenarios, which can be demonstrated on the barrel:

> what happens, in case the horse speeds up or spooks during the exercise? What will it feel like?
> which way will you fall?
> who should jump free and who should try to stay on? why?
> what happens if the horse stops?
> which way do you fall? why? should you get off? who first? etc.

In the 'kur' part of the book I will give some examples of how to train for falls out of particular high exercises. I think it is important for the mental attitude of the vaulters to consider the *fall an integral part* of each exercise. Expecting it means being prepared for the eventuality, and having practised it means avoiding broken bones, as well as being able to vault without fear or panic.

The last thing you train on the barrel is the flow of a complete performance. Teach your vaulters to save time on approaches, mounts, transitions and dismounts. The horse should never run 'empty'. Dismounts in a kur should be away from the next approaching vaulters, who should be mounting as soon as the last vaulter 'disconnects' from the horse. The vaulters and the trainer develop a feeling for the rhythm of their horse's canter stride (or you can use a metronome) and a show becomes much more predictable. The better your team gets, the more they will want to be sophisticated and perform to music, recorded particularly for this show (the mood: a Christmas Show is different from one designed for a Rodeo! The pace: mixture of walk— trot—canter, because you include your beginners, or all in canter for a top-notch performance with your best). Practising the flow of a performance on the barrel does not only save time on the horse and increase the discipline of the team, it is also valuable help for timing run-in and bows, warm-up canter round, performance and run-out for recording the music.

13 *Vaulting exercises — introduction*

We have mentioned before how important it is to plan your vaulting sessions with a great deal of variety. Therefore the following chapters do not suggest the *sequence* of exercises to practise. You will choose from them what is suitable to the expertise of your individual vaulters, always keeping in mind that minimal discomfort be caused to the horse, and maximum safety enforced for the children.

All exercises will first be trained on the barrel. The ones which *can* cause great discomfort to the horse (like scissors and flank) will be transferred to the live horse *only* when sufficient expertise is reached by the individual vaulter, so the horse will not be hurt by the typical beginners' mistakes. (Keep in mind *again* that your horse might decide to become 'unsuitable' for vaulting, if he gets too sorely tried!) You will train all exercises in walk first, then moving on to trot and canter.

Obviously some exercises can not be performed in walk, namely all the ones which are only possible by using the optimum momentum gained from the movement and speed of the cantering horse. Complicated roll-mounts, direct jumps into high positions and series of touchdowns and mounts are examples of this, but by the time your vaulters are good enough to worry about these, they are also good enough to train the necessary grips and hand changes on the barrel, make up for missing momentum by using a small trampoline, and then move directly onto the cantering horse.

As the trainer of a beginners' team you deal with different problems. In compulsories as well as in team kur exercises you want to teach correct technique — and that sometimes means quite a bit of talking! In walk, you have time for this. And of course the children feel safer trying out something new in walk first, before moving into trot or canter. The *amount* of verbal explanation you will use, will again depend on the age level, the understanding abilities and concentration span of your vaulters.

Some exercises are actually more difficult in trot than in canter, but I have always found that it is nevertheless better for the children's psychological attitude to let them proceed walk—trot—canter, because they *perceive* this as safer. The safer they *feel*, the safer they usually *are*.

If you are not a vaulter yourself, just consider this for better understanding of the difference the paces make to the vaulter:

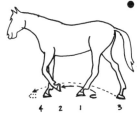

- *Walk*: is a four-beat rhythm. See the drawing for the sequence of hooves. If the horse is active and 'steps under' with his hind feet, the track of the hind hoof will step over and past the track of the front feet. The croup will then move in a more pronounced way than in canter. All exercises other than mounts are easy in walk. With more sensitive horses it is good to give the vaulters a leg-up, to prevent the horse from being thrown off balance by excessive hanging and crawling of the beginner. However the beginner has to get a chance to learn the correct jump-off and necessary hand changes on the grips, before he can try it in canter, so the horse will have to put up with a bit of this. Give the beginners a push though to minimize the discomfort of the horse by taking off some of the weight. Train mounts on the barrel (with a small trampoline if you have access to one) as much as possible.

- *Trot*: is a two-beat rhythm. Since the left front hoof moves with the right back one in an exactly parallel way, the horse's back is very even and straight. The vaulter has to deal only with one movement, namely up-down, which makes trot ideal for practising relaxed knees in the stand. The children get used to greater speed — an active trot is about as fast as a collected canter. The momentum gained for mounts is considerable, though it is harder to train the exact jump-off point for the best action quantum.

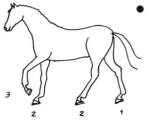

- *Canter*: is a three-beat rhythm. It is the only gait with a 'lead'. Vaulting needs an even canter, on the correct lead (that is, the left lead) where the horse balances himself on the curve of the circle. Hindquarters should be active and step under deeply, so the main weight of the vaulters is supported by them, and the back has an evenly swaying movement. Counter canter or disunited canter can not be tolerated for vaulting. Counter canter produces a 'staccato movement', because the horse is unbalanced around the corner. Disunited canter results in a 'wiggled' line along the horse's spine and a throwing movement, which makes it very hard to stand. (Your lunger must recognize and correct this immediately.)

In all paces, whether walk, trot or canter, the vaulter will pick up the same gait as the horse when approaching and mounting. Other paces, like amble and pace are not used in vaulting.

Compulsory exercises

Compulsory exercises form the ground work for vaulting, demanding the basic skills each vaulter must learn, before going on to more complex free-style movements. They are designed to show off balance, flexibility, jumping power and arm control as well as correct sense of timing in the swing exercises.

You will try to train all of these exercises 'whole—part—whole'. This means that after the introduction (and perhaps demonstration) of the whole exercise you'll take it apart into its components and train those separately. After the individual parts are well understood and the underlying technique is grasped you will re-assemble them and practise the complete exercise. The reason a trainer arranges it this way is that the vaulter can not retain and concentrate on more than two or three things at one time at the most.

The six prescribed compulsories consist of a mix of static and dynamic exercises:

● *Static compulsory exercises*: The seat, the flag and the stand are static. This means the exercises must be fully balanced and held in a quiet pose for four canter strides. It also means that excessive swinging motions to get *into* those exercises are usually seen as a minus point by the judges.

● *Dynamic compulsory exercises*: The mill, the scissors and the flank are dynamic exercises, that is, they consist of motion. Here the maximum action quantum must be used to achieve speed, height and push-off power. Timing is essential in dynamic exercises. Accuracy and arm strength are necessary. However, many vaulters, especially strong males, have a tendency to overdo the strength factor by stopping at the high point, which for them equals the position of the handstand. This is *not* the purpose of a dynamic exercise and will not get the highest scores! Although extreme scope (i.e. height) is rewarded in an exercise, the movement of a dynamic one must be fluid and continuous.

● *One and two-phase exercises*: The compulsory exercises can be grouped into one and two-phase exercises: the seat, the flag, the mill and the stand are one-phase, that is, they are fully performed in one go without pause. The scissors and the flank consist of two parts, and the time spent preparing for the second phase is not specified in the rules. However, the less time is wasted in *any* in-between phases (which also applies to time spent between mount and exercise, or finished exercise and dismount etc.), the better the scores will be (*if* the exercise is performed correctly).

● *Prescibed dismounts: basic dismount and vault-off*: Compulsory exercises have prescribed dismounts, of which there are two: the 'basic' dismount and the 'vault-off'. The exercises in the first block of the compulsories, consisting of basic seat, flag and mill, all are followed by the 'basic dismount', if performed individually. The ones of the second block, the scissors, stand and flank, are followed by the 'vault-off' dismount. In practice sessions the trainer should always adhere to this rule in order to minimize confusion of junior vaulters. In none of the compulsory exercises may the vaulter have contact in other places than the grips. It is a good idea to include this consistently in the training, as bad habits (even if they are friendly: like patting the horse from the backward seat in the scissors) are so hard to get rid of! If your vaulters get used to patting the horse *during* a compulsory exercise, they will have the tendency to do the same during a competition and lose points this way.

- *Consideration of the horse*: In *all* vaulting exercises consideration must be shown to the horse. The trainer must insist that all exercises, starting with the compulsories, be practised in a fashion that any movement, and particularly landings on the horse's back after high swings, are soft. S/he must insist that vaulters stand in the correct spots on the horse's back and don't hurt him in the sensitive kidney area. Vaulters should understand the basic make-up of the horse's body, where sensitive organs are, what the skeleton looks like, and where important muscles are located.

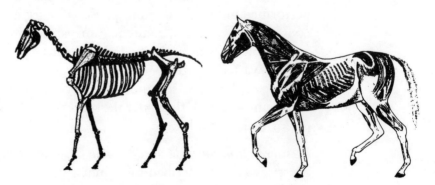

Where is the elbow?
Where is the knee?

Which muscles do we
need to develop for vaulting?

Which sensitive areas
must we avoid?

Before starting *any* exercise on the horse, ensure that he is properly warmed up (as well as your vaulters) on the opposite (the right) lead for at least ten minutes, or until you can see that the horse relaxes along his back and is quiet and prepared in his mood. Check that the equipment is fitted correctly, and sensitive spots protected. In particular make sure that the buckles of the girth do not rub behind the legs and that the withers are covered with some padding under the surcingle. Use only equipment permitted by the rules, excepting different side reins as discussed in chapter 7. Make the vaulters check all these things *with* you, as the horse is their team mate and they carry responsibility for his well-being if they want to use him. If using regular side reins, adjust them to the correct length on both sides, when you turn the horse onto the left lead after warming up. Before the first vaulters go on, ensure that the surcingle is tightened. If vaulters get caught with their feet in the stirrups and the surcingle is starting to turn on the horse, very nasty situations can ensue, where they get dragged under the horse without being able to free themselves.

Now you are ready to start!

14 The compulsory exercises

Compulsory exercises are important for two reasons:

> Through them the vaulter learns the basic prerequisites of good jump, good balance, good swing, good arm work and timing.

> In competitions they provide the judges with a show of performance, evenly measurable and easily comparable for all vaulters of those basic prerequisites for good vaulting.

This does *not* mean that the compulsories are easier or less important than the freestyle exercises. They are the important ground work for all else to follow. It is quite intricate to teach correct technique, and in the description I will mention the things you should in my opinion emphasize at the various stages of your vaulters' development and according to their age and understanding.

Although we here discuss the compulsories mainly in the context of competition, they can't be undervalued, even if you only train your vaulters for show. There are no team exercises where you can disregard a good balanced seat (as practised in the basic seat and mill), a good balanced kneel or stand (as practised in the flag and stand), or well cantered swinging exercises (as in the scissors and flank). The vaulters must learn the correct posture and body control, the timing and balance for all other exercises and a good way to see the progress, is to practise the basics in the compulsories. So the argument that a vaulter does not have to bother with them, since he does not want to compete anyhow, is totally pointless.

In competitions the compulsories carry a lot of weight. Also, for two teams achieving the same end result in marks in a competition, the higher scores in the compulsories decide the winner. The sooner 'your vaulters learn to 'respect' the importance of training for the compulsories, which are always perceived as less fun than the team exercises, the better for the team results in the end.

There are six compulsory exercises in vaulting:

the basic seat ⎫
the flag   ⎬ block 1
the mill   ⎭
the scissors ⎫
the stand   ⎬ block 2
the flank   ⎭

Some countries now offer an easier version of compulsories for the beginner divisions in local or national competition. These are then parts or pre-exercises to the full compulsories (and are discussed in this book as such) like: a free kneel rather than a stand, a series of leg swings over the neck rather than a full mill with backward seat, and pre-swings with consequent vault-off rather than a full flank. Often the scissors are omitted altogether for beginners, as the combination of swing, push, rotation and crossing of legs is a very complex movement. Consult your vaulting association on what is expected of your beginners in which area.

Depending on which competition your vaulters are starting in, these exercises are performed in one go-through or two blocks, and if you plan to go into a competition, they must be trained in that sequence. In team competitions, each vaulter must perform the first block − basic seat, flag and mill − and then dismount (via leg over the front, which will hereafter be called 'basic dismount'). After the last vaulter of the team finishes, the first vaulter will begin with block two, performing scissors, stand and flank. And so on to the last vaulter. In individual competitions, both blocks are performed together, with a touch–down after the mill and direct re–mount into the next exercise, the scissors.

Scores

All exercises will be scored in competitions on a scale from 1 to 10 (including the freestyle exercises, individual as well as *pas-de-deux* and team). These marks mean:

10 excellent	5 sufficient	0 not executed
9 very good	4 insufficient	
8 good	3 fairly bad	
7 fairly good	2 bad	
6 satisfactory	1 very bad	

and the words are somewhat misleading. You get a better idea by considering this: there are internationally three categories of performance, and here we are talking about vaulters who of course perform all exercises in canter:

C category   vaulter (or a team), who has reached the average mark of 5.0 not more than once per year in a recognized competition.

B category   vaulter (or team), who has reached the average mark of 5.0 at least twice per year, but 6.5 not yet twice.

A category   vaulter (or team), who has reached the average mark of 6.5 at least twice a year.

The major considerations in the evaluation of each compulsory exercise are the following seven points:

(1) *Mechanics*: the way to get into, and execute (dynamic) or hold (static) the exercise, and terminate the motion correctly (getting out of), that is, correct position and arrangement of

body parts to fulfil the criteria of an exercise as defined and prescribed. For example: height in the scissors is *not* mechanics, but not truly exercising the scissoring motion or turning the pelvis *is* a matter of mechanics. Under the new rules a basic score is given for the mechanics in each compulsory exercise. This means that even if the 'performance' (the execution) is one hundred per cent wonderful, the mark can not go higher than this basic score given. From this basic score points are then deducted for all other faults. In the discussion of each compulsory exercise it will be explained which faults are 'mechanic' and how they get penalized.

The most important criterion for good mechanics is the correct alignment of gravity point: gravity point is the alpha and omega of balance and control, and equally important in static and dynamic exercises, in compulsories and team kur configurations. If the vaulter's gravity point is misaligned in regard to the horse (taking into account the horse's bending on the circle), and to the speed (centrifugal force) *and* within himself, he will lose balance. This either means a fall or, more often, a hard landing on the horse; it means throwing the horse off balance or pushing your team mates off his back!

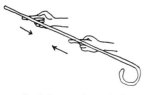

Find the gravity point!

Smaller children especially have no concept of gravity: explain it to them. Tell them, it is the *one* point in their middle, where they are *heaviest* and then let them find out, where that point is. Take any long object and place it over two out-stretched fingers held apart. Move the fingers toward each other, keeping the object balanced. Where the fingers meet without the object falling off, *that* is the location of the gravity point of that object. (Choosing an irregular object, so the gravity point does *not* lie in the middle, makes the point clearer!) Now move to the 'human object' with the exercise we call 'the killer'... demonstrate if you can. Let the vaulters grip as shown in the illustration and slide their legs from a kneel position with pointed toes to the back of the barrel. Elbows must be kept together, knees lift off and the weight is slowly shifted to the front. The legs become fully stretched, and will lift off the barrel as soon as all the weight is transferred to the arms of the vaulter. Note that your gravity point is always *much further behind your shoulders* than you might think. I tell my vaulters that although they wish their brain might be the heaviest part of their body it is usually their posterior... It is essential for good vaulting to understand this sad truth!

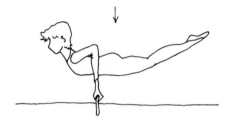

Wrong: alignment too far back, vaulter tries to correct through arching the back

The perfect 'killer'! Gravity point is in the middle of the body

(2) *Essence*: the prerequisite skills without which the exercise can't be properly executed (like sense of balance, flexibility etc.) are matters of essence. They are to be tested. What are we trying to show or prove? Essence expresses the *intent* of the exercise.

(3) *Form*: posture and stretch and straightness of the body, limbs and extremities. Correct position of hands, feet, head.

(4) *Scope*: elevation, width, amplitude of movement (dynamic exercises). In other words: how high can the vaulter lift the leg in the mill? How high can he clear the horse in the swing of the scissors? How high and wide is the flight phase in the flank?

(5) *Difficulty*: of execution, meaning the degree to which the vaulter takes on risks, in order to heighten scope and elegance. For example: is he standing very tall with feet close together, rather than broad-legged and more secure? Is he bringing out leg and arm together to go into the flag, or does he establish safe balance first, before letting the hand go?

(6) *Security*: and balance, shows the level of proficiency of the vaulter's performance. (This applies more to freestyle as the vaulter is not given a choice in the compulsories. In the kur, the vaulter can choose between a more or less secure version of an exercise.)

(7) *Consideration*: meaning soft landings on the horse out of any position in particular, and generally the minimum disturbance to the horse (canter rhythm, throwing horse off balance etc.)

Compulsory and freestyle exercises may be scored in 1/10th of a mark.

Mounts as well as dismounts are counted into the exercises (where applicable). For example: the first mount traditionally counts for forty to fifty per cent of the score for the basic seat. When compulsories are performed in one go-through (as in individual competitions), the touch-down and immediate re-mount count into the *next* exercise, that is, the scissors. And so on.

The next chapters will take you through the compulsory exercises in detail, including approach, mounts and dismounts, and are broken down into phases for more clarity.

15 Approach to the horse and mount

Correct approach and mount are part of the first compulsory exercise of each block, or of each exercise, if performed individually. They are marked into the exercises and therefore very important. The trainer should never let sloppiness pass in approach, mounts and dismounts, but rather explain that the vaulter's 'job' starts with the approach and ends with the running out after the dismount. The basic things in vaulting as well as the whole attitude of your vaulters toward their own performance can not be expected to change three weeks before a competition, but rather must be so familiar to your vaulters that they execute them correctly without thinking about them. In a competition or show they have so many other things to think of! And especially your smaller vaulters will not be able to retain more than three important points in their memory under the pressure or excitement of a show. As the driver of a car must be expected to step on the brakes as a reflex from eye to foot in case of an emergency, bypassing a complicated thinking process, so the vaulter must put his best into each mount, point his toes always, and assume correct seat position in between exercises as a matter of second nature.

With inexperienced horses keep the whip down when 'opening the gate'

The approach

The approach sets the tone for a correct mount. And a wrong approach can set your horse off at a speed, so the vaulter may never catch up with it and get a chance to mount... We mentioned before how the lunger 'opens the gate' to let the vaulter pass. The vaulter then approaches the horse along the lunge line, in the same gait as the horse. The vaulter must never approach from the back. First of all, there is a chance of getting side-kicked by the horse's hind leg, but this is usually also an effect of the following: The horse is a 'flight animal', and this means that anything which seems dangerous or insecure to him will set him running. A vaulter approaching from the back can't be clearly seen by the horse; he might just catch a glimpse of him from the corner of his eye. This can spook him! Also the way from the back is longer, and smaller vaulters will never catch up with the horse that way!

The vaulter's shoulders must face the same way as the shoulders of the horse. This means that the vaulter does not aim straight for the surcingle, but runs *with* the horse *while* approaching. Head is erect and eyes to the front. Emphasize erect and elegant posture (back straight, head up, chest out, shoulders back and down) and correct arm position in the approach. The vaulter's arms should be held calmly, yet not in a stiff line along the body, but rather swing in a natural movement with the motion of walking or running. Excessive waving of the arms during the approach irritates the horse.

Correct approach to the horse: vaulter is on the same lead and in step with the horse, facing the direction of travel. Approach sideways in direction of horse's shoulder, arms in natural running position, head erect

Vaulter reaches for the grips without exaggerated or showy arm movements

Incorrect approach: vaulter does not run along lungeline, but approaches too far back. Arms are 'fishing' for the grips

Once at the side of the horse, the vaulter should not 'fish' for the grips by extending the arms too early. It should not look as

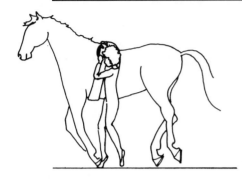

Correct position next to the horse

if the arms are pulling the vaulter toward the horse once the hands are on the grips; rather the vaulter should be perfectly balanced within himself until in the right position for the jump-off. The hands touch the grips when the vaulter has reached the horse with his whole body (not leaning with the torso), i.e. runs along with his shoulders parallel to, and his right side nearly touching the horse. In canter, as the horse must be on the correct lead, so does the vaulter. 'Flying changes' should not occur in the vaulter's approach! It manifests confusion about which foot to jump off on, and can become a nasty habit.

Correct position next to the horse

Correct position before jump-off is *next* to the surcingle, *not* a foot behind! Beginners have a great tendency to run either too far *away* (toward the centre of the circle) from the horse, or too far *back* — or both! One reason for this may be the inborn caution to keep their feet away from the hoof in front of them. Point out that *if* they canter along on the correct lead and with the correct rhythm, they will not be in the position to get stepped on, as their feet always stay parallel with the hooves, and out of their way.

Incorrect approach: vaulter aims straight for the surcingle, facing the horse

Incorrect approach: vaulter is on the wrong lead, with stiff posture of arms in the wrong sequence

In the illustrations of the mounting sequence I have tried to show how the wrong position *before* the jump-off *necessarily* leads into a whole series of wrong moves, so that the mount *must* collapse. And will!

Taking hold of the grips

Once the vaulter has almost reached this position right next to the horse, the arms swing up and the vaulter touches the grips (at this point the judges' stop watches start running, when exercises are timed). There are three 'height adjustments' possible to mount: small vaulters will grab the inside (that is the left) grip with both hands (right hand higher than the left), medium height youngsters might use the leather loop between the grips for their right hand to hold on to, and tall vaulters can reach both grips with both hands respectively (see illustrations in chapter 12 'preparation before vaulting').

Correct jump-off point

If the vaulter's body is positioned right next to the surcingle, the jump-off point lies almost a *full foot* ahead of the body position. Train them to do this correctly even in walk, where it is hard to feel *why* this is correct, as you do not get the benefit of any momentum. But in canter it is obvious: the horse moves quickly and the vaulter's body needs a certain time to 'fly' up, before coming down in the seat. During this 'flying' time, the horse does not wait for you! If the vaulter jumps off *ahead* of the horse's movement, s/he will reach the highest point *above* the horse at the point in time, when the horse has advanced just the distance which the vaulter had gained by 'getting ahead', so s/he is *again* lined up correctly at the surcingle, which means s/he can then land *right behind* the surcingle and sit in the prescribed spot, without any seat corrections.

The correct mount

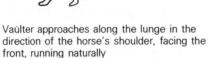

Vaulter approaches along the lunge in the direction of the horse's shoulder, facing the front, running naturally

Vaulter falls back very slightly when reaching the horse to arrive at the height of the surcingle

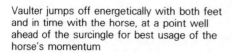

Vaulter jumps off energetically with both feet and in time with the horse, at a point well ahead of the surcingle for best usage of the horse's momentum

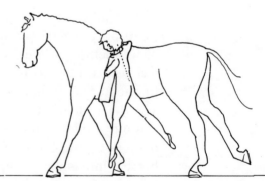

After jump-off, the vaulter immediately spreads his legs, the left leg stays extended to the ground and hips face the front

Vaulter reaches for the grips without exaggerated or showy arm movements

Vaulter finds himself next to the surcingle after taking hold of the grips

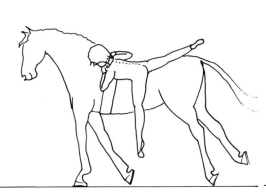

In order for the right leg to achieve maximum height, the head and upper body of the vaulter must stay down

The vaulter starts pushing with the arms

As the horse enters its flight phase of the canter stride, the vaulter reaches his optimum height

Depending on the flexibility and strength of the vaulter, the mount may reach handstand height, but the left leg stays down and fluid movement may not stop

As the vaulter's leg comes down, his upper body comes up. The arms push to assure soft landing, and also direct the vaulter (via pull)...

...into the correct landing spot, directly behind the surcingle

Gravity point must be over the vaulter's hands and straight body line (long spine) maintained...

...regardless of the elevation, which the vaulter can reach

Gravity point of the vaulter must stay over the grips throughout

The correct spot for the basic seat

A typical *incorrect* mount

Vaulter approaches too far back, 'behind the horse's movement'. Apart from the possibility of getting kicked, the vaulter has lost his chance of getting his gravity point over...

...his hands, as the horse is progressing forward. The vaulter gets dragged along, which makes for a very ineffective jump-off on one foot

The vaulter 'jack-knifes' the upper body, pulling his head and shoulders to the outside in an effort to catch up with the horse. All fluidity of movement is blocked

The vaulter must pull himself toward the surcingle

Height can't be achieved like this! The vaulter is clinging and pulling in the attempt to avoid sliding back down. There is no gain from...

...the horse's momentum. This can last as long as it takes the vaulter to crawl on, so nothing is in time with the horse's canter stride any more

Considerable seat corrections are necessary, before he can...

...settle into the correct basic seat position

General mount mistakes

Wrong: although jump-off technique is correct and hips achieve good height, the piked body position barely lets the vaulter clear the croup with the outside foot

Wrong: vaulter does not leave his shoulders down to achieve straight body line, but achieves height with leg by overarching a very flexible back

Wrong: vaulter's gravity point is not over his hands: the arm push will have a backward effect, rather than up, so the arms can't break the body's fall when coming down...

...so he will land hard and too far back

Most frequent mount mistake: the vaulter brings head and shoulders up and over first, which results in a twisted body position and 'jack-knifing'. Only extremely flexible vaulters would ever achieve any height with this wrong technique

Wrong: hips, shoulders and head are turning 'into' the horse after jump-off

The jump itself

The jump consists of a combination of best use of the momentum from the horse's movement (best technique) and the muscular strength of the vaulter. The easier it looks, the better the marks get! But the jump-off has to be energetic and must use feet, ankles and knees for best push-off. For best momentum to be gained, the vaulter must jump off in the moment just before the horse's inner front leg lifts off. At the moment of the jump off, the vaulter is actually leaning back a little, because his feet are aiming to jump off in front of the surcingle.

Beginners have a tendency to demonstrate the effort they are making by jumping a hole into the ground, rather than putting that energy into a lift-off. 'Jump harder' is no useful comment in those cases, as they *are* jumping as hard as they can (but in the wrong direction: down — instead of up). Many waste a great deal of energy in useless 'pre-jumps', hopping alongside the horse in a succession of jumps without results. In beginners this is natural and expresses their indecision (the next moment might be the better one for jump-off) as well as lack of concentration. With older children you can explain the technique, with little ones *always* make them count: 1−2−3−*hop*, and emphasize that the 1−2−3 are *running* steps. (This counting is *so* important later in assisted mounts and other coordinated team exercises.)

Make them jump in the warm-up in the following manner: let them jump into the air as high as they can without arm swing out of a semi-crouched position. This will teach them to use the take-off power they potentially have in their ankles and the ball of the foot as well as in the knees. Then let them do a series of hops, also just from their feet. Apart from the jump, this is a necessary skill for soft landings after dismounts from high positions.

The lift-off

As the body lifts off, the legs immediately separate and the vaulter lowers his head over the horse's inside shoulder, while the shoulders of the vaulter stay approximately at the height of the surcingle. The vaulter's seat should fly as high as possible into the air, but the inside leg (left) stays pointing to the ground – knee fully extended and foot and toe pointed. The higher the vaulter swings his right leg, the more height he can gain in the hips. If the head does not go down, the hips will not reach best possible height.

As soon as the right foot swings up, the vaulter transfers his weight to his arms and pushes to achieve best height over the horse's back. The buttocks must definitely reach greater height than the shoulders of the vaulter.

The weaker the jump-off (of the beginner vaulter for example), the more important it is that the arms are used in the most effective way to assist in the mount. If it could be seen in slow motion, the arm action could be described in three phases: in the lowest phase of the lift-off, the right arm does most of the work: pulling. Then the inner arm (left) starts pushing by working over the elbow, while of course the outer arm continues pulling. As the upper body comes up, the inner arm also lifts up and the arm action changes mostly to the wrist, to extend the arm as much as possible as the torso straightens into the seat position. Small vaulters with a good mount rely on this wrist action a lot, as they usually do not perform a hand change to the outer grip, but rather fly into the seat position, straightening the upper body by wrist action of the inner arm only. Small beginners, who still 'cling' to the horse during their mount, will have to perform a hand change from inner grip or middle loop to outer grip to rely on both arms, the pulling *and* the pushing one, more evenly – otherwise they slide down again, before the right leg can 'hook' over the back of the horse.

With very strong arms (older male vaulters mainly) another increase in height can be reached in the mount after the lift-off and maximum extension of right leg, as shown in the drawing. Many such vaulters mount directly over the handstand: as impressive as this looks, and with all the power this proves, it has no place in the compulsories. The rules state clearly that the 'right leg nearly approach [es] the vertical, as his left leg stretches down towards the ground'. The kick-in of the arm push however is necessary in any case, because as soon as the vaulter has reached his or her highest point in the air, the downward movement starts, and with it, s/he has to get ready for landing...

Let's pretend our vaulter now comes down from airy heights in slow motion: as his right leg swings down on the outside of the horse, and before his seat touches the blanket or back of the horse, the arm action must start to bring the torso up. The torso must be lifted into the vertical position in a *smooth* continuation of the movement of the legs swinging down.

The arm action

The outside (right) arm will pull the vaulter into the correct sitting position behind the surcingle, while the inside arm gives a push to continue moving up the torso (which needs to come up now, as the hips swing down. We are basically striving for a straight body line throughout the exercise). The lifting of the upper body should be a 'smooth continuation of the vault-on, which ends in the seat astride', and that means a lot of arm control. By landing in the seat we mean landing in the *exact and correct position*, that is, the tailbone of the vaulter over the spine of the horse (not right or left of it) and about one hand's width behind the surcingle (not one foot behind!) The legs and feet must also land in the correct position for the basic seat. No weight shifts or seat corrections should be visible after the landing.

The strong arm action is necessary to ensure a *soft* landing on the horse's back. The highest jump is no good, when the vaulter comes down like a ton of bricks. And your horse will start bucking immediately after the first mount, if he has his senses about him — so much for your show or competition! Teach your vaulters to 'work over their inner elbow'. Let them grip the surcingle as shown in the illustration with their inside (left) hand, thumb *under* the grip from the front and the other fingers over top, on the top part of the inside grip. Like this the elbow lies aligned with the surcingle and can help in the push-off, when the torso has to swing up. Wrist action also helps: when the torso is half way up the inner arm starts pushing out of the wrist, because now the torso is already so high that the elbow does not touch the leather any more. Small vaulters, who grab the inside grip with both hands, rely on wrist action more than on the elbow. Their right hand also does more pushing than pulling, as it still is on the inside grip as well. Small vaulters with a good jump-off do not need to switch the right hand to the outside grip until the mount is actually completed. They do all the necessary pushing action from the inside handle.

Correct timing of the arm action in the mount is hard to teach and most vaulters find it out through repetition and practice rather than through explanations. You also can't pin down the exact moment when the arms have to kick in, as that point changes depending on the height of the jump. However it is clear that the vaulter can't exert arm control, if he does not shift his weight (his gravity point) over his hands. Many new vaulters do not understand that the arms do as much work in a good mount as the legs.

With a normal height jump-off the inner arm will do more pushing to assist the torso in swinging up, and the outer arm will assume (along with the pushing) more of the directional control: some pulling in toward the surcingle to assure correct landing position. But the higher the jump becomes, the more pushing the outer arm does, rather than pulling, because the body has more time (during a higher flight) to align itself with the centre line of the horse's body. World champions do the mount over a complete high vertical with arms fully extended. This position should however not be *held* as such. The motion, no matter how high the mount ends up to be, should not be arrested, but be one flowing and continuous movement from beginning to end. Remember: there should be no *stops* in a dynamic exercise!

Directly after the landing the vaulter should immediately check himself for correct seat position, before going into the exercise itself. Especially beginners should take a deep breath here (concentration on a good mount usually takes their breath away...), put their legs to the horse, achieving the correct 'wrap', point their toes, and set their mind for what is to come.

Common mistakes

- *In the approach*: vaulter approaches toward the hindquarters of the horse rather than along the lunge. *Danger*: of getting kicked in the approach by spooking the horse through an approach which he can't clearly see. *Danger*: vaulter falls behind the movement and may never catch up with the horse.

- Shoulders are turned toward the horse, rather than parallel with the horse's shoulders and aligned with the direction of travel. *Danger*: in case of a stumble the vaulter will get twisted into a backward position and will fall.

- Vaulter 'fishes' for the grips, and/or leans the torso toward the horse; vaulter does 'flying changes' out of indecision over the jump-off foot; vaulter runs on the wrong lead; vaulter holds arms (or neck) stiff.

- *At surcingle*: vaulter runs too far away from, or too far back from the surcingle; vaulter twists body.

- *Jump-off*: foot position in jump-off too far back, vaulter is 'behind the movement'; vaulter jumps *into* the ground, rather than *away* and up from it; vaulter does useless and wasteful pre-jumps; vaulter separates legs at jump-off, rather than jumping off forcefully on *both* feet and *then* separating the legs; vaulter does not use *all* the joints necessary for good and efficient jump.

- *Flight phase*: vaulter separates legs too late (if right leg does not 'open', it can not fly up and over); vaulter is too far back with legs. *Danger*: ramming his knees or feet into horse's kidneys, causing great disturbance to horse, resulting in bucks.

- Vaulter has no arm power and lies on the horse, no height achieved; vaulter slips back down, because insufficient height is achieved. Here especially beginners, who have the tendency to cling, rather than separating from the horse, when called for, may twist their upper body and end up touching the ground in a backward position. *Danger*: this results in the vaulter being dragged under the horse, in particular when the vaulter only lets go at the very last moment. Never allow your vaulters to cling this way. If a mount fails, they must bring their legs back down quickly and actively jump away from the horse.

- Vaulter keeps head and shoulders up.

- *Landing*: vaulter 'jackknifes', moves head to outside shoulder of the horse in an effort to crawl over to the right side. Most beginners feel that if the head is up, half the battle is won! Explain to them that they are up when their heaviest part is up — which in most cases is the bum, not the brain... By jackknifing, he blocks his own movement by his right arm. A very bad habit, which must be trained *out* of him right away! Hard landing: vaulter slams down on horse, no arm control; vaulter lands too far back and needs strong positional corrections; vaulter's legs are down, but torso does not come up.

16 *The basic seat*

The exercise of the basic seat consists of the mount, discussed in the last chapter, the seat itself and the basic dismount (if performed outside the block), which will be described in the next chapter. Train your vaulters to understand this sequence as a *whole* right from the start.

As mentioned before, the judges traditionally count the mount into this exercise with about forty to fifty per cent. The exercise of the seat itself is mainly judged according to mechanics (the way to execute the motions) and essence (suppleness, elegant posture).

In the basic seat the vaulter must be able to show balance and suppleness (especially in the waist and the hips), to pick up the motion of the canter stride while holding the upper body still (not stiff!) at the same time. It is of course a static exercise, and must therefore be held for four full canter strides. The judges start counting the strides, when the exercise is *fully built up*. It is very important to teach your vaulters this concept, otherwise they will lose points in competitions.

'Sitting' on the horse sounds like such an easy thing for a vaulter, but nevertheless even the best most often do not achieve the best scores in this exercise. In order to understand what is mechanically correct in the seat, one must understand a bit what we sit on.

Basic score

The judge will give a basic score of not more than 4.0 for an extreme 'fork seat' and of not more than 5.0 for an extreme 'chair seat' from which then all the other performance faults are deducted. In order to understand what the judges are seeing here, we must first have a look at the bones which we are sitting on. There are often great misunderstandings when we say 'seat bones'. The lower part of the seat bones is formed like a runner on a sled or on a rocking chair, and the pelvis can tilt around an axle point to accommodate various movements from standing to sitting. The leg rotates around the hip joint and the lower part of the spine curves more or less, according to the position of the other body parts.

The ideal basic seat will distribute the weight more or less onto the middle part of the seat bone 'runner'. In the illustration you can see how the pelvis tilts with the upper leg stretching down – this is of course the position of the leg which we are striving with to achieve the correct alignment of 'head-hip-heel'. So if the back is held straight and the knee pushed down to make a 'long leg', the weight will end up on the right part of the 'runners'! If the upper leg is pulled up, the pelvis will tilt back, and in the 'extreme chair seat' the vaulter will 'fall off' his seat bones and end up by sitting mainly on his buttock muscles. In the 'extreme fork seat' the vaulter tilts off the front part of the 'runners' and ends up supporting his weight on the inside of his thighs, rather than the seat bones. Both positions are very wrong – and make it hard to balance correctly in a seat position.

In the correct seat the vaulter will slightly rock forward and backward on these 'runners', as his pelvis follows and absorbs the movement of the horse's canter stride. (This applies of course just the same in walk and trot.) As the weight must remain on the seat bones, there will be no extreme movements to either front or back, and therefore also no extreme curvature of the spine either way. The legs must be extended down as far and as long as possible, turned slightly outward at the hip to correctly 'wrap' the horse's belly. They should be turned out as little as possible, to allow the feet still to be positioned in a forward direction: the top of the foot should show to the front and the

Seat bones: correct alignment in the basic seat

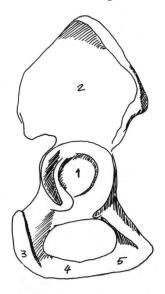

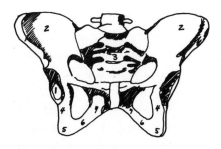

1 socket of hip bone
2 haunch bone
3 front of seat bone
4 seat bone (lower branch) 6 to 8 cm long
5 back of seat bone

Pelvis from the front

1 hip bone sockets
2 haunch bones
3 os sacrum (tail bone)
4 upper branch of seat bone
5 front of seat bone
6 lower branch of seat bone
7 back of seat bone

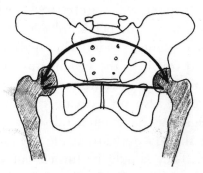

Distribution of weight in a standing body: over hip bone sockets into the legs

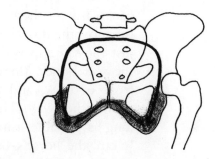

Distribution of weight in a sitting body: over the sacrum into the seat bones

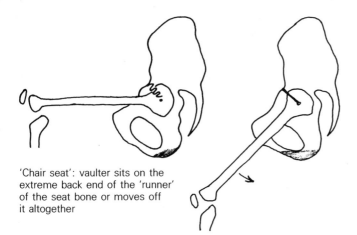

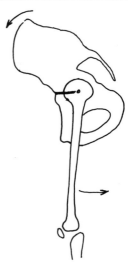

'Chair seat': vaulter sits on the extreme back end of the 'runner' of the seat bone or moves off it altogether

By pushing the knees down, the pelvis will tilt to distribute the weight more over the centre of the seat bone

Knee all the way down: vaulter sits on the front of the seat bone. If he tilts off it altogether, the weight rests on the upper legs only: 'fork' seat

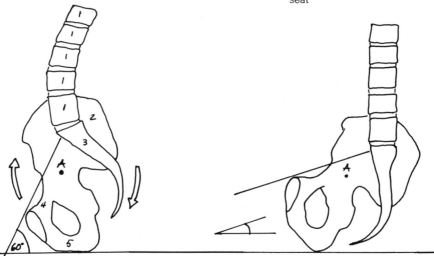

Normal position of pelvis in standing body

1 lumbar vertebrae
2 haunch bones
3 sacrum (tail bone)
4 upper branch seat bone
5 lower branch seat bone

Position of pelvis of sitting body A: axle around which we can tilt the pelvis

heels to the back. The inner seat bone will take on a bit more weight than the outer, to make up for the horse's curvature on the circle, so watch that the vaulters do not pull up the inner leg. This is a typical beginner mistake, in which the vaulter clings with his inner leg to counteract centrifugal force, rather than 'balancing', which means distributing his weight correctly (putting more weight on the inner seat bone) to remain with his gravity point aligned directly over the horse's centre line.

The correct position for the buttocks is as directly behind the surcingle as possible, without the knees hiding the sides of it. The toes must point down, the heel to the back. This means that the seat is positioned approximately one hand's width behind the surcingle. The back must be straight, neither slouching nor hollow, overemphasizing any pelvic tilt. The alignment seen from the side is basically the same as in riding: a vertical line runs from the head, through shoulder and hip to the heel. Seen from the front the vaulter must be centred on the spine of the horse, without any kinks in the hip.

The legs touch the horse's belly lightly (not clinging!) but stay in contact constantly and in the same spot. The legs may not swish along the horse in the rhythm of the canter stride. It is *only* the pelvis, which rocks with the canter movement. Many other-wise very flexible people are very stiff in their pelvis — tell them to belly dance at home... If the pelvis absorbs the movement correctly, the upper body will be perfectly still, pony tails will hang limply, legs will be quietly resting in one place and shoulders and head will move around on a circle like on a record player. You should be able to position a glass of water on the vaulter's head and not lose a drop. The only problem is to get the water up there in the first place!

As boring as little vaulters find these sitting exercises, as important they are for the understanding of the concept of balance. If the movement of the horse is not absorbed (and this by the joints closest to the contact: the pelvis in the seat, ankles and knees in the stand, wrists and elbows in the handstand), the vaulter will bounce, and start sliding to one side or the other. This in turn will throw the horse off-balance, who will then start falling out of rhythm and cramp his back muscles! Which in turn will throw the vaulter off even more and get bouncier...and so on. Make it clear to your vaulters that the horse must counter-balance each of their mistakes as well — that in fact two living beings are balancing together to make a perfect vaulting exercise work.

The seat is considered fully built up when the arms and hands have reached the prescribed position. The hands should rise in a direct line from their position on the grips to the end position, which is at eye level and square with the shoulders. Arms are extended outward in a straight line (elbow, hand), the hand with fingers together and palm facing down. Arms, neck and shoulders should be stretched elastically, not rigidly. This means that although the hands are held up, the shoulders must stay back and down in a relaxed manner, making the neck long. Right and left arm and hand should be at the same height, seen from front and back.

The highest level for the hands you should ever permit your vaulters is that of the top of the head, the lowest at shoulder height. Correct height is eye level and the face should look straight ahead, eyes parallel to the ground. Don't tell your young vaulters to 'keep their chin up', as they then often kink their neck to stick the chin out. The image should rather be that someone has a fish-hook in the crown of their head and is pulling them up to the ceiling. That way they will look straight ahead and the chin will be in the correct position with a long, straight neck.

After holding the exercise for at least four complete canter strides (five is better than three and a half, so the judges have no doubt about the count), the arms are taken down back to the grips, again in a direct line. If the compulsories are not performed in a block, the basic dismount is then begun without wasting time.

The basic seat

Correct alignment: vertical line from head through shoulder, hip and heel. Arms straight out sideways, correct height, palms down

Wrong: 'chair' seat: vaulter sits on buttock muscles only, not on seat bones. Therefore the back curves and the knees are pulled up to keep balance. Legs cling, feet are too far forward, arms are bent and too low, and too far to the front

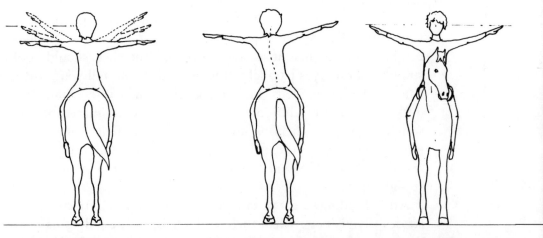

Correct alignment from the back vertically and horizontally. Minimum and maximum height of permissible arm positions are shown, ideally the fingertips should be at eye level

Wrong alignment of seat: vaulter bends spine to compensate, shoulders are tense and pulled up, arms at uneven height

Correct alignment vertically and horizontally, seen from the front: shoulders and legs are relaxed

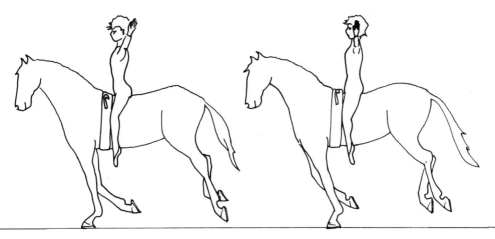

Wrong: 'fork' seat: vaulter falls off the seat bones to the front: therefore overarches the back and holds the arms too far back to keep balance

Correct alignment: the vaulter stays in the vertical regardless of the horse's up and down movement by gently absorbing it in his own pelvic movement. Upper body stays still

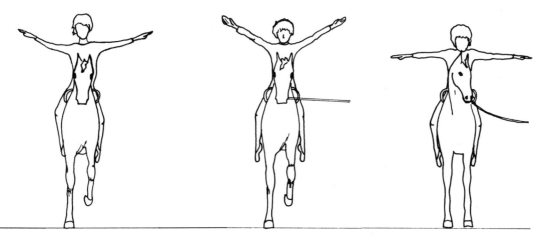

Wrong: twisted seat: spine is bent sideways, one arm kinked to make up for mistake

Wrong: arms too high, palms not down, shoulders pulled up. Bad 'wrap' of the legs, feet are not to the horse

Wrong: cramped shoulders, chin and hands too low, tense back

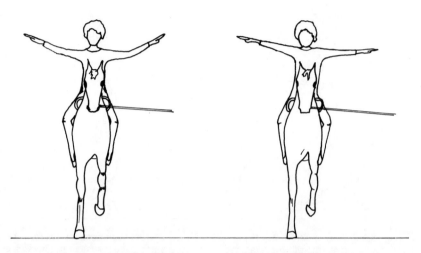

Wrong: bad posture, insufficient body
tension, arms bent, head tilted, knees
pulled up

Wrong seat off centre: inner knee
pulled up, shoulders cramped, arms
uneven height

Arm position for basic seat and stand

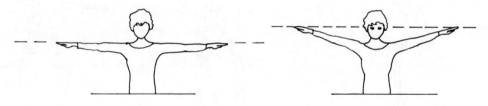

Lowest arm position at shoulder height

Ideal position: at eye level

Correct hand position:
fingers together, palms
down, thumb at the side

Wrong alignment

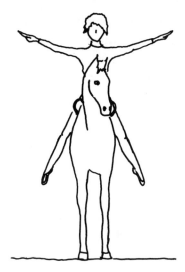

Practise balance and alignment by
stretching the legs away from the horse

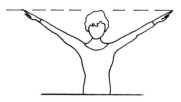

Highest position: top of the head

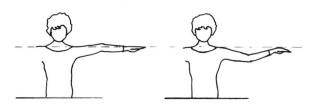

'Double jointed' elbows   Lacking tension

Before and after *each and every* exercise which does not end in a direct dismount itself (like the flank), the basic seat position (without arm extension) should be assumed for a split second. No exercise should be started out of an incorrect seat position.

Exercises to improve: Belly-dancing — no joke! Let the vaulters sit straight and extend the legs away from the horse, first in walk, then canter, to find their gravity point and align with the horse. Later let them close their eyes when practising this. In the beginning they must do the 'pelvic push' quite actively, if they are stiff. This movement must go down straight from the back and forward. The idea is *NOT* to overcurve the spine to the back and stick out a 'duckie bum'. It must feel as if the pelvis pushes the horse into the next canter stride.

Common mistakes

- *Curved back and round shoulders*: slouching posture, shoulders forward, or cramped back. This often occurs with beginners, when they are still afraid of losing their balance. Let them rest their open hands on the grips lightly (this gives them a sense of security) and tell them to breathe. Since beginners are anxious and tense (which leads to uncomfortable bouncing and hence to more cramping), let them do pelvic pushing movements downward and forward with their hips (practise this in the warm-up time), sit behind them or run along holding on to their leg, if necessary for reassurance. Young girls in puberty often curve their shoulders forward to hide developing breasts — they have to overcome this awkward period somehow...chest out! They have to get used to it sooner or later...

'Duckie bum'!

- *Arched back*: thereby producing what I call the 'duckie-bum'. Goes along with overdone pelvic tilt to the front. Tailbone of the vaulter lifts off and correct vertical alignment is not achieved.

- *Light seat*: bouncing, a sign of lacking suppleness in the hips, occurs when the vaulter cramps up and pulls up his knees. Also gets more pronounced the further back the vaulter sits. Correct for long legs and right position on the horse's back.

- *Pelvic tilt*: tilting forward on the crotch results mainly from lack of suppleness. Usually it goes along with an overly curved back and lower leg positioned too far back. It indicates evasion of difficulty, as the vaulter tries to get around having to catch the motion in his hips. Correct all of the above. Use images for small children. Pelvic tilt to the back goes with rounded back (see above) and pulled up knees. It is often an indication of soreness or back pain, especially in the young child. Ask about this! They may be too shy to mention it...

- *Off centre*: Usually a kink in the hip. Many vaulters (and riders) have a tendency to lean to one side, which is usually a mannerism and a very bad habit. Often goes along with other ways to make up for the resulting imbalance, like twists etc. Becomes dangerous when vaulters start to lift and carry as undermen, so don't let it pass even at the beginning. Look at vaulters from front and back too to determine the problem.

- *Uneven height*: in arms and hands. Often lack of concentration, but also an indication of lacking directional awareness. Can your vaulter touch the tip of her nose with eyes closed? Can he make the two index fingers meet with outstretched arms and eyes closed? Many vaulters, especially little ones, don't have a clue where their own body parts are in space in relation to each other. (More about this when we discuss rolls, hangs and jumps later on.) Let them train even height in front of a mirror, then repeat with closed eyes, then open eyes and check. Children love these exercises, and it usually corrects the mistake quickly, as soon as they get the feel for it. Also check the previous point, uneven height can result from a combination of hip kink plus lacking directional awareness. Correct all points in older vaulters, use images for children.

- *Arms*: *too far back*, often in very flexible children. They should be able *just* to see their wriggling thumbs out of the corner of their eyes when looking straight ahead. Let them check this way often! *arms too low*: often sign of insecurity; *arms too far to front*: also insecurity. Let them test in walk how quickly they can reach the grips from the correct arm position, to prove to them that they are not safer through persisting in the wrong one! All these things are purely in the mind and must be dealt with accordingly.
- *'Riding'*: another mistake which is often to be seen, is the vaulter *riding* the horse. This is *not* his job (unless you ask them to help you with training a new horse), and looks very bad in vaulting. Neither should the vaulters hammer their feet into the side of the horse (as the horse *must* learn to listen to the lunger!) nor should they overtly push with pelvic movements. (This becomes very evident in many vaulters when they later have to sit backwards on the neck in kur exercises — vaulting should not look like a mating dance...). The pelvic movements should be just pronounced enough to catch the movement of the horse's motion, not go over and beyond that. When suppleness turns into slackness, it will diminish the vaulter's strength for lifting or supporting partners.

  Of course the vaulters can help the lunger invisibly by squeezing their legs to the horse, if the horse has a tendency to slow down or fall into trot. Their main help however will be to keep themselves perfectly centred and aligned, as many inconsistencies of the horse stem from disturbance of the vaulters throwing their weight around up top.
- *Head down*: is a sign of insecurity with young vaulters. Teach them that looking at the surcingle does not make an exercise more secure, that potential trouble rather manifests itself in the horse's ears! Make them repeat exercises in walk grasping the grips with closed eyes, until they believe you that looking is not necessary to find them. Use the example of a driver looking down to find the brakes in case of emergency...

17 *The basic dismount and the vault-off*

The basic dismount

Before starting the dismount, the vaulter sits in the correct seat position, back straight and head up. The right leg is then carried over the neck of the horse in a wide and high arc, fully extended and foot and toes pointed, to the inside. Greatest scope is desirable, but extra height should not be gained by making up for lacking flexibility through curving the back or excessive leaning. The leg should be lifted from the stomach muscles and pass by the vaulter's face (as close as possible) with a quick release and retake of the grips, as the leg passes the hands. The leg movement should be fully controlled and balance maintained. The upper body may lean a bit (as little as possible), but the back must stay straight. The left leg must stay long and stretched and not change out of the 'basic seat' position, and the weight must rest on both buttocks.

Other than in the mill, in the basic dismount the eyes and the shoulders of the vaulter remain pointed into the direction of travel! The legs are then brought together and both stretched (pointing slightly to the front, to where the leading foreleg of the horse touches the ground) and in a fluid continuation of the movement, the vaulter pushes away and slightly back from the horse (without curving the spine into a hollow back!), while dropping his legs to the ground. The movement should *not* come to a dead stop here, but the vaulter should absorb the impact elastically in his knees and continue to run in the same direction as the horse to let the momentum of the motion peter out.

Correct basic dismount

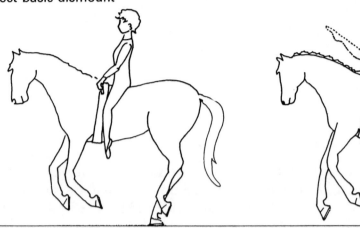

From correct basic seat (erect posture, back must stay straight throughout)...

...the vaulter passes the outside leg over the horse's neck, releasing and retaking the grips as the leg passes by

Basic dismount mistakes

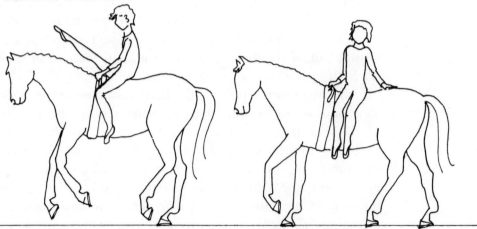

Wrong: curved back, clinging inner leg, insufficient height with other leg, head too low

Wrong: touching the horse's back with the hand, turning to the inside, legs apart

In the sideseat the vaulter faces the front with head and shoulders...

...then pushes off and away from the horse (slightly to the back), lands softly and continues running in the direction of travel of the horse

Wrong and dangerous: dismounting sideways! The horse's movement creates a turning momentum...

...which may lead to twisting, and in combination with getting dragged (if the grip is released too late) results in sliding to under the horse

Common mistakes

- rounded back to make up for lacking height and flexibility
- gliding down the side of the horse without push-away
- hanging on to the grips too long and getting dragged (this is often a sign of feeling insecure; explain that getting dragged is always more dangerous than pushing away!)
- turning shoulders and/or head toward the lunger
- dropping head to look for landing spot on the ground
- twisting either way and not landing in direction of the travel (correct this immediately, it is dangerous! If a vaulter twists and therefore stumbles upon landing, he can end up under the horse)

The vault-off

When compulsories are not performed in blocks, the scissors and the stand are followed by a vault-off. In the compulsories the vault-off is always executed to the inside of the circle. In team kur exercises one often prefers it to happen to the outside, so the dismounting vaulter is immediately out of the way of the other mounting team mates. The technique of inside and outside vault-off is basically the same.

- *The 'pre-swing'*: The vault-off is a symmetrical exercise. Both legs and arms perform in the same manner. It begins with an up-swing of both legs, which should be carried to the maximum possible extension for the vaulter, while remaining balanced on his buttocks. To achieve this, the upper body leans back slightly, but with straight back, and the grip of the hands becomes lighter. The motion does not stop at the highest point, but reverts into the down-swing at once and in one fluid motion. This motion has to be quick enough to fit on the canter stride. No energy can be gained for the swing if the up-swing goes against the horse's canter stride. If the up-swing is limp, no energy can be gained from it at all. If it stops at the highest point, very little can be gained from it.

- *The down-swing*: If any use is to be gained from the down-swing, it must accelerate, achieving the fastest speed at the lowest point, just like a golf club. It is very clear that the energy which the vaulter does *not* put into acceleration of the down-swing, can also *not* come out of that swing at the other end. Note on the illustration how the upper body follows the motion of the swinging legs: when the legs are down again after the swing the weight is transferred to the arms, so the vaulter must lean forward to bring his gravity point over the grips. Otherwise he can not be in control of the movement and stay with the horse.

- *The through-swing*: After the down-swing (to the lowest point) follows the through-swing, during which the vaulter must already have his gravity point over his hands. Here the arm action must kick in with a strong push. This is about the point indicated on the drawings on the hindquarters of the horse. Up to this point the swinging curve is basically a circle with the same radius around the hand-hip-point.

- *The up-swing*: But now, as the arm push kicks in, and the up-swing starts, the curve gets flatter, with a larger radius, the more the arms extend. Straight body line must be preserved − the legs may not gain additional height from a curved back. The legs can only come up to best height, if the shoulders go down. For training purposes I consider it better if the vaulter first collapses on the neck of the horse, rather than cheating his way around the push! The highest extension possible is the handstand position, but even if this can be reached, the motion should *not* stop here. Remember: there should be *no stops* in dynamic exercises.

- *The push-off, flight phase and landing*: As the apex of the swing is reached, the vaulter releases the grips with an energetic push and starts the third curve pattern. There must be a definite flight phase within the vault-off. The vaulter keeps his

Correct vault-off

From the correct basic seat position...

...the vaulter goes into the up-swing.
Bodyline stays straight, back may lean slightly

The vaulter keeps his weight over his hands while pushing,
also retains straight bodyline from head over spine to toes

As the momentum of the horse's canter
stride is used for added height...

In the down-swing the legs accelerate

The vaulter must have his gravity point over his hands for an effective arm push

...the vaulter may gain handstand elevation. But the movement must not stop...

...as the vaulter pushes himself away from the grips energetically to achieve the prescribed flight phase. He then lands softly on both feet and continues in running motion in the direction of the travel of the horse body straight during flight and lands with an erect upper body, absorbing the impact of landing in bent knees through supple ankles and feet. After landing, approximately at the level of the horse's hindquarters, the vaulter must continue the forward motion, running in the same direction as the horse.

Common mistakes

- Rounding the back in the pre-swing phase to make up for lacking flexibility.

- Moving the seat back behind the basic seat position to facilitate the pre-swing (all exercises should be started out of the correct basic seat position).

- Keeping the shoulders up during up-swing of the legs, thereby overarching the back, to avoid arm push (evasion of difficulty).

- Collapsing onto the neck of the horse, leaving out the arm push. Lacking arm strength! Let them do push-ups for home-work... Train assisted swings into handstand, mainly on the stationary horse. The assistant sits on the back of the barrel and catches the vaulter's legs in the up-swing, to then push him into the handstand. The vaulter must learn to keep his weight as much as possible over his own hands during the whole exercise; he should feel *light* to the assistant! He must use good body tension, and keep his back muscles tensed to achieve the straight back line. If he sags into a hollow back, the intent of the exercise is missed. This conveys the way it *should* feel, once they have built up the strength in their arms, and motivates them not to try to cheat their way around this difficulty. Encourage a lot, and tell the beginners *not* to expect exercises with this difficult arm push (difficult in strength *and* timing), such as the vault-off, the scissors and the flank, to work well in a matter of weeks. It took us all longer to learn...

Swing and push

Gravity point
must be over his hands

'Nose plant'
means lacking arm strength

- Leaving the left leg down and swishing the right one around to join the other one: this is the worst mistake, and you should never let it pass! *Both* legs must swing up symmetrically, join in the air, and come down together and closed.

- Clinging to the grips, omitting the push-off at the apex of the movement. Small vaulters in particular will make this mistake, because they fear the landing from high points. Train soft landings, vault-offs in walk and on the stationary horse, and lots of jump-offs from standing position (first in walk, later canter) to get them used to height.

- Twisting the body (usually because the inner grip is not released) and coming down sideways. *Any* landings, in which the vaulter does not face the direction of the movement, are potentially very dangerous. Vaulters can not continue the running motion when facing sideways or backwards, they then stumble and sprain their ankles or might get dragged under the horse: as I tell my kids: *the number ONE place where you DON'T want to be as a vaulter! Never* let this pass in training! Facing the front after landing out of any position must become second nature. (There are very few exceptions, like the sideways roll-off dismount, but these are performed much later, when the vaulter has already very good spatial orientation and can twist into the right position quickly during the landing phase.)

Vault-off mistakes

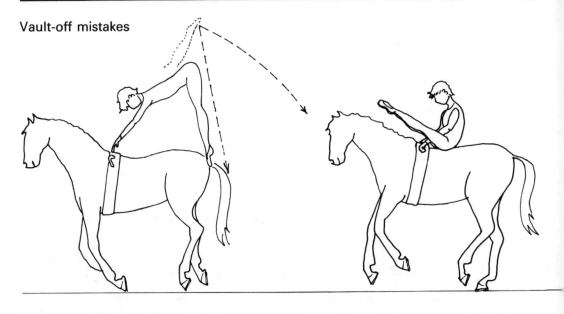

Excessive piking: although good height is achieved and the vaulter pushes off, the flight curve is interrupted and the flight phase shortened

Wrong: curved back to achieve greater swing with legs

Worst mistake: vaulter does not swing up left leg at all, just slides the outer leg around to join the other. This is *not* a vault-off!

Wrong: overarched back

Wrong: head down during swing and push phase

Wrong: overarched back to achieve greater height with feet: interruption of straight body line

Wrong: collapse of supporting arms

Wrong: no push off: clinging to grips, vaulter gets dragged along. This often results in a fall (touching the ground with hands or knees counts as a fall in competition)

Wrong: vaulter twists in anticipation before landing.
Clings to grips and 'fishes' for the ground

Wrong: the legs separate during or after the
up-swing

Wrong: collapse of the supporting arms so vaulter does not clear the horse, no flight phase

Wrong: vaulter twists during flight phase

18   *The flag*

The flag

The flag is one of the first movements every beginner learns, because it is considered easy, and the one which is most often taught the wrong way. When executed correctly it is quite difficult to hold, as alignment with the horse must be perfect and balance well developed. The flag is a static exercise. When performed outside the block it is followed by a basic dismount. The essence is concerned with posture and balance. There are three support points: the right hand, the left knee and the left foot (except that these two points are not really separate, as the weight should be evenly distributed over the whole shin of the left leg), and these are arranged in a triangle configuration. This gives the exercise good stability when performed as prescribed.

Basic score

The basic score is always given according to the worst mistakes in terms of 'mechanics' in a given exercise. In the flag those mistakes are:

- *A broken arc*: below we will describe what the correct unbroken arc should look like. Very flexible vaulters will show an extreme kink in their vertebral column in the attempt to achieve greater elevation for leg and arm. A flag like this can not be scored higher than a basic mark of 5.0 (from which all other performance faults are then deducted).

- *An extremely rotated hip*: this is the most common attempt to get the leg as high as possible, but not one that pays off! For an extremely 'open' hip, the vaulter will not be scored higher than again a 5.0 as basic score. Insist on the correct hip alignment from the start, so the vaulters can enjoy the feeling of success as they increase the leg elevation successively with practice — rather than having to put it a foot lower when somebody corrects their open hip after years of performing such a nice (but unfortunately incorrect) flag!

The build-up

As in all exercises the build-up should happen as soon as possible after the mount (or after taking down the arms from the basic seat). From the correct seat position, the vaulter moves himself *into the kneel position* via a slight swing or hop (not dramatic enough to make it look like the start of a dynamic exercise) with *both* legs simultaneously. (Failure to execute the kneel costs a full point.) For this he needs to support his weight with his arms, as consideration must be shown to the horse and the legs must touch the horse's back softly, first landing with the flat top of the feet, then settling down over the shin to the knees. The knees should land immediately in the correct spot for building up the flag. This point is determined according to and depending on the vaulter's size, but lies approximately one to two hands' width behind the surcingle. When the flag is fully and correctly built up, the supporting thigh should be almost at a right angle to the horse's back.

Position of the supporting leg

The left lower leg is then crossed diagonally over the horse's back, with the left foot on the right side of the horse, the knee on the left of the horse's spine, and the weight evenly distributed along the whole flat contact surface. The vaulter must move his gravity point far enough backward, so half of his weight is over this shin. There may be no airspace under the foot, and absolutely no toes dug into the horse's kidneys. In this position, the triangle support configuration is achieved, which, as everyone

The correct flag

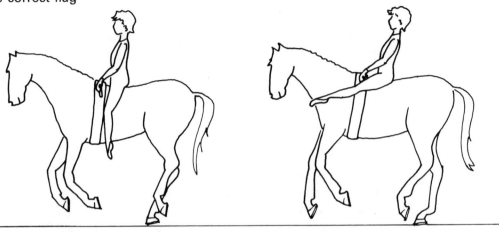

From the correct basic seat...

...the vaulter takes a moderate swing to elevate the legs into...

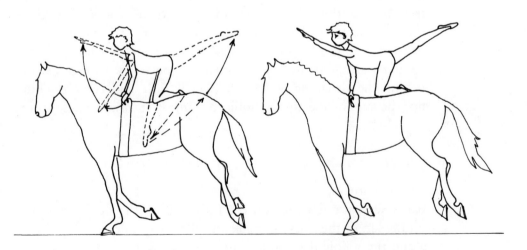

...the vaulter (either extends his outer leg down, which is optional and by some judges not considered proper for competition) stretches his outer leg to the back simultaneously with the extension of the inner arm to the front, both to above a horizontal line over the top of the head

Correct: hand and foot about the same height, soft unbroken arc of the bodyline, hips flat (not rotated) shoulders parallel to and vertical above the grips. The vaulter looks over the back of the extended hand

...a kneeling position. Gravity point must be over the hands to settle down softly over the arch of stretched feet. Both legs must kneel in the diagonal position across the horse's back before the flag

From a balanced bench position, with the thighs approximately at a right angle to the horse's back (shoulders vertically above the grips)

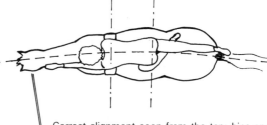

Correct alignment seen from the top: hips and shoulders are parallel, and square to the horse's spine. The extended arm and leg are parallel to the horse's as well as the vaulter's spine. The supporting leg lies diagonally over the horse's back

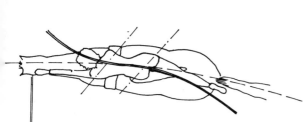

Wrong: vaulter is twisted, cramped and unbalanced. The leg points too far in, shoulders and hips are not aligned with the surcingle, head is turned out

remembers from geometry lessons, is the most stable configuration that exists.

Bringing up the right leg

When this 'bench' position (kneeling on both knees and supported by both arms) is assumed, there are different ways to lift the right leg into the flag position. Only the second one is presently considered correct in competition, and the scores get higher with added elegance, fluidity and difficulty of execution. I will group them from easier to more complex.

- Beginners should slide their right leg directly from the kneel into the extended position, then establish their balance over a strong right arm, and only when they are sure that the balance can be maintained should they extend the left arm into the fully built up position. They get penalized less like this, remember: in competition, for leaning onto the horse's neck with the hand (without loss of form) the vaulter loses a full point, and for retaking the grip (because of loss of balance) s/he loses two full points! Retaking the grips twice causes a compulsory exercise to be scored as zero — so repeated loss of balance is never worth the risk. No vaulter can afford that... so train them accordingly. Undue delay to get into the exercise is penalized, but the beginner especially should always take the time and concentration s/he needs to get fullest satisfaction out of his/her own best possible form.

- The better way is to extend the leg in the same fashion, but simultaneously with the left arm. This increases of course the level of difficulty, as the risk of losing the balance is higher this way. Although elegance in vaulting is subject to different trends over time, this seems to be the way for compulsories, which judges want to see at this time in competition. Arm and leg should reach their end position at the same time and in the most direct way possible — no fancy moves in between!

- The third option is to extend the right leg *down*, fully stretched and pointed, before swinging it up in a controlled motion; at the same time the arm swings up, also fully extended. Hand and foot again reach their respective highest points simultaneously. This looks quite elegant and is acceptable within the international rules at the time of writing this book, but harbours the danger that the vaulter omits the full kneel before swinging the leg into the flag position. This omission will cost the vaulter a full point in competition.

Correct arm, shoulder and head position

The extended arm should be lifted to about the same height as the leg (the right foot should be *slightly* higher than the left hand); ideally to above the horizontal line running over the vaulter's head. Fingers should be together and palm down with the thumb against the hand. The shoulder of the extended arm should *not* stretch forward, rather both shoulders must stay square with the shoulders of the horse. The head should be erect, face and eye forward, looking over the back of the extended arm, but without resulting in a kinked neck.

The vaulter's top line should describe an even, smooth, unbroken arc from fingertips to toes along the hand, arm, back, leg and foot. With correct alignment (see next point) it is not easy to reach a higher leg extension than the above mentioned horizontal line. But very flexible vaulters achieve it: take care that the head (the eye should look over the extended arm, which is almost as high as the leg) is not lifted to the extreme that proper breathing stops during the exercise.

Alignment

So far it sounds easy, but here comes the tricky part. The flag needs to be aligned in two ways for correct performance:

lengthwise: with the spine of the horse, and
parallel to the horse's back (or the ground)

- Lengthwise, or seen from the top, the spine of the vaulter must follow the exact line as the spine of the horse. All twisting action in the vaulter's body is easily detected and should always be corrected. (Push the little ones into the correct form, rather than explaining, so they understand the *feeling* of it.)

- Parallel to the ground is much harder...when the flag seems easy to a vaulter, this is where he is doing it wrongly. Explain to your young vaulters that you must be able to rest a full glass of water on their tailbone — to keep them from 'opening' their right hip. The back of the pelvic bones *must* be flat, both buttocks at the same height. The sole of the right foot will then point to the sky, the knee straight down, not sideways as in dancing. Otherwise the flag is technically not correct. As soon as you correct their opening hips, all legs sink...the balance is lost, the right arm collapses...the body starts to twist... The extended leg must be lifted from the muscles in the vaulter's back, and holding the balance like this actually requires a lot of strength, apart from flexibility.

Stillness of the exercise

Unfortunately this flag is one which is not allowed to flutter in the wind; the name is not logical...

Once the extended arm and leg position are established, the flag must be held as still (not stiffly) as possible for four full canter strides (start counting after it is *fully* built up) because it is a static exercise. The supporting knee, very slightly bent (with the seat of the vaulter as high off the horse as possible) and the supporting elbow are both 'greased' and ideally move just enough to absorb the motion of the horse.

Although the flag should be held calmly, it may never look stiff. It is better if the leg waves a little, because the vaulter swings with the motion of the horse, than if the vaulter holds himself completely stiff in his attempt to keep still, cramping up and working against the canter stride. Watch especially that the left shoulder and the neck stay relaxed. And remind your beginners that the cure against losing your balance is not hanging on harder, but shifting the gravity point back where it belongs: over the spine of the horse (and ever so slightly to the inside of that point to make up for the centrifugal force).

Take-down

After holding the flag for four strides, the extended leg is taken down, fully stretched, at the outside of the horse, at the same time as the left arm returns on a direct arc to the grip. With equal arm support on both sides, the vaulter executes a little lift-off from the supporting leg, which is then also fully stretched, as s/he slides in one fluid motion into a soft landing on the horse's back, immediately into the right spot for correct seat position, without any necessity for seat corrections. If no other exercise follows, the correct way off is the basic dismount.

Common mistakes

The length of the list shows the difficulty!
- exaggerated hop or swing into kneeling position
- build-up, forgetting to go over the kneel (one full point deduction)
- sitting on haunches: collapse to the back
- supporting knee too far back, combined with weak arm: collapse to the front
- supporting knee too far to front: flag can't be properly extended upward, stays low
- supporting leg not positioned diagonally over horse's back
- toes of supporting leg dug into horse's back, airspace visible (this means too much weight on the knee, not enough along the shin, and/or clinging with the left foot)

Common flag mistakes

Wrong: the supporting leg is too far back. Bad posture generally, lacking body tension

Wrong: right hip is 'open', i.e. the hip rotates to facilitate gaining height for the outer leg. The supporting leg is too far to the front. No alignment, inner shoulder is dropped, arm is too low because balance is lost

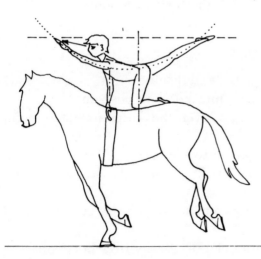

Correct alignment

Wrong: supporting leg is too far to the front. The weight is not distributed evenly over the entire shin, as can be seen by the air under the foot. The arm is not stretched, head is too low

Correct way for beginners to extend the leg: extend leg before the arm. Establish balance securely before lifting the arm into position

Can you see the mistake? The supporting leg is not diagonal across the horse

Wrong: twisted alignment: left shoulder is drawn to the front, right hip is 'open'. Leg and arm height are very uneven

Wrong: overarched back! Hip is 'open', supporting leg is too far back. Arm and chin are too high

Wrong: left shoulder too high and cramped

Wrong: excessive swing to get into the flag. This may *not* look a dynamic exercise!

- twisted shoulders
- open hip, turned out right leg (knee facing out) (this is the most common evasion of difficulty!)
- arm too low (often with left shoulder pulled forward)
- touching the horse's neck with extended arm (one full point deduction)
- head too low, and/or looking down onto horse
- overarched back (usually with open hip), head too high, restricted breathing
- broken arc of the top line (especially at waist)
- low right leg, missing flexibility
- bent knee in right leg, toes not pointed
- stiff supporting knee and elbow, bouncy, wavy flag
- stiff and/or twisted shoulders
- missing alignment along horse's spine

19 *The mill*

The mill

The essence of this exercise is balance, flexibility, scope (height of legs) and timing (sense of rhythm). The mill is so called because the exercise should evoke the picture of an old-fashioned windmill: (the wind being the horse, who hopefully 'blows' in a regular fashion, keeping an even canter stride). The wings of the mill must have even height, even rhythm, even appearance, even straightness and even speed. The whole exercise must have a fixed point for an 'axle'.

Position

The mill is a *sitting exercise*! In order correctly to execute a mill, the vaulter has to be able to sit in a balanced fashion! Like in the basic seat, he will need to absorb the movement of the canter stride in his pelvis, only this time also sideways and backwards.

The exercise is of course started out of the basic seat position. I tell my vaulters to imagine that they are sitting on a *small* cookie plate, the exact centre of which is pierced by their tailbone. This is the fixed point, or the axle, of the mill. This centre point must be directly over the horse's spine (about one hand width back behind the surcingle), and the vaulter's bottom must turn on the cookie plate. So there is really no option of where to sit, and *no* sliding around − no seat corrections should occur in a well executed mill.

The mill begins (unless a mount counts into it, when performed outside the block) from the seat astride. In this exercise the vaulter performs a complete rotation on the horse's back in sitting position (left turn), which is executed in four evenly timed phases, with the dismount started in the same rhythm.

Rhythm

In canter each (except the last leg over) phase lasts four canter strides (when you practise in trot let them count at least to six, otherwise it is too fast). As soon as your vaulters are able to well maintain their balance in all side and backward seat positions, and are actually starting to perform a full mill, *always* insist on their counting the beat (loudly for beginners), as *not* keeping the rhythm in the mill is the fastest way to lose points! *Each* rhythm fault (and you can commit up to five) is good for a one point deduction, and they are cumulative.

Beginners and little vaulters especially will count and stop at their convenience at the stages where the exercise becomes more difficult (and they need more time to complete leg movement and hand changes). It must be quite clear to them that the *horse* with his rhythm sets the rhythm for this exercise, and *not* the vaulter!

'First leg' into inside side seat

From seat astride the vaulter lifts his right leg (and *all* the legs in the mill must be perfectly straight and toes pointed) and carries it over the horse's neck, in an *arc as wide and high* as possible. The leg which does *not* travel stays long, pointed down, so it is positioned under the vaulter's hip (like in basic seat), and *to* the horse. Each grip is released and retaken quickly, as the leg bypasses the hand. The upper body stays erect, the torso may *slightly* lean backwards, but the back may not be rounded to facilitate the lifting of the leg. The control of the leg's movement and height must come from the stomach muscles! The eye should follow the foot in the air, the head should 'lead' the movement.

When the right leg comes down on the inside, both legs are immediately closed (whole length). They should be as long as possible, both put *to* the horse and kept still (not swish along the horse's body with the canter movement). Shoulders are now pointing towards the lunger, hands are still in the original position.

'Second leg' into backward seat

Now the left leg is lifted to be passed over the back of the horse. All the above mentioned criteria apply. *Both* buttocks should remain in contact with the horse's back. As soon as the vaulter reaches the backward seat (and not before or during the movement), the hands are quickly changed. The seat should be erect, with legs long. Don't forget to move the pelvis to avoid bouncing.

'Third leg' into outside side seat

This is the move most affected by centrifugal force — and where beginners often involuntarily dismount! So the weight should be shifted very slightly (and invisibly to the judges) to the inside of the horse's spine to counteract it. So run along with the little ones, when they do the mill in canter for the first time, to ensure they have sufficient balance to maintain control in this position. It could be dangerous for them to fall during this turn, as they are either backward or half turned and in a sideways, twisted position and might land under the horse.

The right leg is lifted again and carried over the croup and the vaulter lands in the outside seat, where his legs must be immediately closed (all the way). This 'third' leg is for many the most difficult one to lift, because of the wide straddle backwards position, so teach your vaulters to pay special attention to bringing it as high as the other legs. It is also the turn, where most buttocks lift off, because the vaulter tries to facilitate lifting the leg by transferring weight onto his arms. Indeed, a good mill should not need the help of the hands at all, it should be fully balanced out of the sitting position. The hands stay in previous position, until the rotation of this leg is almost finished, then they are quickly changed. Shoulders face the outside.

The correct mill

From correct basic seat...

...the vaulter carries the first leg over. Hands release and retake grips as leg swings by. The 'down' leg (here the inner leg) must not cling, but stay long and relaxed. Upper body stays erect and in near vertical position throughout, the eye follows the foot. The smaller the angle between torso and leg, the better. All legs should achieve the same height

Balanced backward seat: legs are long, pelvis absorbs the movement, head stays erect

Shift weight very slightly to the inside before passing the next leg over, to counteract centrifugal force

Establish balance in the side seat: shoulder, head and hips face the lunger. Legs are long and together touching the horse's body with their full length

The right leg must not cling, and stay still. The seat is never shifted from its centre position. Hand change happens *after* the leg is passed over

Both buttocks stay in contact with the horse's back as leg lifts over. Hand change happens *after* the leg movement, when outside seat is reached

Balanced outside seat: shoulders, head and hips face the outside, knees and feet are together legs long and relaxed

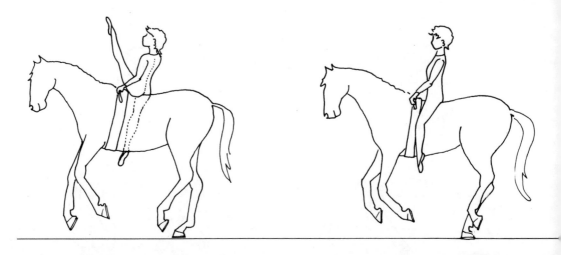

Hands release and retake grips as leg moves by. Outer leg stays long, both buttocks stay on the horse's back. Eye follows foot

Back in the basic seat, but the vaulter continues to count in the four-beat rhythm

. . .this time the vaulter keeps his shoulders to the front (direction of travel) to dismount

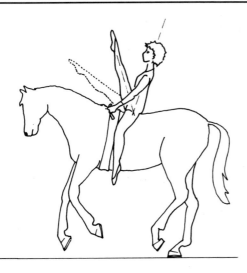

The 'fifth' leg moves like the first, but...

Then follows a slight push away from the horse
and to the rear, soft landing, and continuation
of the forward motion after the dismount

'Fourth leg' back to seat astride

In the outside seat the legs must again touch each other for the whole length. The 'fourth' leg, again the left one, is then lifted over the front, landing in seat astride as when s/he started. In this move the vaulters most often 'leave their shoulders behind', meaning that they do not turn the torso and the hips together. (Try it without taking the grips.) Insist on balance, rather than pulling on the grips with force.

'Fifth leg' and dismount

Now don't forget that the 'fifth' leg (the right one going into the dismount), although not part of the mill, *must* be started on the *same* beat rhythm as all the others. This is where most rhythm mistakes occur, because the vaulter has the impression that the job is done, once landed back in seat astride. Not so... But the vaulter does not have to sit out four strides, the dismount should be performed fluently and in one movement, as any delay in the sideways seat will receive deduction points in competition.

The dismount is carried out as described in the 'basic dismount', or else, if all the compulsories are performed in sequence, this dismount ends in a 'touchdown' with immediate remount (which counts into the next exercise).

The balance

If beginners are always gripping the handles, they may not really understand the necessity of balance in the mill. A good way to train for this understanding is to let them do the mill with arms crossed in front of their chest — first on the barrel, then on the horse in walk. More advanced vaulters should then practise in canter to let go both hands immediately after swinging the leg over and then sit the three following canter strides with arms crossed — and fully balanced.

The height of the leg in the mill largely depends on the

flexibility of the vaulter, but even many very high mills are nevertheless not achieving good scores, because the vaulter can't 'sit' the mill. The vaulter should learn that balance is the beginning of everything in this exercise: only when fully balanced can legs be lifted and carried around with ease and in good rhythm and equal height, only then can the other leg stay down and long without clinging. Only then will the shoulders rotate with the hips evenly and the buttocks not lift off, when the leg comes up. And the list goes on.

A well executed mill in canter should look as if the hands were not necessary to perform the exercise. The vaulter must express in his body posture that he is indeed independently balanced and straight throughout the exercise.

The rule says that each leg must be carried 'fluently without rushing and without interruption'. There is no set rule concerning *how long* the vaulter should *keep* the leg suspended in the air. However, it is clear that it is easiest to throw the leg around in a quick motion (on the 'one' beat) and then sit for the next canter strides (two to four). This can result in quite a nice looking mill, especially with very flexible, but rather weak children (weak in the stomach muscles). Best scores are naturally never achieved by evading difficulty: therefore an experienced vaulter tries to *carry* the leg in a controlled fashion on the canter beats one to three, and only uses stride four for hand changes, while sitting still. In a high-scoring mill the body and the head are turned *while* the leg is travelling through the air, not via seat corrections, when the leg is already around. This is the part that makes the mill difficult, as it requires the excellent balance and control, which is needed to make the vaulter look perfectly at ease during the turn.

If the compulsory exercises are performed all in one block, the vaulter will dismount and re-mount via a touch-down directly after the mill. The technique for the touch-down is very similar to that of a correct mount, the jump-off is the same. So the vaulter will slide off the horse with both legs stretched and

Basic score in the mill

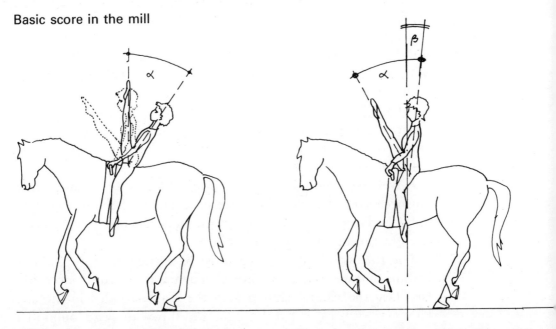

Angle α means angle between torso and up-leg, i.e. is a measure of flexibility   Angle β measures the leaning of the torso, i.e. the deviation from the vertical

Same angle α between torso and leg will be scored higher here, since leaning angle β is smaller

extended slightly to the front, to hit the correct jump-off point approximately one foot ahead of the surcingle. The re-mount will count into the next exercise.

Basic score

Obviously it is very desirable to reach very high leg elevation in the mill, as one of the essence points in the mill is flexibility. The main faults in the mill stem from putting too much emphasis on high legs alone — the vaulter tries to make up for lacking flexibility by introducing more mistakes.

Excessive leaning of the torso is one of them. The angle alpha in the illustrations is an indication of the vaulter's flexibility, but the angle beta shows how much s/he leans from the vertical,

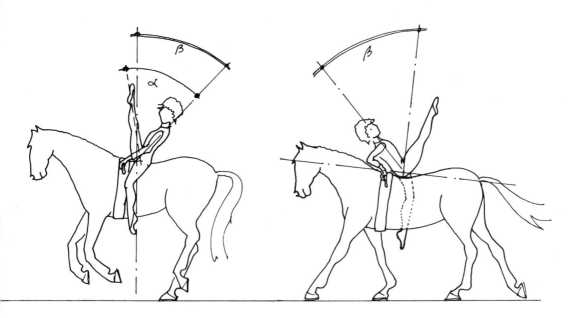

Although the vaulter has excellent flexibility (small α) and legs are near split position, basic score can't be higher than 7.0, because of leaning angle β at 45 degrees — a full 3.0 point deduction

Excessive leaning angle β of 45 degrees or more

approximately perpendicular to the horse's back. (This line will depend on the horse's position according to the canter stride, but is more or less parallel to the ground.)

The basic score can not be higher than 7.0 at the most, if an excessive leaning angle (beta) of 45 degrees is reached, as this constitutes a full 3.0 points deduction. (If this is the only mistake!) The basic score will vary between 4.0 and maximum 6.0 points if two or more of these main faults are committed:

the resting leg is lifted (clinging to the horse to facilitate the lifting of the other leg)

side seats do not rest on both buttocks

upper body does not rotate with the legs (shoulders lag behind the movement of the leg rotation)

buttocks lift off while leg is carried around

Typical mill mistakes

Rounded back means evasion of difficulty
It is easier but wrong to gain height for the leg
this way. Inner knee comes up and clings to
make up for loss of balance. Dotted line shows
what is considered insufficient height

Wrong: excessive leaning and clinging 'down'
leg. Vaulter is off-centre

Wrong: facing front direction in outside seat

Wrong: cramped posture and insufficient
height of leg. Clinging inner leg is a typical sign
of lack of flexibility

Wrong: slouched back, vaulter will bounce.
Lack of absorption of the horse's motion: stiff
pelvis. Head is too low

Wrong: excessive leaning of torso. Right
buttock lifts off

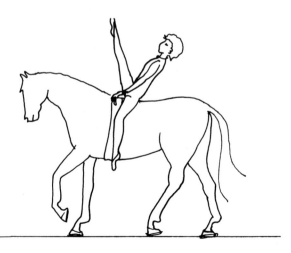

Wrong: excessive leaning, right buttock lifts off

Common faults

- rounded back to make up for lack of flexibility in the legs
- rhythm mistakes in the count
- seat corrections, because the vaulter slides around, following the movement of the legs with his seat
- losing balance to the outside, because centrifugal force was not taken into account
- lifting off with one buttock when leg is passed around
- head dropped
- lacking scope (height of the leg)
- *uneven* elevation of legs in the four phases and the dismount
- lacking posture: chest not out, shoulders pulled up, head down
- lacking form: knees kinked, feet not pointed
- shoulders not turning with the hips in rotation and seat
- shoulders turning to the centre when dismounting (when they *must* stay facing the front)
- arc of the leg not *wide* enough, or asymmetrical 'slicing'
- stopping at top of arc (interruption of fluid motion)

20 *The scissors*

The scissors start block 2 of the compulsory exercises. When the two blocks are performed separately, the mount counts into the scissors. When both blocks are performed in sequence (as in an individual competition) the mill ends with the last leg over the neck, then a 'touch-down' is performed, meaning that the vaulter touches the ground only very briefly and rebounds directly into another mount. The mechanics for the touchdown are the same as for the mount at the jump-off point. This touchdown counts into the exercise of the scissors — so practise it often, as the scissors are difficult enough themselves, without getting deductions for a failed touchdown (or 'ground jump'.)

The Scissors

When training for the scissors with beginners, tell them *not* to be discouraged if it does not work right away...it never does!

What is the scissor movement?

Even among good vaulters there is a lot of confusion about what the judges are really looking for in the scissors, as it is a complex movement. Explain it to beginners as shown in the illustration, in a standing position.

Any scissoring movement will be entered into by turning the pelvis first. This means that the legs, which were in a *straddle position* before the first 90-degree pelvic turn, are now in a *step position*. The shoulders have not moved yet, but the legs look as though they are walking. Now they *do* walk, and this is the actual scissor movement. The vaulter's legs are again in a *step position*, but the other leg is in the front now. Then the pelvis completes the 180-degree turn and the legs are again in a *straddle*

Step 1: person seen from the front: legs are in straddle position

Step 2: upper body stays the same. Only hips turn 90 degrees. Feet are in the same spot, but legs are now in step position

Step 3: upper body stays the same. But the feet have taken a step (exchanging position). *This* is the scissor movement proper. Legs are again (or still) in step position

Step 4: hips turn another 90 degrees. Feet stay in the same spot, upper body turns and person is seen from the back. Legs are therefore again in straddle position

What is the scissor movement?

position. In the scissors on the horse he will now be sitting backwards.

Small children in particular find this a very difficult movement to *understand,* so let them lie down onto the barrel and turn them, by keeping their legs straight. Little vaulters very easily get confused about the direction, and this *is* one of the things that they *must* learn correctly, right from the beginning. Once they have the 'wrong turn' in their system, it will take ages to set them straight again, and confusion will last a long time.

- *Direction*: In competition a scissor exercise, which is performed in the wrong direction, counts as *zero*, just as badly as not performed! It is a mistake that nobody can afford... *The turn is always executed with left leg over the right*, that is, the stomach of the vaulter turns toward the lunger in both turns. Or in other words the vaulter turns to the back seat over the inside of the circle, and then *back* again, *not* performing a full rotation in this exercise, but rather two half ones.

- *Height and pre-exercises*: In order to be able to turn his body in the prescribed way, the vaulter must get his seat into the air, and this again implies a lot of arm work and good balance.

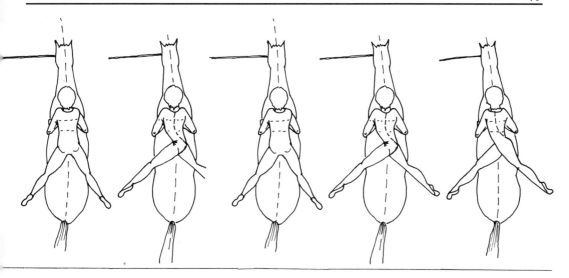

| The straddle position seen from the top on horse | The first step position, preparing for the scissor motion | Here the scissor movement has been completed. Right leg is now inside | Pelvis has performed the second 90 degree turn | Shoulders follow and vaulter settles into backward seat |

The scissors performed by beginners, especially heavier ones, can be a great discomfort to the horse, if the vaulter does not yet manage to position his gravity point over his hands in the swing and has the strength to maintain arm control for a soft landing after the turn. I believe that this is an exercise that should be thoroughly trained on the barrel before trying it out 'for real'. Under 'common mistakes' in the vault-off (chapter 17) we mentioned how to train the arm strength via assisted swings into the handstand on the barrel. The same thing applies to the scissors and the flank. The correct leaning over the hands to be able to maintain body control during the flight and landing phases, and the timing, of *when* to start the arm-push, are essential.

It is a common misconception that in order to perform the scissors correctly the vaulter has to be able to achieve great height above the horse. In fact the height which must be

If you could see the scissors in slow motion, you would see the vaulter swing up, legs in straddle position. The following drawings show the scissor motion broken down into its components

The pelvis now turns 90 degrees toward the lunger, therefore the legs are now in 'step' position. Left leg, the inside leg, is still on the inside.

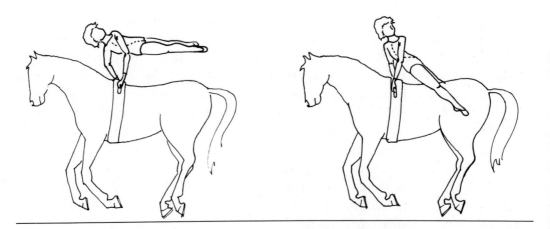

The pelvis performs a second 90 degree turn and now faces upward. Right leg is on the inside and...

...the vaulter is in the correct position for the backward seat. Only the handchange must take place to free the shoulders for completion of the turn with the upper body

Here the legs have taken the 'step' which *is* the scissor motion. Now the right leg is on the inside

While this step is being taken, the shoulders will start to turn. The rotation must however be initiated by the pelvis

reached for a technically correct turn is only a clearance of the horse — and even, if beginners do in fact not yet clear the horse at all, the same technique applies. The illustration shows a technically correct exercise without great elevation. What can't be demonstrated in the drawings is that the rotation movement of the pelvis is of course not stopped at any point: so the scissoring motion must be performed while the pelvis continually turns — but it should be quite evident that the hips lead the movement and the shoulders follow. It is not desirable to chop the various parts of the motion apart, but rather all movements, the lifting and turning, should be executed simultaneously. The image to keep in mind is that of a 'Gothic arch', meaning that the feet should meet (or come together as closely as possible in the scissoring movement) at the highest point of the lifting and when the hip is at a 90-degree angle.

The basic score for the scissors

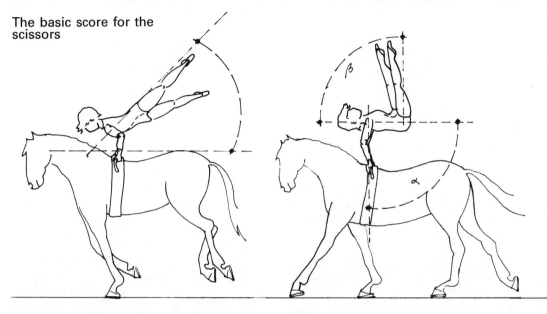

If the vaulter does not achieve an angle greater than 45 degrees, the basic score for the first half of the scissors can't be higher than 7.0, even if all else is perfect

Reverse scissors: If angle $\alpha = 90°$ and $\beta < 90°$, this means perfect basic score of 10.0 for this phase

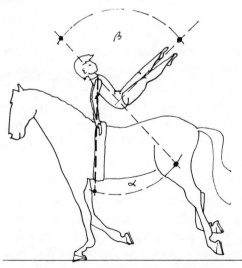

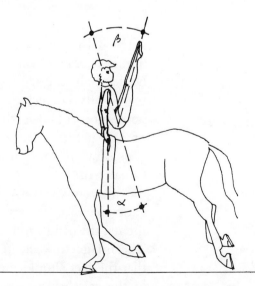

If angle $\alpha = 45°$ and angle $\beta = 90°$ then the basic score (as shown) will be ± 6.5

If angle $\alpha < 45°$ and angle $\beta < 90°$ then the basic score (as shown) is not higher than 6.0

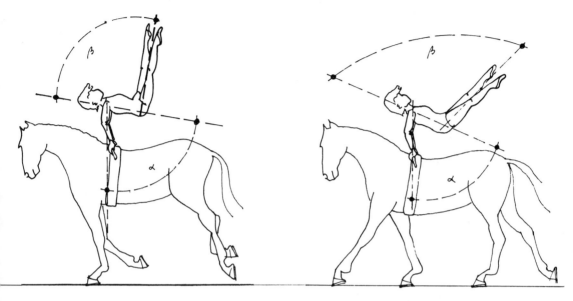

If angle $\alpha < 90°$ but $>45°$ and angle $\beta = 90°$ then the basic score will be (as shown) ± 8.0

If angle $\alpha > 45°$ and angle $\beta > 90°$ then the basic score (as shown) will be ± 7.0 to 7.5

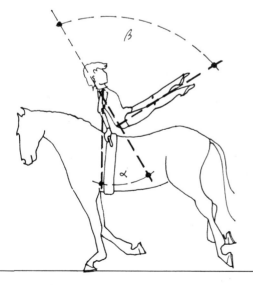

If angle $\alpha < 45°$ and angle $\beta = 90°$ then the basic score (as shown) is not more than 5.5

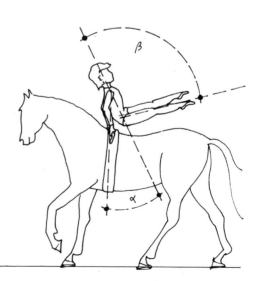

If angle $\alpha < 45°$ and angle $\beta > 90°$ then the basic score (as shown) will be 5.0 or less

Basic score

The basic score, which the judge will give for the two distinct phases of the scissors, will depend on the mechanically correct motion of the scissoring as well as timing of the rotation and angles reached in the height, in relationship to the vaulter's body parts and the horse. This is best shown by illustrations, as follows.

- If the vaulter does not perform the scissor movement ('helicopter' scissors), that is, keeps the straddle position of the legs throughout the turn, the basic score for mechanics can't be higher than 5.0 (then minus deductions for performance).

- If the vaulter does not reach an angle of at least 45 degrees or greater in relation to the horse's back, the basic score can't be higher than 7.0 for the first half of the scissors.

- If the pelvis rotates too early or too late (slicing scissors) the basic score will not be higher than 7.0.

In the second phase of the scissors we are dealing with two angles:

- If angle alpha reaches 90 degrees (that is, the vaulter's back is parallel to the horse's back) and angle beta is 90 degrees or smaller, the basic score will be between 9.0 and 10.0 (the smaller angle beta, the better).

- If alpha is a minimum of 45 degrees and beta a minimum of 90 degrees, the basic score will be between 7.0 and 8.0 (the smaller beta, the better).

- If alpha is smaller than 45 degrees and beta around 90 degrees, the basic score will be between 5.0 and 6.0 (the smaller beta, the better).

- If alpha is smaller than 45 degrees and beta larger than 90 degrees the score can therefore never be higher than 4.5, or worse.

Keep in mind that these basic scores are concerned with the mechanics of the exercise only and from them will be deducted all other performance faults. Lacking height off the horse as well as a collapse on the elbows because of incorrect gravity point (a deduction of up to 3.0 points) are examples of performance faults.

Training 'whole–part–whole'

As the scissors contain the most complex movement of all compulsories, it is very important to train this piece by piece on the barrel. Start with the previously mentioned assisted swings into handstand and then introduce the first 90-degree turn of the pelvis into the swing. Tell the vaulter to swing up, keeping the shoulders facing to the front throughout, but performing the hip turn and landing with the legs in a clear 'step position'.

Now let some speed come into play, to train for precision. Tell the vaulter to execute the previous exercise, but rotate the hip *back* into straddle position before landing in the basic seat again. This introduces the feeling for moving the legs independently from a complete turn, and thus avoids getting into the bad habit of performing 'helicopter scissors'. (This means turning the whole rotation with legs in straddle position – no real scissoring movement.)

After these pre-exercises are mastered, perform the whole first part of the scissors. Keep in mind that this is the way to train your advanced vaulters! Don't bore your little ones with such detail, just make sure they turn in the right direction and maintain balance.

First phase

- *The pre-swing and downswing*: The vaulter starts from the basic seat position, then leans his upper body backward very slightly, but without rounding the back, to lead the legs (stretched and toes pointed) into the pre-swing. At the apex of this swing the legs do not stop, but reverse direction in a fluid, ongoing motion. Greatest possible acceleration should be achieved in the downswing, and the vaulter should understand that the highest and most flexible pre-swing is of no use, when the down-movement is performed in slow motion, or when the legs are *guided* down. Maybe the vaulter's parents play golf: compare the swing of the club with this action of the legs: the momentum you want to get out of the swing, to aid you to gain height for the turn, *must* come out of the acceleration of the leg downswing. The arm push then helps raise the body and sustains the height achieved.

- *Through-swing*: In the through-swing phase the shoulders start to come down. Again, we are basically aiming for a straight body line throughout the first half of the turn, and if the shoulders don't come down, the legs can't come up, at least not without overarching the back (which is wrong). The approximate point as shown on the drawing, where the through-swing goes into the second upswing of the legs, is the latest timing of where the arms start pushing. In training I prefer the vaulters to collapse on the neck of the stationary horse (realizing that the arm strength is still missing), rather than avoiding the difficulty of the arm push by keeping the torso (the shoulders) up too high.

- *The up-swing*: The gravity point of the vaulter must stay *over his hands* during the whole flight phase. If this point shifts too far to the front, the exercise will collapse onto the neck, even if the arm push is strong. If it shifts too far back (which is common), the vaulter will push himself onto the back of the horse, rather than *up*, and land very hard approximately right in the kidney area of the horse. If the gravity point is not controlled and *over the hands*, the vaulter can not break his fall, and for both reasons, the going up as well as the coming down, the pre-exercises of swinging into the handstand on the barrel are essential.

- *The turn*: To explain the turn in the scissors we have to understand the concept of 'scissoring motion'. When the vaulter does his upswing, his legs are in a straddle position. As soon as he clears the horse's back the hips start rotating and the legs assume the step position. At the highest point of the upswing they interchange places, bypassing each other closely, and again are in step position — this motion resembles the opening of a pair of scissors, hence the name. Throughout, the hips continue their rotation so that the legs resume straddle position again just before landing back on the horse. You will experience that if you open your 'scissors' with a strong emphasis of 'left leg over right' opening, the correct turn will follow almost automatically. It will greatly diminish the confusion about the right direction of the turn. It is incorrect to straddle the legs wide and turn in this position. Also, if the vaulter just flails his legs through the air and lets the body follow, the rotation will usually not be terminated by the time the vaulter lands on horseback again. The rotation of the pelvis will start as soon as the vaulter clears the horse's back, and the scissor motion of the legs should happen at the highest point of the flight phase, and with the hip at about the 90-degree angle turn. In the scissor turn the left leg should cross over the right, forming said 'gothic arch' at the highest point — legs stretched and toes pointed, of course! As the hips complete the rotation, the arms continue pushing all the time to assure a soft landing in the backwards position.

I keep pointing out to my beginners that there is *no* danger of their body *not* coming down again...it is very important to train them for the continued push after reaching the apex of their upswing. Only this, in conjunction with the *control* through keeping their weight over their hands, can assure the soft landings you want for your horse. If a vaulter crashes down onto the horse — back to the barrel! Don't let your most important team mate suffer unnecessarily.

The correct scissors: first phase

From the correct basic seat position...

...the vaulter goes into the up-swing. Body line stays straight, back may lean slightly

The vaulter keeps his weight over his hands while pushing, also retains straight bodyline from head over spine to toes...

...as the momentum of the horse's canter stride is used effectively for added height

In the down-swing, legs accelerate

Vaulter must have his gravity point over his hands for effective arm push

All stages of the scissor movement must be executed in one fluid, continuous, simultaneous motion. The vaulter swings up, legs in straddle position, gravity point must be over the vaulter's hands throughout with strong arm support

The pelvis starts to turn, left leg is still on the inside, (shaded leg in background) legs are in 'step' position

While gaining more elevation, the scissor movement was performed and the right leg is now on the inside, still in 'step' position. Legs come close together at the apex of the flight. Hips are at 90° rotation, this is the tip of the 'gothic' arch

The vaulter continues arm support while coming down. Legs change into straddle position again, while the pelvis continues the rotation

...the correct backward seat position

After 2 to maximum 4 canter strides, the vaulter commences phase 2 of the scissors

The pelvis is now rotated 180° and legs are back in straddle position. Legs should not be apart wider than the width of the horse's body

The pelvis must be fully rotated before the vaulter settles down into...

Second phase

- *Back kick and upswing*: The backwards seat position should be straight, chin up, legs long, pointed down and to the horse. The time delay before going into the backwards turn, although there is no prescribed canter stride count, should be as short as possible, which of course heightens the difficulty. Very good vaulters start phase two right after landing in the seat. A delay longer than four canter strides before phase two is considered too long for international vaulters, but for beginners it is important to draw a deep breath and briefly concentrate, and this delay can last as long as half a round on the circle. Longer than this shows great indecision: they must learn to make up their mind within six canter strides!

Phase 2 starts with a back-swing of the legs, for which the stomach is stuck out to achieve greater extension (arc tension). The further the vaulter can take his legs back, the more momentum he can get out of the upswing of the legs.

- *Pre-exercises*: For this phase we also do pre-exercises during training. For the pre-exercise the vaulter swings both legs up and clicks them together over the croup of the horse. He then separates them again and lands in the same backward position. This is necessary for the beginner, because the action of the swing alone is difficult enough (without the turn.) and must be good and high, before an effective turn may be attempted. The more thorough the training in these pre-moves is from the beginning, the better and faster the vaulters will learn the complete exercise.

  During these pre-swings, train for a complete weight transfer onto the hands. A new vaulter can usually only feel the extent of the necessary shift (to the front of the horse) if he goes beyond it a few times and collapses backwards onto the neck. It also makes clear to them the required strength of the arm push, as we are aiming for a moment of suspension in the air.

  This 'leaning and pushing' motion, which must result fluidly out of an efficient swing, is very difficult. Little vaulters must literally lift their bottom over the step which the surcingle forms behind them. All vaulters have the conception that their torso is leaning much further behind the vertical than is actually the case. Use a video camera during barrel session, if possible, then stop the motion at the high point during replay.

  The leaning brings the vaulter's buttocks off the horse and is quite independent of the achieved leg elevation. In the basic score both aspects are addressed separately. Bringing the legs high is much easier than bringing the back into the ideally horizontal position, parallel to the horse's back. But swinging the legs up vigorously of course helps gain elevation for the back as well.

  It helps the vaulter to look at the point in the air where the toes should arrive at the highest point − imagining them there, brings them there. It also keeps the vaulter's eye level up, which is essential for the success in this exercise. If the back curves and the chin drops onto the chest, no height will ever be achieved in the back scissors.

You must train for soft landings (with strong arm control) in these pre-exercises, before the vaulter should attempt the actual turn.

It is important to notice that the leaning angle of the back will greatly determine the scores which your scissors might achieve later. The more you lean your back to the direction of the horse's neck, the more difficult the exercise becomes. However, it is the *only* way to achieve greater height, as the performance progresses. It requires an optimum sense of balance, control of your gravity point precisely over your hands, and exquisite timing to 'lean' in step with the horse's canter motion, because the vaulter does not have much time to spend on this 'lean—push—turn' motion!

- *The second turn*: Once the pre-exercise works, the vaulter will train for the second phase of the scissors. The rotation of the pelvis again 'leads' the motion, and pre-exercises can be similar to those described under the first phase. The weight transfer onto the inner hand (the right hand), which makes for an easy and clean turn, can be practised by trying to release the left hand during training.

  At the apex of the swing, where maximum height over the horse and maximum scope of the legs is achieved, the legs will perform the scissoring movement and pass each other as closely as possible, while the arms must push strongly to sustain the height. The weight must shift onto the right (the inside) hand at the highest point of the turn. (Tell your vaulters to shift it even earlier, because they always have the time lag between thinking of it and doing it, and correct timing is of the essence.) The pelvis completes rotation before the upper body does, and the lower body must be fully rotated before landing in the seat astride at about the point when the weight shift onto the right hand is complete.

- *The weight transfer*: Vaulters with strong arms can actually let go with their left hand during the last phase of the turn, although they should not do so in competition. (The rules are

Correct scissors: second phase

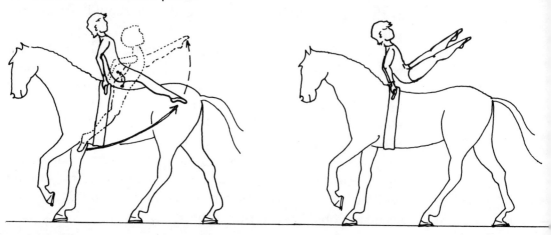

From an up-swing (out of good arc tension) the vaulter leans and lifts: gravity point must be over the hands again to be able to bring torso and hips up via arm push

The pelvis starts turning as soon as the legs come up. Legs are still in straddle position.

Scissor movement was performed at approximately the point of highest elevation. The right leg is now on the outside, still in 'step' position, hip at 90° and continuing the turn

The pelvis has turned nearly 180° again, legs are in straddle position (left leg inside). The weight transfers to the right hand. Let hand go in training only

Torso and hips continue to move up while the pelvis starts to turn

The hips have nearly reached the 90° turn, right leg still inside in 'step' position — now the scissor movement

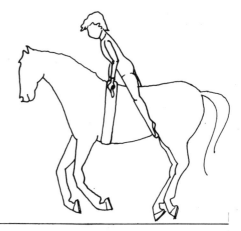

The gravity point must be over the hands throughout. The arms continue pushing until the very end to ensure a soft landing, and the legs (straddled no wider than the width of the horse's body) help in the braking action

The hand change is performed during the end of the turn or immediately after landing softly in the correct spot for the basic seat

Common scissor fault: 'helicopter scissors'

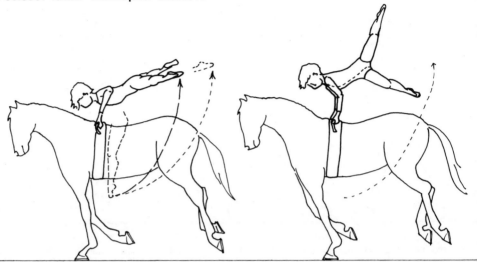

This is a common mistake, where the vaulter swings up in straddle position and then turns, retaining the wide straddle throughout. The actual scissor motion is never performed. The legs turn *with* the pelvis and never make the independent step movement.

Although good height can be achieved, this performance will never reach a good score, because the mechanics of the exercise are wrong

and the same applies backward

Common fault: 'slicing scissors'

The legs, instead of the pelvis, introduce the turn. The hips come too late

The right (outside) leg is trying to slice by to the inside, although the pelvis is not yet sufficiently rotated to permit a free scissor movement

The vaulter lands with the legs before the hips have completed the full 180° turn

With incomplete rotation the vaulter lands off-centre and therefore usually hard

The legs have scissored long before the apex of the flight was reached. The 'gothic arch' with a tip is not achieved

The rotation of the pelvis lags behind

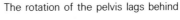

Especially in the second phase this means that considerable seat corrections are necessary

Slicing backward: at the apex of the height, the legs have already scissored and are fully back in straddle position

General common faults in the scissors

Typical beginner: collapse of supporting arms, trying to 'cheat' the right leg under the left which is made even more difficult by bending the legs (first phase of the scissors)

Wrong turn (first phase)

Collapse of supporting arms in the second phase, buttocks don't clear the horse

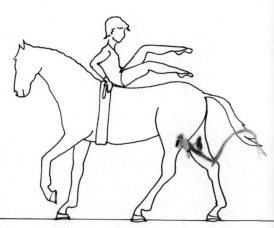

No arm push, the weight is not over his hands, bad form with bent legs

Upper body does not lean back, hips don't come up sufficiently

The vaulter pushes himself toward the croup: a sure sign that the gravity point is not far enough forward over his hands

The upper body did not go down in the swing of the first phase of the scissors, no straight body line. Overarched and kinked back try to make up for the mistake. The right leg never came up in the swing

The gravity point is too far back. This will result in a hard landing in the kidney area of the horse's back

not very explicit on this point.) Most vaulters hang onto the grips the way they did in the backwards seat, until they have landed fully rotated. This does *not* however mean that they omit the weight transfer. It only becomes less obvious. Upon landing — controlled and soft — the hands quickly change grips and the vaulter finds himself in the correct basic seat position again. In conjunction with the continuing arm push, both thighs should help evenly to break the vaulter's impact of landing. This means that the legs should not be straddled wider than the width of the horse's body at the landing time — in both directions. Seat corrections should not occur, if the gravity point was over the arms, so they could exert their power of pushing and guiding the vaulter back into the correct 'landing spot'.

Common faults

hard landings on the horse (consideration of the horse)

motion too slow, or working out of sync with the canter stride

shoulders kept high, while legs swing up, in the first phase of the scissors

turning the wrong way

crossing at the wrong moment

no acceleration in downswing, no momentum as result

no arm push, body not raised off horse

rotation not complete before landing, off centre

seat shift to the back of the horse before starting turns, rather than starting from basic seat position (evasion of difficulty)

flailing legs rather than controlled quick rotation

extended time lapse between two phases of scissors

sticking: interruption in coming to erect position astride

not enough height achieved

gravity point not over hands, push goes to back of the horse

stopping in the high (handstand) position to show off arm strength (motion must be continuous in a dynamic exercise)

21 *The stand*

Optimum mechanics for the stand is interpreted at this point as 'to be in a balanced position', that is, not to fall off. Therefore the basic score in terms of mechanics is a zero in case of a fall. However new rules also provide for the case where a zero can be given by way of deductions, so it does not necessarily mean 'not performed'.

The discussion as to whether a 'stand', which is in fact never still, but rather a 'walk' on the horse's back, can be counted as such, is ongoing. If a vaulter is continually walking (losing balance) for the prescribed four canter strides, he is, according to the rules as they stand at the moment, 'mechanically' standing, but with a deduction for 'major fault' between 2.0 and 3.0 points for each full step; this will nevertheless land him very close to a zero. It is very important that you point out to your vaulters at an early stage that taking steps during the stand is not a minor thing: it is much more than a bad habit. Therefore you must always make sure that the vaulter stands on the full surface of his feet, and no tilting to the toes or the heel should be permitted.

Over the kneel into the crouch

To go into the stand, the vaulter hops into the kneel from the basic seat position via a small swing. The height of the swing should not be exaggerated, as the stand is one of the *static* exercises, and even the hop into it should possibly express that. It is wrong to jump straight away into the crouch; the buildup *must* go over a full kneel position. (One full point deduction, if the kneel is omitted.) When swinging up into the kneel, consideration must be shown to the horse: the landing on the knees must be as soft as possible (so don't gain more height than absolutely necessary), the toes should not be dug into his kidneys, rather the flat top of the vaulter's feet should touch the horse's back first, then the ankles, then the knees. The face should be up and looking straight ahead the whole time.

Building up the stand

From the kneel position (or bench position, since the hands are still on the grips) there are two permissible ways to build up the stand: experienced vaulters do a small jump (with very soft landing) into the crouch, with both feet simultaneously, which looks more fluid and elegant, but there is nothing wrong with standing up with one foot first, then the other following. Remember that the judges (and a good trainer as well) watch for the consideration shown. If you have a jittery horse it does not make sense to upset him by a hard landing or pain in the kidney area, before you expect your vaulters to stand. And younger vaulters *feel safer* putting one foot up first — and half of the standing exercise happens in the head. If the vaulter is not confident that he can do it, it will not work, and elegant posture will never be achieved. In none of the compulsory exercises does self confidence show as much as in the stand...

From the crouch position the vaulter raises the upper body, arms fairly straight and still pointing in the direction of the grips. Tell young vaulters to stay low *in the knees*, if they feel insecure, but they *must* come up with their shoulders. Balancing is much harder when the child stays bent down, eyes fixed on the grips (because that is how he perceives security), since it shifts his gravity point out of the vertical to the front. In this way, it will take him unnecessarily long to experience the wonderful feeling of accomplishment, when he can stand the prescribed four strides for the first time. The gravity point must be aligned: we try for a straight line from head to shoulder to hip to ankles, just as in the seat.

Before we actually go into our stand, a word about beginners

The stand is what every beginner wants to be able to do. The scissors are much harder, but the glory is in the stand! If you want your children to stick with vaulting, you must satisfy them in this. Start them with the stand early: first in walk of course, and holding their hand (don't hold on to their legs). Always let them jump off out of the standing position in the beginning, the little ones to the inside holding your hand, the bigger ones to the outside by themselves. (Pre-exercises are jumps with soft landings from a chair as mentioned in the warm-up.) Never let a beginner sit down again, because if you do, it will take him forever to lose the reflex of bending down to the grips. Security in the stand, which is so important later for an 'underman', comes — if not from the soft knees and balance alone — from the feeling of being able to *separate* from the horse at any time in a controlled manner, of landing softly and on your feet always, and of not perceiving the given height as a threat.

It usually takes my beginners not longer than two months to jump off out of a crouch in canter. I ask them for the jump off (first in walk, of course) much earlier than for a stand. As soon as they feel that they can jump off and run safely from that height and speed, they can *all* stand. Their eyes are up (looking for the landing spot after the jump rather than looking at the surcingle) and their posture is more or less erect. Offer a sitting partner (in front of the surcingle) for added security — and your beginners have reached their glory very soon!

The stand: correct build-up

From the correct basic seat...

...the vaulter takes a moderate swing to elevate the legs into...

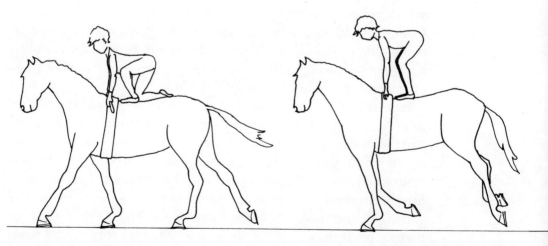

Beginners should stand up on one foot first to ensure avoiding discomfort to the horse

More advanced vaulters jump directly into the crouch with strong arm support for gentle landing

...the kneel. The gravity point must be over the hands to ensure soft landing. Both legs must kneel before the stand

From a balanced bench position the vaulter stands up

The vaulter brings the upper body up, establishing his balance. His back stays straight

With beginners the knees may stay bent low, but the back must be straight and torso must be brought to near vertical position for good balance

Building up the exercise

Coming up from the crouch, and having established his balance, the vaulter then extends his arms into the same position as in the basic seat, hands flat and palms down, ideally the finger tips at eye level. The movement into the stand should be smooth and fluid, without any disturbance of the harmony of movement with the horse. The stand must be held for four canter strides, *after* it is *fully built up*; that is, with arms fully extended and hands in the prescribed position and elevation.

Keeping balance in the stand

The stand really happens in the knees. All the movement, which arrives at the vaulter's feet from below, should be caught in his knees. In *actively* soft knees, I tell my vaulters, meaning that in

When this position is fully built up, the arms are extended. The correct arm position is the same as in the basic seat

The weight must be on the full flat soles of both feet throughout. The stand is taken down slowly and with a slight hop...

the beginning phases I let them *move* their knees *actively* themselves with every step the horse takes. This makes for an exaggerated motion, but it gets grease into those knees, stiff with concentration or apprehension! Of course the ankles catch some movement too, but it is not important to mention this, because the ankles are not usually held as cramped up. Better vaulters, who are already able to stand in canter, should look at a line on the wall to determine how much their upper body moves: it should ideally not move at all. The head (as well as hips) travels on a very quiet orbit around the riding ring...with the proverbial glass of water on top!

In training, especially in trot, we try to get the vaulter to make his stand independent of having his eyes glued to the grips... when they are secure enough, and if your horse is safe enough, make the vaulters count the cars that go by...or the clouds in

...the weight is shifted onto the arms and the vaulter slides with stretched and straddled legs back into the seat

The gravity point must be over the hands to ensure a soft settling down onto the horse's back

the sky. My better vaulters close their eyes to concentrate on their balance. The intent is to train their instinctive response to any interruption or disturbance in the regular canter movement: with slight disturbance the reaction should be to 'give' even more in the knees and 'shock absorb' even better. In case of major interruption (spooking etc.) the instinctive reaction should be to separate from the horse in a controlled manner, self-determining the direction of the fall, which will be more of a jump in that case, with a planned landing spot. The correct response would not be to get the hands back onto the grips: retaking the grips in competition costs too many points (full 2.0 the first time, and score of zero if retaken twice) — and in team exercises it can cost a 'flyer' partner an accident!

To get a little vaulter used to the correct body alignment right away, bring up their upper body into the vertical for correct balance and train them with an assistant sitting backwards on the neck. This person can hold the beginner around the hips, and the vaulter can rest his hands on the assistant's shoulders and feel safe without keeping his eyes glued to the surcingle.

Slight loss of balance may occur due to an inconsistency in the horse's gait, and this is often corrected by the vaulter by taking a little step on the horse's back to regain control. In case of competition, this is better than a fall or re-taking the grips of course, but do not let it become a habit with your vaulters during training. Teach them to be ready for slight changes in speed and make up for it with their shock-absorber knees — not through walking around.

Coming down from the stand

The torso is then bent down, the hands retake the grips, and the vaulter slides smoothly and softly back onto seat astride, after putting his weight on his arms and lifting it off the feet with a little hop. Feet are then pointed and legs fully stretched. The whole length of the legs should break the movement of sliding down, the motion must be fluid and elegant.

Don't let even beginners get away with falling back onto the horse! As long as they lose their balance, they should jump off. When they are able to come down out of the stand in a balanced and controlled manner, they are also able to do it softly and elegantly. Instil in them the notion that the stand is not over *before they are back down* — and this *elegantly!* If the stand is not performed within a block of compulsories, the exercise is terminated by a vault-off dismount.

Common mistakes

upper body not brought to vertical
'walking' on the horse, that is moving feet to make up for loss of balance
stiff or arched back (which I call 'duckie bum')
standing on toes, rather than whole foot
feet too wide apart, knees too low, or knees bent outward
faults in alignment: vaulter twists his body sideways or has arms at uneven height etc.
vaulter holds himself off centre
feet too far back behind surcingle
head too low, not looking straight to the front
building up the stand over one foot from the kneel (for competition only, for training this is ok)
going into the stand via direct hop into the crouch (omitting the kneel)

Common mistakes in the stand

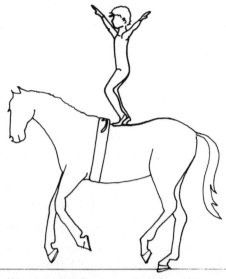

Wrong: 'Duckie bum'! Overarched back, arms too far to the front, feet too widely apart

Wrong: weight is not on whole foot, the vaulter walks around to keep the balance, arms are uneven

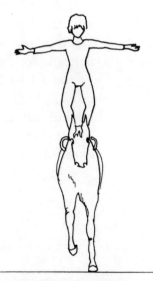

Wrong: the pelvis is tilted too far to the front. The back is rounded (poor posture) arms too far to the front and head low. The torso is behind the vertical, which will result in loss of balance and walking, or a fall

Wrong: the arms are too low, head down, palms showing to the front. The legs are too far apart

Wrong: feet are too far back. The insecure vaulter tries to stay close to the grips: the torso does not come to the vertical. Arms don't come up, head is low

Wrong: feet are too far back. Loss of balance to the front is counteracted by extending arms too far back

Correct stand: seen from the front. Hands are at eye level, knees close together, good posture

Wrong: unbalanced stand. The vaulter leans to inside, kink in the hip to make up for uneven legs. Thumbs are not to the hands

Beginners should be assisted to get used to correct posture from the start, i.e. straight back close to the vertical, eye up. Security given by a partner makes it possible to concentrate on softly absorbing knees

22   *The flank*

The last of the six compulsory exercises is the flank. It is a two-phase exercise, and the beginning is the same as the moves to go into a vault-off. I will dissect it into different pieces to explain the mechanics in their correct sequence.

Basic score

For the first half of the flank the basic score is set similar to the criteria in the first half of the scissors. If the angle which the vaulter achieves in the up-swing is smaller than 45 degrees, the basic score can not be over 7.0. (The necessary soft landing counts as performance mark.) In the second part of the flank it is the height achieved which sets the basic score, as well as the flight phase: if there is no flight phase after leaving the grips, but the flank was a good height, the basic score can not be over 8.0. A 9.0 needs a good height during the flight phase, and a perfect 10.0 needs a gain in height after leaving the grips. If your vaulting club is just starting out, this will not be your immediate concern...

Pre-exercises in training

Important pre-exercises in the flank are the swinging into the handstand with and without partner on the stationary horse. As consideration to the horse is such an important factor in vaulting, I believe that the exercise must be performed quite well on the barrel, before moving onto the live team mate! Those hard landings can really turn a horse sour...and beginners need considerable time for building up the necessary arm strength, as

Good position   Lacking arm strength

well as for learning the correct technique and timing of the coordination of leg swing and arm push.

A good pre-exercise to coordinate the swing and the arm push, as well as to learn to position the gravity point over the grips correctly, is once again the assisted swing into handstand on the barrel. If the vaulter does his 'nose plant' at the beginning of the swing, he does not have enough strength in the arms yet. If he does it when the assistant pushes him into the handstand, he has a gravity point problem, or both: this makes for the hardest landings on the live horse! The worst mistake (typical beginner's fault) is to swing up without moving the gravity point over the hands − forward − whereas the beginner tries to get his feet up, because this is how he perceives he should gain height, and the feet are in the back! If the gravity point is too far back, the arms can't push up, but will rather push the vaulter backward. So he is in the wrong position, has *no* arm control and crashes into the horse's sensitive kidney area. To avoid this, you must explain to the vaulter that we are much more concerned with the hips coming up than the feet. So we train what we call the 'pop-up' exercise.

Here the vaulter takes a quick and precise pre-swing and downswing, with acceleration in the downswing. The movement of the feet stops abruptly behind the surcingle and propels the hips up into the air. This means that the upper body, which tilts with the swing motion, has tipped enough at this point so that

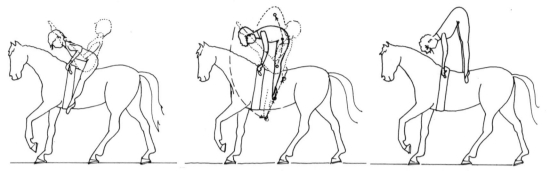

At the lowest point of the down-swing, the weight is transferred onto the hands

Pre-exercise for scissors and flank (all swing exercises) the 'Pop-up'

Hips have 'popped' to the highest position, the gravity point is entirely over the hands. The vaulter can stop in mid air

all the weight is over the vaulter's hands: theoretically the vaulter could hold this position without leaning the legs against the horse's side. It is a handstand position, although the legs are not extended. Later the vaulter will learn to extend them by straightening the legs in the hip joint, but this will not change the technique of bringing the gravity point over the hands at the correct moment in the swing.

When the vaulters have practised this enough, they will be able to land their feet on the horse's back by leaving them extended in a relaxed manner. First they will land them toward the croup, then be able to bring them toward the surcingle closer and closer. The swing will bring their hips up (which is their main weight) and the arm push will be able to maintain them in this position, because the gravity point is exactly over the hands and the position is balanced.

The second pre-exercise takes this arm control one step further. It is really the proof to the vaulter of whether he actually *has* his weight (his gravity point) over his hands. Make him perform a regular up-swing as described under the first half of the flank, then, sometime *after* he has piked in his hip joints, clap your hands to make him stop in mid air! With a correctly aligned gravity point the vaulter will be able to hold such a position at any given point during the phase of coming down. This is of course necessary for controlled soft landings.

First phase

- *The pre-swing*: Note that a deduction of up to 2.0 points is possible (for performance) for moving the buttocks back too far, to evade the difficulty in the swing. The swing must start out of the seat position. The flank begins with a pre-swing of both legs, which should be carried to the maximum possible extension for the vaulter. To achieve this, the upper body leans back slightly, but with straight back, and the grip of the hands becomes lighter. The motion does not stop at the highest point, but reverts into the downswing at once and in one fluid motion.

- *The downswing*: If any use is to be gained from the downswing, it must accelerate, achieving the fastest speed at the lowest point, just like a golf club. It is very clear that the energy which the vaulter does *not* put into the acceleration of the downswing, can also *not* come out of that swing at the other end! Note on the illustration, how the upper body follows the motion of the swinging legs: again the vaulter must shift his weight to move the gravity point over his hands during the swing, so he can exert an arm push straight up (not backward) and maintain control of the movement and body weight throughout the whole flight phase. Otherwise he will not be able to land softly.

- *The up-swing and arm push*: After the downswing (to the lowest point) follows the through- and up-swing, the arm action must kick in with the push. This can happen as soon as the vaulter has transferred his weight to his hands. Up to this point the swinging curve is basically a circle with the same radius around the hand-hip-point.

  But now, as the arm push kicks in, and the up-swing starts, the curve gets flatter, with a larger radius the more the arms extend. The legs can only come up to best height, if the shoulders go down. For training purposes I consider it better if the vaulter collapses on the neck of the horse, rather than cheating his way around the push! The highest extension possible is the handstand position, but even if this can be reached, the motion should *not* stop here. Remember: there should be *no stops* in dynamic exercises.

By the apex of this up-swing at the latest, and while the vaulter has his weight fully over his hands and supports himself only with his arms, the legs must be closed, and must now stay together and fully stretched with pointed toes, until the very end of the exercise. The vaulter now bends sharply in the hip joints and the legs (still together) fold down and point to the ground. The weight is over the hands, so again, theoretically the vaulter should be able to stop the down motion at any given time! If not, the gravity point is not in the right spot and there is no arm control to break the landing impact.

To come down into the inside lady's seat is therefore not a fall: the vaulter can control the speed and breaks the impact by first touching the horse's side with his right foot, then gliding down over calf and thigh. His shoulders continue to face the front, and the hips will rotate ideally just a moment before he softly settles into the inside lady seat. To achieve this, he must continue a strong arm support all the way down! The seat must then be erect and the weight must rest on both buttocks evenly, the head must be high, legs long and together and both to the horse.

(*Please see the drawing on pages 144/5 for the up-swing before the pike of the hip.*)

Second phase

- *Pre-exercises*: As in the first phase, the most important aspect is the correct weight transfer of the gravity point to over the vaulter's hands. Since this feels very different for beginners out of a sideways seat, train 'whole—part—whole' again. To achieve height is much easier if the vaulter leans slightly over the outside shoulder of the horse, while his shoulders, aligned with the horse's, come down. In the pre-swing the vaulter rolls onto his right hip and stretches both legs. Exercise this swing without the push-off: let your vaulter swing both legs, together and closed, to the point over the croup, then separate them to settle down gently into the riding seat again. The push-off for the flight phase can be trained separately by a simple vault-off to the outside.

- *The swing*: The second phase of the flank is begun with as little delay as possible after the first one. Try to teach your vaulters from the beginning that the whole flank should be fluid, so they don't waste too much time in between the two phases, but insist with beginners on one deep breath and a second of concentration! If they hurry going into the second phase without any mental preparation, it will most likely not be well performed. Experienced competition vaulters however should not delay for longer than approximately four canter strides between the two phases.

    The second phase begins with a forward swing of both legs, straight and together, upper body leaning only slightly and back staying straight. The more height can be achieved in this pre-swing, the more momentum can be gained in the downswing, which again means more height in the up-swing, just as we discussed in the first phase. As the vaulter is now sitting sideways, he has to take care to balance and exert arm control, so as not to slide off to the inside. The technique of the weight transfer is the same as before. The arm push kicks in as soon as the vaulter has shifted his weight sufficiently to the hands, and continues to the apex of the flight and beyond (as already explained in connection with the vault-off and the scissors), but this time the vaulter leans his shoulders slightly over the outside shoulder of the horse, to make up for the sideways seat. The legs must stay together the whole time; they may *not* separate in the second up-swing to gain additional height! Separating the legs means evasion of difficulty, and a

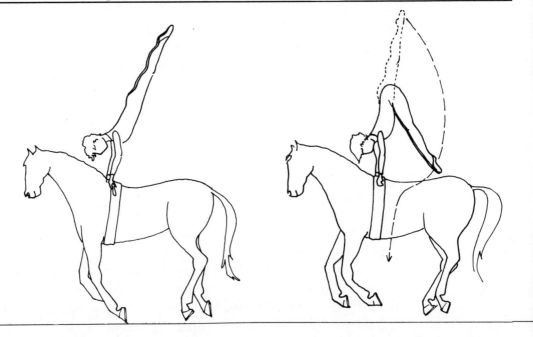

The fluidity of the up-swing should not be arrested in a static handstand. (This is not a static exercise)

At the highest point the body is piked and all the weight must be directly on arms and hands

The hip is turned sideways only briefly before landing in the side seat

This hip movement must then be executed quickly to be fully rotated into side seat...

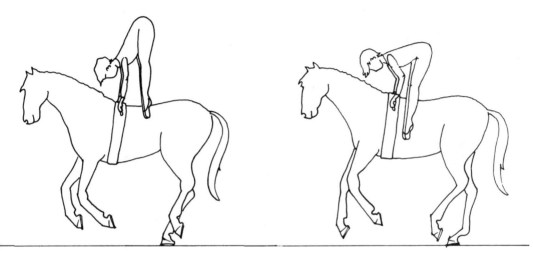

The vaulter must have such control to break the down movement that he can glide down slowly and gently, touching first with the right foot...

...then slide along the outer side of the right leg. Ideally the vaulter should be able to stop the movement anywhere in between on command — that is the arm control which ensures the horse's comfort

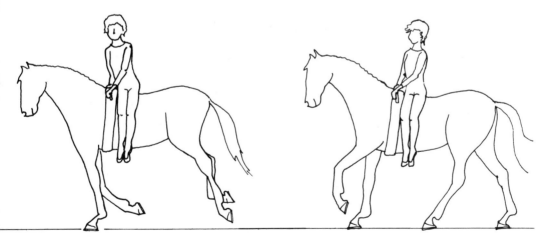

...before settling down. Correct side seat in the flank is different from the mill. Shoulder and head must face the front. Both legs are closed and to the horse alongside the surcingle. Supple hips absorb the movement of the canter stride

The correct flank: second phase

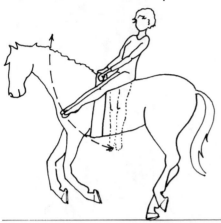 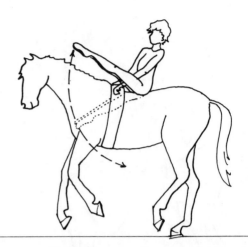

While going into the up-swing, the upper body may lean only slightly and the seat may not be swished back to facilitate the swing

The vaulter must sit on both buttocks while swinging, then roll onto his right hip

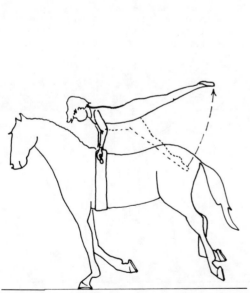 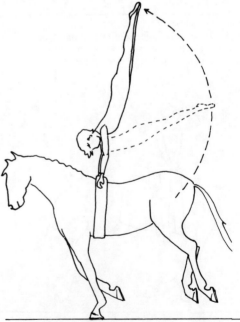

As the legs are swung up, the bodyline must be straight

Good vaulters reach handstand position, but fluid movement may not stop

The legs must accelerate in the down-swing and the weight is transferred onto the arms as the buttocks lift off

The gravity point must be over the hands, the arms and hips are stretched to full extension in the up-swing

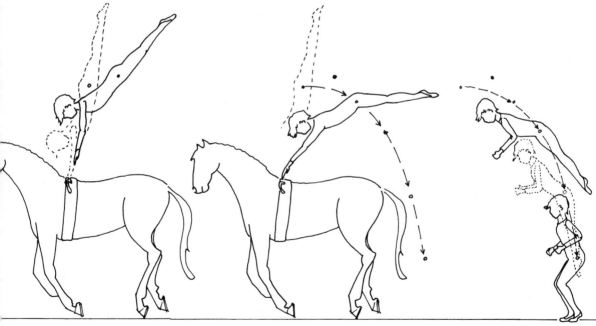

At the apex the vaulter must push away from the grips energetically with both arms to achieve a flight phase. For best scores additional height should be gained here

In the flight phase the body rotates around its gravity point. The vaulter lands softly, absorbing the impact with feet, ankles, knees and hips, and continues forward running motion. The vaulter should land on the outside and away from the horse, approximately at level with the hindquarters

flank will be scored better, if the height achieved is not quite the handstand position, but the legs were together, rather than the opposite!

If the height of a handstand position is reached, which good and very strong vaulters achieve quite frequently, that position should nevertheless not be held, the fluid motion of the flank may not be stopped to show off strength! The flight phase with the push-off must start immediately after the highest point in the up-swing is reached, in one fluid and smooth motion. Note how through the whole up-swing we are basically aiming for a straight body line, although at the beginning the vaulter is slightly kinked in the hips to get the most out of the kick, and toward the end he may arch his back slightly to help the arm push. Hollow backs however are not permitted to gain additional height for the feet!

- *Flight phase*: At the apex of the up-swing then, the flight phase starts, which is similar to the one described in the vault-off. The legs must still be (and stay) together and stretched, feet pointed. The arms now push away from the grips with an energetic movement and the body describes a curve in the air before landing clear of the horse and on the outside, with an erect body and soft knees. The vaulter absorbs the shock of the landing by using *all* joints involved (balls of the feet, ankles, knees hip), and then continues running forward in a fluid motion.

  You will frequently see vaulters gripping the lower part of the outside handle for the push-off in the flight phase. There are no rules about how to grip the handles — let your vaulters try out what feels best to them, and how they think they can achieve best push-off and height.

Common mistakes

not bringing the shoulders down to swing the legs up, and arching the back to make up for it

gravity point not over the hands: arms push the vaulter
toward the croup, rather than up

hitting the horse with a hard landing after the first phase of
the flank, not carrying the weight on the hands and absorbing
it over the right calf

not sitting on both buttocks in the side seat

twisting in any part of the phases

too great a lapse of time between the two phases

separating the legs in the up-swing of the second phase to
gain more height

insufficient height in either phase

clinging to the grips too long, rather than going straight
into the flight phase after the apex of the swing is reached

landing hard into the ground with a dead stop after the
flank off or stumbling and touching the ground with the
hands after coming off

With the completion of the flank, the blocks of the compulsory
exercises are finished. In a normal competition, this will be
followed by the kur after the horse gets an adequate break. This
is the case in Individual Vaulting Competitions, as well as for
Team performances. Only *pas-de-deux* performances do not
include compulsory exercises in the requirements.

Common flank mistakes

Wrong: gravity point not over hands: the vaulter pushes himself toward the croup. No arm control, therefore hard landing, too far back

Wrong: weight not over hands, hard landing

Wrong: gravity point too far back, legs separate during landing. Seat corrections will be necessary

Wrong gravity point in the second up-swing: the vaulter pushed to the back, rather than up

Wrong: hard landing too far back, hip turned in too early

Wrong: vaulter settles in from too far back, no arm control. Arched back and hard landing

Wrong: motion is not controlled: the legs continue to swing past the surcingle after landing

Wrong: full height can't be reached as the weight is not over the vaulter's hands. Legs are separated

Wrong: gravity point is slightly back, over-arched back in an effort to make up for lost height

Wrong: legs separate in the up-swing. Evasion of difficulty

Wrong: separated legs meet only over the croup

Wrong: vaulter turns to inside during swing: twisted bodyline, bent and separated legs

Wrong: vaulter twists during flight phase

Wrong: no arm push, vaulter does not clear
the horse. Arched back

Wrong: excessive piking during flank-off

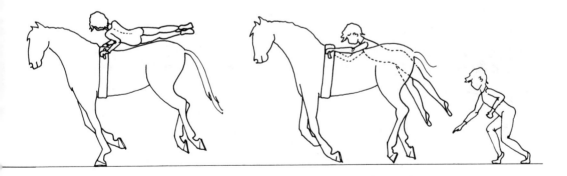

Wrong: collapse of supporting arms, vaulter
does not clear the horse and twists in an
attempt to make up for it. No flight phase

Wrong: clinging to the grips instead of push-off:
no flight phase, vaulter gets dragged. This often
results in a fall, i.e. touching the ground with hands
or knee

23 Training — difficulty of team kur exercises

Before your vaulters drop out because of boredom with the compulsories, you have to start adding some variety by introducing kur, which are freestyle exercises. But if you are not a vaulter yourself, you might need some guidance in how to pick the first team exercises for them to try. This chapter will help you make this decision, according to the ability of your vaulters, the difficulty of the exercises and the potential dangers to avoid.

There are over 300 vaulting kur exercises shown in the catalogue at the end of this book, many of them team exercises. It is not necessary to treat them individually in this chapter, because once the underlying principles are understood, the determination of difficulty follows logically.

double decker flag

- *Freestyle exercises* are grouped into the categories of singles, doubles and triples, within which are:

  Static exercises: seats and splits; kneels, flags and benches; stands, arabesques, high benches; lying exercises; hangs; shoulderstands and handstands; exercises with push-ups or supports; statics on top of statics; flyers (supported without contact of the flyer with the horse)

  Dynamic exercises: mounts, dismounts, transitions; flips, rolls, leaps, jumps; as singles, doubles or triples; assisted or unassisted

  And any combination of the above: for example one sitting and one standing partner (static) lifting a flyer and turning him in the air, while supported (dynamic)

- *Criteria for difficulty*: The classification of difficulty for these exercises is determined by the following criteria:

security of holding points:	whether the vaulter is holding on by the grips, the back of the horse or the neck. It is obvious that the grips are most secure!
the number of holding points:	whether the vaulter holds with two arms, one arm, or free. This is also applicable for a team configuration: the more holding points *all* three (or two) vaulters use together, the more secure the exercise.
the direction of the movement:	in relationship to the horse's travel direction. Most exercises are most difficult backwards and more difficult sideways than executed in the direction of travel.
the direction of the vaulter in relation to the horse:	having your head up is easier than looking at the world upside down, especially on a cantering horse. Outside mounts are more difficult than inside ones, because of the effect of centrifugal force.
the distance/ height above the horse:	the higher the exercise gets, the more precarious the balance, the stronger felt are the swaying movements from the motion of the horse. Obviously, the nearer the vaulter's gravity point(s) stay to the horse, the safer the position.
the size of the contact surface:	when the vaulter lies across the horse with his belly, or sits on both buttocks he is naturally more secure than supporting himself on one shoulder, or standing on one foot!
the complexity of the movement:	changes in direction make an exercise more difficult. Simultaneous turns around the vertical and side axes heighten the complexity further.

All kur exercises are grouped into three different classifications in terms of difficulty by the International Vaulting Rule Book (FEI): they are EASY (class 3), MEDIUM (class 2) or DIFFICULT (class 1). This results directly from the above mentioned criteria. For *training* purposes I will classify the exercises differently. What you want to know as a trainer, who might have to learn this out of the book, because you are not an ex-vaulter yourself, is how difficult and *potentially dangerous* certain exercises are, because your team will largely rely on your judgement in what they are able to perform. And if your judgement is wrong, there could be accidents — and you might be found negligent in your role as a coach. This is what you must avoid. It is too simplified to say that an exercise is potentially dangerous, because it is high. It is also wrong to say that because an exercise is classified as difficult, it is necessarily dangerous. Both statements are untrue and I will show this with examples.

The main reason for an increase in potential danger lies of course in *height*, which is a major factor for four reasons: *the higher the exercise gets* the higher the potential fall; the more unstable it tends to get (at least one partner standing, and lifts on extended arms); the more strength it requires (high means lifts on extended arms); the more important cooperation, timing and technique become; the less the coach can spot or help the vaulters. This does not mean that the lower exercises are by nature easier. The difficulty for *performance* is dependent also on other factors:

in dynamic exercises: the power for the height of the jump, the agility, quickness and precision for complex movements (twists and turns), the sense of coordination and timing; *in static exercises*: the stability of the configuration (number and security of holding points) the demand on flexibility (splits and extensions) demands on strength; quietness and precision in general; talent for artistic expression in general (elegance). In combinations of static and dynamic all of the above apply.

Exercise 145 in the catalogue of vaulting exercises, a 'horizontal lying hang', is an excellent example of this. It is classified as a number 1 (highest level of difficulty) and extremely hard to perform in canter as it requires great strength and control. However it is not in the least dangerous: if it is not well performed and the vaulter can't hold the position, he will simply come down feet first from insignificant height, and will neither twist nor fall, because he has both hands on the grips.

So when assessing a trainer's capability, we have to take his or her experience into account in terms of capability of training vaulters for the case, when an exercise *does not work*. As we are dealing with a living partner (with a mind very much of his own), unforeseen circumstances, such as the horse stumbling or spooking, may come into play at any time. As a good coach you must prepare your vaulters for such eventualities, because they must be able to react fast and 'bail out' in a safe and controlled manner.

For explanation's sake I will group exercises into different 'storeys' as an indication of the height achieved in them:

- *A 1st storey exercise*: is often classified as easy, has usually at least three support points and has the carrying (one or two) partners sitting.

- *A 2nd floor exercise*: is often classified easy to medium, has a mix of sitting, kneeling and/or standing position in the carrying partners; one flyer may be lifted off completely, but usually with at least one sitting underman and the flyer will have three to four support points (or *potential* support points!).

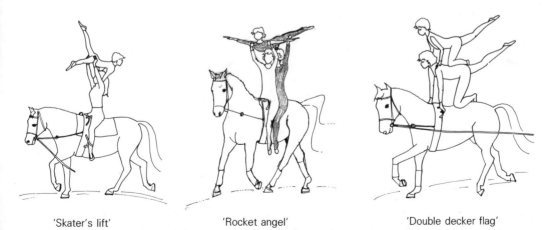

'Skater's lift'   'Rocket angel'   'Double decker flag'

- *A 3rd floor exercise*: will be classified medium to difficult, will have one carrying partner standing; the flyer has no contact with the horse and has fewer holding points to the undermen; the security of holding points is decreased and the general stability of the configuration is more precarious.

'High handstand'   'Statue of Liberty'   'Flag with flag on high bench'

'Superhigh rocket'   'Superhigh handstand'

- *A 4th floor exercise*: may have up to two carrying partners standing (no. 299c); the flyer is lifted *and* pushed high (no. 285).

Please note for reference to the quoted exercise numbers that numbers in the FEI rule book (edition 1986) and the rule book translated from the German Regulations (edition 1987) are not the same as in our Catalogue of vaulting exercises.

Correct 'bail-out' training

We have mentioned before that a fall does not, and should not, mean an accident. A *dangerous fall* is an *uncontrolled fall*. Vaulters must be taught always to expect and *plan* a fall, and must be ready to jump *into* it when the necessity to bail out arises.

Some of the ground rules are: you should never lose your balance to the back, when standing. From stand, you either jump into the fall straight, and run, or you actively fall into it and *roll*. You should not bend down or cling! The trainer should play through the three most common scenarios of falls: the horse suddenly speeds up — what happens?; the horse slows down, or stops — what happens?; the horse spooks, jumps sideways, or stumbles — what then?

In a team kur configuration, the trainer must determine, and *teach*, who should try to stay on the horse as support for others. The main supporting underman must be fully aware of his responsibility, and *anticipate* and brace. Train him like this: where will the exercise fall to, when the horse suddenly stops? Are you bracing against weight pushing you to the front, or pulling you to the back? Where will the flyer pull you to, when the horse stumbles? (Usually to the outside, because of centrifugal force.) How do you anticipate and guard against sliding off in a case like that? Let's look at some different exercises:

- A standing partner will usually bail out, because he is not given much choice, as he can not really brace himself or pull himself back into position.

- A sitting partner at the surcingle will cling and brace and counter-pull, as he is the fixed point of the configuration and has to steady the others.

- A solely supporting underman will try to cling until his flyer has had a chance to slide off, since the top vaulter's fall would be so much higher.

- The only case, when none of the ground rules hold true, is, when for some reason the surcingle comes loose and starts to turn. In that case clinging is the wrong solution for all vaulters, since several children may end up *under* the horse this way. *All* vaulters should separate from the horse as quickly as possible, fall and roll.

I will try to explain further with some examples of how to train for bail-out. However, all exercises are different, and the coach must look at each one individually to determine how to prepare the vaulters for the eventuality of having to get out of it. Some exercises (like a sitting flyer on top of a standing partner's shoulders with 'locked' feet) do not really allow a bail-out for the flyer, and these should *never* be attempted by inexperienced vaulters, not even in walk, *even if* they are classified as easy. And again: discuss the fall scenarios with all partners involved and ask them if they feel confident that they could handle it. Train the bail-out of high exercises in walk, trot and canter, and *never* entice your vaulters to do things they don't feel ready for!

'Draped lift'

When you read the following examples, you might think that the falling scenarios are much too difficult to be remembered by a vaulting child in case of a real fall. If you train with bail-outs in mind, however, you will find that the vaulters are very well capable of letting this sink into their subconscious, and reacting the correct way, if they have the chance to practise it often enough! Indeed they should do a bail-out every second time, when they attempt the exercise in walk, and even in trot, during practice. Although you can never guarantee that they will actually have the time and presence of mind eventually to bail out in the prescribed manner in case of a real emergency, you will at least have taught them that falls are an integral part of high exercises and no need to panic. With this alone, you will have increased the chance of avoiding accidents by at least seventy per cent! Anxiety causes cramped muscles, which in turn causes broken bones — if your vaulters are confident and relaxed, they have a very good chance of getting out of any fall without injury.

Examples of various difficulty in 'bail-out'

(Numbers refer to the Catalogue of vaulting exercises).

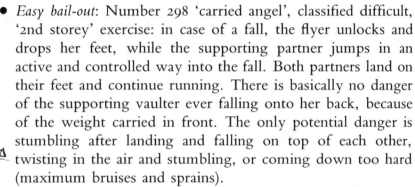

'Carried angel'

- *Easy bail-out*: Number 298 'carried angel', classified difficult, '2nd storey' exercise: in case of a fall, the flyer unlocks and drops her feet, while the supporting partner jumps in an active and controlled way into the fall. Both partners land on their feet and continue running. There is basically no danger of the supporting vaulter ever falling onto her back, because of the weight carried in front. The only potential danger is stumbling after landing and falling on top of each other, twisting in the air and stumbling, or coming down too hard (maximum bruises and sprains).

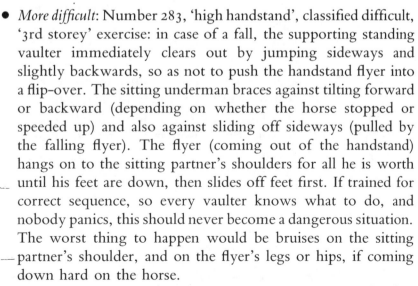

'High handstand'

- *More difficult*: Number 283, 'high handstand', classified difficult, '3rd storey' exercise: in case of a fall, the supporting standing vaulter immediately clears out by jumping sideways and slightly backwards, so as not to push the handstand flyer into a flip-over. The sitting underman braces against tilting forward or backward (depending on whether the horse stopped or speeded up) and also against sliding off sideways (pulled by the falling flyer). The flyer (coming out of the handstand) hangs on to the sitting partner's shoulders for all he is worth until his feet are down, then slides off feet first. If trained for correct sequence, so every vaulter knows what to do, and nobody panics, this should never become a dangerous situation. The worst thing to happen would be bruises on the sitting partner's shoulder, and on the flyer's legs or hips, if coming down hard on the horse.

'BW wheelbarrow on bench'

'Shoulder arabesque'

'Free stand on shoulder'

- *Bail-out with necessary twist*: Number 201(b) similar 'backward wheel-barrow on FW bench, supported from bw seat' and similar: here the supporting sitting partner must tilt off the flyer in case of an imminent fall, preferably to the outside and in such a way that the flyer will come down feet first…and facing the direction of travel, so he can run or roll easily, and with centrifugal force, away from the horse. The kneeling partner should try to cling until the flyer's feet are down, and because of the security of his holding points (both hands on the grips) and the forward direction, he should be the last to come off. If he can manage to help and steady the partner, who is at this point falling off the neck in a backward position, which is much more dangerous, this would be great!

- *Double-height bail-out*: Number 258, shoulder arabesque, or number 234, more difficult with extended leg, is a situation where the supporting underman must be fully aware of how difficult the bail-out would be for the flyer, and must do his utmost to prevent strong jerky movements to any side during the performance. It looks as if the flyer can just jump off — from up high certainly — and land on his feet or roll. In fact, falls out of these exercises are more complicated. Any movement, which the underman experiences due to a stopping or acceleration of the horse, or a sideways spooking, is felt in a much aggravated manner by the flyer up top. This means that he will rarely come down feet first. An experienced and courageous flyer will immediately roll into the fall to the outside. But most flyers will tend to cling, which is dangerous, because then the direction and course of the fall become quite unpredictable. So here prevention is definitely the best solution: if the underman is fully aware of the possible consequences of *his* loss of balance, he will be more attentive and anticipate, therefore being able to counteract any such movement by the horse more effectively.

- *All-standing bail-out*: Number 299(c) shows a 'rocket angel' supported by two standing partners. In such exercises it is very important that the vaulters have an idea of where they will go in case of a fall. The flyer should get a chance to come down feet first, if at all possible. So train the back underman to drop him quickly in case of loss of balance (not by throwing him, but by flexing the knees). Teach the vaulters, in high standing exercises to rely on their own balance only — no shoving or pushing of the other partners is allowed to save their own neck! Standing partners on the croup should try to bail out to the rear, to make room for the others to come down elsewhere. It is painful for everybody to all come down in the same spot... vaulters should always try to land in the direction of travel, and preferably to the outside — centrifugal force helps you to avoid getting under the horse! Always roll, if you are not coming down in a position, where you can continue the motion by running. Teach your undermen to take on true responsibility for the flyer — the youngest and the highest one! — to try to save him or her first.

'Superhigh rocket'

- *feet locked + height*: no real bail-out! Number 243, 'Totem pole', is one of those exercises to be performed only when all vaulters involved, as well as the horse, are truly solid and experienced. Falls in interlocked positions usually have nasty results. Don't overestimate the stabilizing effect, which a sitting partner can exert! Especially when sitting in front of the surcingle, as is often the case in such exercises. The flyer can neither freely jump off out of the sitting position, nor go into a roll, and usually all three vaulters tend to cling and come down in a twisted heap. So if your horse tends to be nervous around applause these exercises are not for your team!

'Totem pole'

No fall can ever be predicted totally accurately! However, know your horse (and his limitations!) and judge the ability of your vaulters correctly! Prepare them for the eventuality of these falls mentally, so they are relaxed and don't panic in unforeseen circumstances, and most problems can be avoided. At least by coaching them this way, hopefully nobody can prove you negligent.

24 *Training for first freestyle exercises*

When you are first starting out with children who have never vaulted, you will train the compulsories for quite a while to teach them the basics, then, to introduce more variety, you will start them on some individual freestyle exercises. These don't have to be discussed in this book at any length, as the progression from simple to complex is logical and you can choose the appropriate exercises from the catalogue at the end of this book.

The basic difference between the compulsories and the individual ('single') freestyle exercises lies in the open choice of:

The Handstand

- *Security and number of holding points*: A simple example of how a beginner will progress is to move from a free kneel (large support surface: both shins; basically four support points: feet and knees; symmetrical exercise) to a 'Prince's seat' (smaller support surface: one shin and only the foot of the other leg; basically three support points; asymmetrical exercise). An example for the progression to difficult would be to move from a forward arabesque in the stirrup (three secure support points: two grips plus one stirrup; plus leg support leaning against the horse; low elevation) to a free arabesque on the horse's back (one very small support point, that is, one foot. Greater height, that is, more impact of motion; requires excellent balance).

The Hang

- *Possible changes in direction*: In freestyle we introduce a great variety of directional changes, forward, backwards, sideways, upside down, inside and outside the circle, and combinations of these (like a SW shoulderhang). Difficulty varies with direction: a BW stand is of course more difficult than a FW one, which, as a compulsory exercise, does *not* qualify for a kur!

The swan

- *We also start using different parts of the horse's body*: And the impact of motion, and width of support surfaces varies greatly with that. Standing on the croup for example heightens the difficulty in three ways: it is harder to get there — it is more slippery (no pad) — and the movement is more pronounced. Standing in front of the surcingle on the horse's shoulders is even more difficult as the surface to stand on is very narrow and slants steeply. Also motion is more pronounced than in the middle of the horse's back.

- *The last significant difference lies in the possibility of making movements more complex*: In freestyle the vaulter can include (in exercises, mounts, dismounts and transitions) such motion as twists, rolls, jumps and complex swings. Here he needs not only good body control and strength for precision, excellent timing to stay in sync with the horse's canter stride, but also good spatial orientation. Get your vaulters used to this concept early. You'll find that many children (especially when they still confuse left and right) are quite lost when they hang upside down! They need to learn some sense of spatial orientation first, before they attempt rolls and twists. When a vaulter later performs a sideways roll-off dismount in canter (from lying on his back) he will roll *and* twist in the air to land in the forward direction to be able to continue running in the direction of travel as required.

The vaulter should progress logically from easy to difficult, from simple to complex. He should be acquainted with some directional changes and some transitions, as well as freeing one or two hands to support a partner, before attempting 'double' or team exercises.

Your vaulters must always train new exercises first on the floor (where applicable, like handstands) and then on the barrel.

Later you will try them in walk on the horse — walk along and spot the children, where necessary. For each freestyle exercise they do they must be aware of and practise the correct procedures to get out of it in case of a mishap (round-offs from handstand, roll-offs, jump-offs from kneel and stand, etc.). When they start these exercises in canter later, always practise the easier form first (that is, without letting the hands go, or holding with one hand), even if the exercise already looks perfect in walk.

I like to start young vaulters on double exercises early, as soon as they are reasonably secure, because it is really what they want most, and offers new aspects of vaulting. For some this point in time may be after the sixth lesson, for others much later. It depends on their age, their state of mind, their balance and their experience in related disciplines, such as gymnastics.

New criteria for the introduction of team exercises

When you start out your children on team exercises, several new criteria come into play, which you did not have to deal with while practising compulsories or other single exercises. Namely:

- *Trust in the partner* becomes essential: this will of course grow over time, but it can only grow in a positive and effective way, if things do not go wrong — so take great care to start out with simple exercises, first on the barrel, then in walk. Assess the abilities of your vaulters correctly, try out their strength slowly — and emphasize the fun of team exercises! An experience of success is essential in the first team exercises, as it is hard to rebuild trust in a flyer, who once got dumped head first into the sand from a height of six feet!

- *Cooperation between partners* becomes necessary. Refer also to chapter 5 for the difficulty which might occur between vaulting children. Take likes and dislikes between the children into account — it is always more fun to cooperate with a friend

'Double jump'   'Draped lift'

You *are* in someone else's hands!

'Lifted FW split'

Variation of 'the star'

first; more professional feelings of cooperation will be developed later. Explain that cooperation means discussing things; if they don't work − never let the children abuse each other or lay blame! If you do not stop such practices (and sometimes the parents get into the picture too!) right from the start, you will not be able to build an efficient and consistent team.

- *Coordination between partners*: each grip should be repeated until it has become second nature. The sequence of grips you demand should be logical, as simple as possible − and always the same for each exercise! This greatly adds to the safety of any exercise, it establishes training routine and it saves enormous time in mounts, transitions and the build–up and take–down of exercises − phases, which should be executed accurately and quickly to leave more time to show off the exercise itself. (In competition you will have to deal with time restraints!)

- *Timing* of moves, coordinated between partners. It is best to establish clear rules for the whole team of how to count: for mounts behind a partner for example we count 'one, two, three, hop', as this gives a beginner enough time to prepare for the jump off, and more proficient vaulters count 'three, hop'. We use the same principle for all exercises. It saves a great deal of confusion. Don't allow one vaulter to jump on hop, the other on three etc.; your team will take twice as long to get coordinated!

There are certain basic principles in team kur exercises, which must be followed to guarantee safe and successful performance.

Basic principles for team kur exercises

Basic techniques of static team kur exercises: Since we can't analyse all static team kur exercises, we'll just explain the most essential techniques, which apply to most of them. Basically, we are always striving for a straight, strong body line. This applies to handstands, bench positions, wheelbarrows as well as lying positions of a flyer.

(A) Exercises with handstands, wheelbarrows and arabesques

To all of the above the same principles apply. In the correct handstand the vertical line through the vaulter's gravity point will run exactly through the support surface of the hands. Eyes should be directed onto the hands and the back should be long and straight, as if pulled upward.

The most common handstand mistakes are:

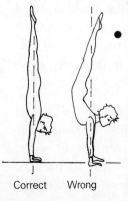

Correct   Wrong

- (1) *Overbent hollow back*: results most often from lack of strength in the back musculature, or lack of ability to tense those muscles adequately. Often the very flexible children find it 'cool' to show off how they can bend their backs, totally unaware of how wrong that posture is. This may also result from fear of losing orientation, so the vaulter tries to look into the forward direction, thereby overextending his neck. Loss of balance, through strong deviation from the vertical line, is then made up by overcurving the back.

- *Correction*: looking onto the hands; pulling stomach in (the shorter the stomach muscles are contracted, the straighter the back will be); imagine someone pulls your toes to the roof. If the hollow back is a result of lacking body tension, try to correct with the following exercise: the vaulter in handstand will be tilted back and forth between two partners, while tensing his stomach and back musculature.

- (2) *Combination of hollow back and bent arms*: could result from deficient arm strength, sometimes combined with stiff shoulders frequently stems from trying to make up for loss of balance by 'walking'.

- *Correction*: tense stomach muscles against hollow back; push-ups for arm strength; exercises to increase shoulder mobility practise handstands against the wall.

- (3) *S-shaped handstand*: often results from fear of flipping over or lack of spatial orientation: not feeling where the legs are in relation to the vertical. Since the legs do not reach the vertical, the vaulter has to shift his butt the other way (opposite the feet) to move his gravity point back onto the vertical line.

- *Correction*: stretching in the hip, practising handstand against the wall, practising handstand to complete vertical, and then rounding off sideways.

Correct   Correct   Wrong

The basic position, the technically correct one, might change a little, as the aesthetic aspect is introduced into it. Some leg positions require that the back is hollowed slightly more than shown before, but an overbending of the back should always be avoided.

The same principles apply to all supported handstands, whether executed on the horse or on the partners, as well as for all wheelbarrow and lying flyer positions.

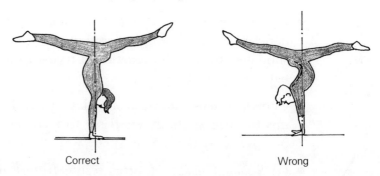

Correct   Wrong

(B) Technique of the carrying underman

There are many books which depict and explain in anatomical terms how the positions of the bones (shoulders, spine and pelvis) should look in a healthy body, and how to relieve the strain on the spine by using stomach and back musculature correctly. The way our spine is built it is obvious that the less we curve it, the less strain we put on the discs. As a trainer you should have the basic knowledge to be able to teach correct posture and determine whether a vaulter has sufficiently developed back and stomach muscles to be used as a carrying underman.

As participation (at least in competition) in team exercises is limited agewise to eighteen years and under, most carrying undermen are still growing, and it is extremely important to insist on correct technique to avoid damaging their backs. They often have to lift flyers not much younger and lighter than themselves and on top of that they have to absorb the motion of the horse in canter, so the load and strain can be quite significant.

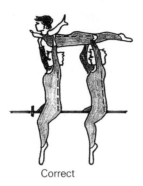
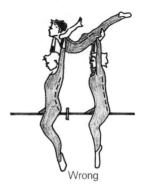

Correct   Wrong

The posture of a strong straight spine, where the weight of the lifted flyer is carried by the muscles (and not by bone and disc compression!), is necessary in all lifting exercises, whether executed in sitting, kneeling or standing position.

When the underman is sitting, all the principles of the basic seat (as discussed previously and in the chapter about compulsories) apply. The underman can only do his best in supporting someone else, if he is perfectly balanced himself and maximizes his strength by assuming the technically correct posture. This means: weight balanced on both buttocks evenly, no slouch, no hollow back, no pelvic tilt out of the prescribed position, no bend in the torso, no drawn-up knees.

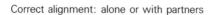

Correct alignment: alone or with partners

When the underman is kneeling, the rules are the same in an upright kneel. In a bench position, take care that the angle of the upper leg to the horse's back is less than 90 degrees, so the weight is evenly distributed on the entire surface of the lower leg of the underman. Otherwise, with the added weight, he might press his knees into the back of the horse and cause him great discomfort.

Correct   Wrong

Wrong   Correct   Correct

There must be no rounded back − the top vaulter would slide off! If a vaulter rounds his back in these exercises, it may be a sign that the weight is too much for him and he is instinctively trying to evade possible pain. Do not let someone stand in the middle of his back then! He may be able to support the weight well if the top man stands further back, toward his hip bones.

Correct a hollow back, as this position is the worst for carrying a load. The vertebrae are forced together, if the underman lets his back sink, and damage of bones and discs may occur.

Correct forced shoulder positions either way: shoulders should neither be squeezed together at the back (this means stiff arms, trying to get the weight off the elbows) nor rounded to the front (usually in conjunction with a rounded back).

And get the stiffness out of their elbows! Remember that it is always the joints closest to the horse, which must stay most 'greased' to absorb the motion of the horse, i.e. here the knees and elbows! This is particularly important, when supporting someone else at greater height as the motion is felt more strongly, the higher the position gets. Stiff elbows may suggest lack in arm strength to support the added weight – more push-up training and give the vaulter time to build up the needed strength. An underman will often hollow his back in an attempt to offer a better standing surface to the vaulter on top, and this is also frequently a sign that the arms are not strong enough for the added load yet.

When the underman is standing, a lack of balance would be even more drastically felt! Therefore, whether supporting a mount, carrying an 'angel' or holding a wheelbarrow, the same principles apply. No rounded back, straight spine with erect head, and soft knees to absorb the motion.

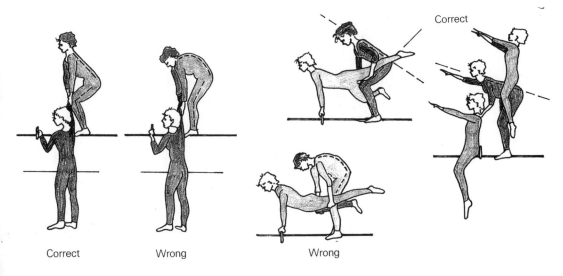

Correct

Correct   Wrong   Wrong

(C) *Technique of the carried 'flyer'*

Wrong

Correct

Wrong

It is important to explain to your flyers that being lifted by your undermen does not mean 'hanging' there like a limp rag! A potential flyer must learn to carry himself, and to have optimal body tension in his back, arm and leg muscles. The flyer has to see himself as executing the exercise himself, only that he is being lifted as he does so. He also has to take care that his own gravity point is close to the support points, and he must balance himself. A flyer who hangs limply and wiggles will indeed feel like a sack of potatoes: he weighs twice as much as the same person holding himself! As the vaulters' performance improves, the flyer will often jump directly into a lifted position, which presupposes even more, that he 'creates' his position by using his muscles actively, rather than just being carried.

Very flexible flyers again have the tendency to over-arch their backs — many people see this as beautiful. For artistic expression a back may be somewhat arched, as long as all the muscles are tensed sufficiently so that the flyer holds his position by himself.

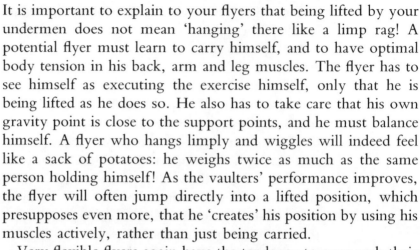

Wrong

Correct

Another fault is forced over-extension of a fellow vaulter, which often is seen in flyer positions. The extended leg of the flyer must be held by his own strength rather than being pushed into a further extended position, out of which it would sink immediately, if the partner stopped pushing. Forced body positions can damage the muscles of the growing child, especially when jolted through the canter stride. Also think of the added danger in case of a fall: a 'hanging' flyer can not roll off actively or jump out of a lifted position. See chapter 23 for reference to 'bail-out' situations.

Good   Wrong   Correct

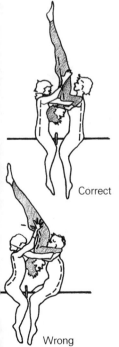

Correct

Wrong

In any of the team kur exercises which you will attempt, whether on the barrel or on the horse, it must be the strength factor of the weakest link in the configuration which determines what the partners will be able to do. So see to it that your juniors (who will grow into the show team later) learn these correct techniques right from the start, and introduce them to these exercises slowly, so they can be useful when they become the reserve vaulters for the show team.

A vaulting team undergoes constant change, as during the crucial years the children grow rather quickly, and the change from flyer to underman can happen within one or two years! Don't forget that fast growth also affects strength! There is often a time when you can't use a vaulter for either — he has become too big and heavy to be a flyer, but is not yet strong enough to lift his partners. Sometimes vaulters can very well be undermen in kneeling positions, but not lift with their arms. Always discuss with your vaulters what they feel comfortable in doing, and watch that they don't overexert themselves to show off.

If you have reflected on the difficulties of various exercises and the appropriate bail-out, it will be quite simple for you to decide how to build up the progression from simple to complex for your vaulters. But you must teach them correct technique right from the start, and disciplined cooperation on the horse: so just a few words about that.

Since it is much easier to correct a double rather than a triple, start with that. Because now you have to train your eye to detect the mistakes made by two (and later three) vaulters in relationship to the horse! Does the exercise fail, because the supporting vaulter is unbalanced on the horse, or the flyer on him, or both are off the gravity point in relationship to the horse? Is the routine insecure, because they grip each other the wrong way, or have the sequence of grips mixed up?

Wheelbarrow   Double stirrup arabesque

Of course you start them in walk. But always keep in mind that the goal is to perform in canter. Therefore it is of the utmost importance that the sequence of grips, which you (in conjunction with your vaulters) decide to be the most logical and most secure one, be followed consistently by the whole team and in every repetition of the exercise. Should the horse spook when you later perform in canter, then every vaulter knows exactly where to grip, one partner knows what to expect of the other in terms of the next move, and this greatly adds to your chance of avoiding accidents.

The 'shoulder sit'

One of the first double exercises will be the 'shoulder sit', if you have a team, which is mixed in size and age. The underman has to be strong enough to support the flyer, so choose them accordingly. When you first correct them on the barrel, mention straight body line and upright spine to your underman again; don't let him slouch. Refer to chapter 11 for correct body posture in exercises. The flyer also has to sit straight, so as not to throw his partner off balance. Let them do it *wrongly* on the barrel and make them *feel* what it does to the balance of the whole configuration!

It is important that the underman learns to feel whether the person on top is the cause for his imbalance, because he can then mention that to his flyer during training, or if it is a result of his own difficulties in relationship to the horse's motion.

These doubles are the beginning of the vaulters' understanding that they cease to be individuals in a team exercise. As mentioned before, laying blame on the partner for failures of a team exercise is out of the question. Never allow fighting! If an exercise does not work, it simply means that one must find the mistake: you as the trainer have to be able to see it, and where it is hard to determine visually, you have to be able to get it out of the vaulters through discussion. In any case, it has to be solved. So now you explain the position of the gravity point of a configuration, rather than a single body on the horse. This must be aligned just like a single, down in a straight line from the top onto the horse's spine, and sideways neither right or left of it.

Again explain what the underman has to anticipate in terms of unexpected motions from the horse. Simulate on the barrel by giving them a gentle push, what it will feel like, when the horse suddenly stops — the height extension of having a flyer sit on top of you really makes a difference. It's a bit like doing a brake check, while driving with a heavy trailer for the first time... Gently push him from the front to simulate a sudden acceleration, from the side of sideways shying of the horse. There are many ways to prepare your vaulters for reality, before they perform something in canter.

- *The sequence of grips*: Depending on the exercise, there might be no sequence, but rather just one grip. But the example of the 'shoulder sit' is a good one for more complex moves, although the exercise is very simple. After vaulter number two has mounted, she hangs on to the shoulders of the underman in front of her to stand up. This should be done gently over the kneel and without digging pointed toes into the kidneys of the horse. She then stands with feet turned slightly outwards directly behind the underman, whereupon he holds up his hands to support her. An inexperienced flyer will then take the underman's inside hand and hold onto his head with the outside hand. (Experienced vaulters don't hang on to people's heads any more!) The underman lets his outside arm sink, to make room for the flyer, while she is passing the outside leg over his shoulder. She then 'locks' this foot behind his back, by turning the toes toward his spine. Now the hand positions get changed: the underman reaches up with his outside hand and supports the flyer, while she grabs onto his head with the inside hand, to pass the inside leg over the other shoulder, while he lets that arm hang down. She then locks her foot, balances herself, and lets both hands go to stretch the arms to the side. Depending on how balanced and strong the underman is, he does likewise. Don't instruct the underman to let go, if the horse is jittery or the vaulter insecure. In walk, again make them simulate sudden stops and accelerations of the horse. Halt the horse, while the exercise is still built up, and get him going again. Once the vaulters have understood cause and effect, they just need to be reminded of the eventualities and can start to let anticipation become second nature to them.

Why should the outside leg go over first? In walk this is not evident, but in canter the vaulters begin to feel the effects of centrifugal force. It is safer to stand on the inside foot, while lifting the first leg, because this moves the flyers gravity point to the inside — less chance of losing her right away! This is why they should also dismantle the exercise the same way: inside leg comes off first, then the vaulter has a secure foot to stand on with her weight counteracting the force of gravity. The sequence of grips will be the same.

The 'double hang'

In the double hang one vaulter completely supports the other, and the weight of the two vaulters must be distributed very evenly on both sides of the horse — otherwise the configuration might slip to one side. The first vaulter mounts and immediately slips his outside foot through the stirrup. Then the second vaulter mounts, and as soon as the first has passed his inside leg over the neck to assume the outside side seat, he starts going down into the cossack hang. He then securely grips the second vaulter with his right hand on her (inside) leg, passing his arm over her shin and grabbing her with the hand from the back, in the hollow of the knee. Now the second vaulter shifts her weight slightly to the outside to feel some pull on the leg, then passes her outside leg over the front to the inside, and lets herself down into the hang as well. When the weight of the two is evenly distributed, both free legs of the vaulters go up to cross in a V shape over the horse.

'Double hang'

Some word of caution, before you do this in canter: check the tightness of the surcingle. Check whether on your surcingle the stirrup loops do not come up too high, so vaulter number one hangs too low — this exercise can not be done with every surcingle, if the vaulters can not freely balance over the horse's back. If the loop is high, the vaulters must be small. The two vaulters must be matched in size *and* weight and must hang evenly and in a balanced fashion on both sides of the horse. (In other words: this is not an 'underman—flyer' exercise!)

- *The sequence of grips*: Here of course the sequence is very important, especially when coming up again. The outside vaulter comes up first, the inside (first) vaulter *must* stay down until receiving a sign (little tap) from the second vaulter, signalling that she is up *and* has regained her balance in that position (sitting in seat number 2 without hanging on to anything can *also* be pretty bouncy!) *Only then* will vaulter 1 release his grip of her knee and come up himself, to proceed by swinging his leg back to the inside. When the outside vaulter (number 2) starts coming up, the weight on vaulter number 1's hand becomes less, and this is often the point when junior vaulters think they can now let go. But vaulter number 2 still has her buttock way on the outside of the horse's side and has therefore no means of balancing herself without being supported. And if *not* supported, she will of course go down head first!

  If this sounds very dangerous to you, let me reassure you: the double hang was always considered an easy exercise, and really *is*, if executed correctly. But the point I want to drive home is, that *all* exercises are potentially dangerous if taught in an incorrect or negligent way, and *none* have to be, if practised with proper technique, foresight and the anticipation and correction of potential trouble.

  There are many double exercises and a great variety from easy to very difficult. In many doubles a third vaulter can be added to decrease difficulty by adding more support, and when you first start training them, this is most advisable. In triples don't forget the rule that at least two partners must stay in contact with the horse! And quadruples are simply not allowed.

Not too difficult with light-weight flyer, as holding points are secure: 'Skater's lift'

Very difficult to balance. Requires excellent body tension and precision of the flyer: 'Diver'

Requires secure balance of supporting partner: 'Carried angel'

More complexity in direction: upside down and backward: 'BW assisted handstand'

'Free stand on shoulder'

Third partner for added support and security: 'Shoulder arabesque'

Not permitted — why? (two of the three vaulters must stay in contact with the horse)

25 *How to write a kur*

Now that your vaulters are not totally inexperienced any more, you will be preparing for the first demonstration show or stable competition.

In a show you have complete freedom over what you want to do. Ask the organizers about how much time they wish to allot for your performance and write your show accordingly. If they want to see a longer show (and don't do shows longer than maximum fifteen minutes! Your audience will get bored...) you will include parts in walk, trot and canter. If the time allowed does not exceed five minutes, you might want to show an all canter demonstration with only your better vaulters. Don't forget that most people in your audience are new to vaulting — they will not see the fine distinctions between exercises! Each demonstration should kindle new interest in this sport, and hopefully recruit a few new members for your club, if you're showing near home. So keep in mind that many exercises, although different in difficulty and variation of direction, look very much the same to the untrained eye. Don't include too many of those! For example: a lifted sideways split with a partner sitting backward on the neck looks much the same as a forward lifted split supported by two forward sitting partners. Although quite different in direction and complexity, don't show them both.

A brief note about making up names. You will find very soon that the lengthy official names in the rule books make it almost impossible to put a show down on paper. You have to write the show and make copies for your team, so they can learn it well in advance of the show. Invent names! Make them short and precise, even like this the documents get lengthy enough...

'Lifted SW split'

'Lifted FW split'

The way you start writing the show is simple: six weeks ahead of the show you choose the members of the club who will be allowed to participate. A normal show consists of eight vaulters, but depending on what you're aiming for, you can include more (which gives a nice chance to show off your 'babies' in the walk part) or, if you only have six vaulters for that top notch five-minute show, do it just with them. Less than six gets tricky: your vaulters get too many turns in a short time and get exhausted. Twelve should be the upper limit. I find it looks a bit strange to have twenty-six vaulters run in after one horse...

In our club the chosen vaulters then have to commit to not missing any training sessions during those six weeks, come hell or high water. You can not adequately train with half a team! If someone (or their parents) lets you down − rewrite the show quickly immediately and exclude them. The vaulters and parents must understand that in terms of quality you mean business. Remember that your demonstration will or will not pave the way for this sport in your area or country. Shows should be worth seeing. *Never* show things that do not work! Children, especially beginners will usually perform slightly worse at a show than during training because they are nervous, the horse is nervous, and applause and music distract both.

So everything must be bombproof! They, the horse, and you, have to be able to feel at ease. Choose the exercises for the show accordingly. A show which has a lower level of difficulty, but is executed really well and cleanly, will make a much better impression than attempted daring exercises (which the spectators don't recognize as such anyhow) that collapse. The worst scenario at a show is an accident. You would turn other potential vaulters away from this sport for the next ten years!

In a competition it looks different again: here you have to push for the difficulty a little, and you will have a defined time limit, but also include in the final show *only* what really works. By the time your team gets into competition, where difficulty really matters, they are also experienced enough to swallow a change of sequence in the show and relearn quickly: take out the things which still don't work two weeks before the competition. For the last two weeks your team should only solidify and polish what has been trained before.

The run-in: Refer to the next chapter about the design of the run-in. Here, let me just mention that you should allow an additional two minutes for run-in, salute and run-out at the end of the show.

The kur itself: An optimal kur includes the following, always keeping in mind that you are choosing from exercises of an adequate level of difficulty for your vaulters:

diversity: static and dynamic exercises with a differing structure
highlights: and accents in motion
direction: diversity in direction (in regard to the direction of travel), using the whole horse, forward, backward, sideways
relation: direction in relation to the horse, diversity of inside, outside, up and down, front and back of the surcingle and the horse's back
originality: in the choice (or invention) of exercises, as well as fluidity and flair of the composition and choice of music
mix: a good use of all vaulters, and not the same group of people on the horse for too long at one time
harmony: with the horse and its movements, also with the other team mates. No hurried impression!
music: the music must fit the mood of the show. World-class teams actually perform precisely *on* the music, in which case the exercises have to fit in rhythm and speed, as well as mood, but this is very hard to achieve and can not be the goal for a beginning team.

- *Variety*: This basic rule applies to all kinds of kur, whether individual, *pas-de-deux* or team routines. The kur must be designed so that the horse never runs empty. Usually one vaulter will get two to maximum four turns in a row (in which he should have changes in direction and variety in activity, not just be a forever forward facing underman!) Include many double and triple exercises, and only a few singles. Otherwise it does not seem like a team kur. Vaulters in one configuration mount and dismount at different times, so the group actually on the horse is never the same for any length of time. But keep in mind that mounts take up a lot of energy — and time. So don't include more than necessary to assure a good flow in the kur.

- *Number of turns*: See to it that all vaulters in the show get more or less the same number of turns, or at least the same number relative to their experience and stand on the team. It is the first thing all my vaulters have always done, when a new show comes out: they count and compare their number of turns. By under-using a good vaulter, just because you can't arrange the flow of the show with enough expertise, you can really hurt the feelings of a team mate. In a 'long show' an experienced vaulter will have eight to maximum nine turns (not all in canter) and a beginner about four. In a five-minute all-canter show (with good vaulters of the same level) each vaulter will have about six to maximum eight turns.

  So this is where the difficulty of writing a good kur begins: for fairly young teams, usually only certain vaulters are able to do particular exercises. Some are strong undermen, others flyers, some are courageous and experienced enough for lifts, others not yet and so on. The more even the performance of the team members, the easier to achieve equal turns. If you have three flyers and three undermen, who can take each other's place, the design of the kur will be much easier.

- *The flow of the kur*: But if not, to create this flow in the kur, where vaulters get up to three turns in a row, adequate breaks in between and an equal number of turns, is a hard job. You have to be able to visualize the transitions in between exercises too! Often you have finally bunched the right groups of exercises together, but find out that the vaulter, who needs to stand on the back of the horse, has ended up in front — how to get him to the back? (Reshuffle on your wordprocessor...)

- *Use of different mounts and transitions*: The more proficient your vaulters get, the more easily this can be solved. They will be able to do assisted mounts into the middle of a configuration of two already on the horse, mounts to the front of a sitting partner, mounts *under* another partner, mounts in reverse onto the neck. Transitions *on* the horse will be made easier: one can jump over the top of another to get to the front, or roll over backwards to get behind their team mate. The variations in transitions are pretty endless. And in a good kur they are refined and taken quite as seriously as the exercises themselves. With beginners you should try to minimize the number of transitions. They are usually quite difficult for the vaulters and look very unbalanced and awkward. (Exceptions are a few easy ones, like the 'flea', where a sitting partner grabs a little one around the waist and swings him around to the front, or back.)

Flag on high bench over flag

Designing different parts of the kur, example of a 'long show'

In competition, each static exercise must be held for at least three strides, but I always find that this is a bit short for a show. Your spectators don't have the judge's trained eye, and if the exercise is held for only three strides, they have not really begun to understand yet what it is all about, let alone been able to take a good photograph for you! I train my vaulters to hold them at least four strides, and the really nice (and bombproof ones) for five, especially the spectacular lifts. It is better to have a show with fewer exercises, but these held nicely and in an unhurried manner, than a show crammed full of rushed brief things that nobody can really see.

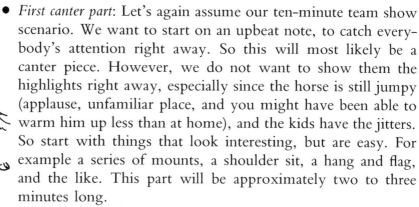

- *First canter part*: Let's again assume our ten–minute team show scenario. We want to start on an upbeat note, to catch everybody's attention right away. So this will most likely be a canter piece. However, we do not want to show them the highlights right away, especially since the horse is still jumpy (applause, unfamiliar place, and you might have been able to warm him up less than at home), and the kids have the jitters. So start with things that look interesting, but are easy. For example a series of mounts, a shoulder sit, a hang and flag, and the like. This part will be approximately two to three minutes long.

Hang and flag

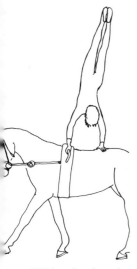

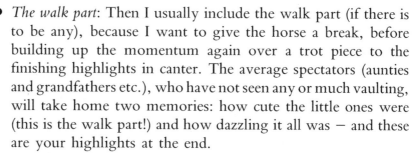

- *The walk part*: Then I usually include the walk part (if there is to be any), because I want to give the horse a break, before building up the momentum again over a trot piece to the finishing highlights in canter. The average spectators (aunties and grandfathers etc.), who have not seen any or much vaulting, will take home two memories: how cute the little ones were (this is the walk part!) and how dazzling it all was — and these are your highlights at the end.

In the walk part I include my beginners, who are allowed to perform in a nice summer show (especially when this means an interesting trip with billeting and so on — nothing builds team spirit as fast as these travels together), but are not really safe in any lifts, or useful as supports in highlights of any kind. Keep in mind that mounts in walk are difficult, especially for beginners, and use as few as possible. Don't show *only* beginners: if you have a gymnast, who can do a handstand-flip over the croup, show that as well. Keep the interest going! Roll dismounts are easy in walk, somersault over the croup, full splits, leapfrog over the croup etc. (*If your horse never kicks!*)

SW free handstand

'Skater's lift'

'Carried angel'

'Double jump'

In this part you also include the more difficult lifts, which you might have practised well in walk, but which are not safe in canter yet. (Fully supported lifts, like the rocket angel, in trot are pretty bouncy stuff, so you usually show them in walk or canter.)

The walk part should not be too long, up to a maximum of ten exercises, because otherwise you lose the momentum of the show to a degree which will make it hard to build it up again. Once you have lost the spectators' interest, they leave to get a drink instead...and they won't come back.

I will include a copy of one 'long show' and describe the vaulting quality of the performers at the time of that show in Appendix B, so you see more clearly what I mean.

- *The trot part*: In the trot part you show mainly exercises with standing partners which don't work in canter yet. All stands are much easier in trot because of the even up and down movement of the horse's back, as mentioned before. So this part can well prepare the audience for the highlights soon to follow, because it can be very interesting! But in some of the easier exercises (like the 'family round', that is, 'sitting, kneeling, standing') you can again show off your junior vaulters. Make this part short: it is no real break for the horse — rather a kind of transition, which allows you to show certain things which would not shine in walk, but don't yet work in canter. About six to seven exercises should be the limit.

- *The second canter part*: By now your horse is not fresh enough to buck any more...but he is also not fresh enough to make this part too long! Maximum ten exercises should do for the highlights. Try to build exercises up in height toward the end, if your team is able to do lifts and stands. The very end should be whatever draws the most gasps — it need not be the most difficult exercise. If you have good flyers, use something like the double jump (over sitting partner), which spectators always see as particularly courageous...

- *The salute and run-out*: The run-out is not as important as the run-in, but the salute even more so: this is when most pictures are taken! If your horse is quiet enough, build up a pyramid. If not, align the children in a decorative way on both sides of the horse, with one little one up top, some standing with leg extended into the air, kneeling next to it, and doing full splits or the like. (Not if you are showing outside in potentially muddy weather!) Prearrange with the organizer, if and when a small gift (chocolate bar, anything will do) will be given to the vaulters as thanks for the show. (I always insist on this; it can be done very quickly and sets a festive end to your performance.) This means that your team has to align in a neat row again, and should receive such gift with equal bows or curtseys. It makes a very professional impression when one can see that all this has been thought of and practised for in anticipation, and does not throw your embarrassed youngsters into a fluster and confusion.

'Pyramid'

Writing a kur for a competition

In competition you are dealing with different kinds of kur, depending on whether you put together a single (individual vaulter), a double (*pas-de-deux* vaulting) or a team kur.

In most countries rules are set for recognized competitions. In any competition on a higher level, all exercises will be shown in canter. But if such rules do not exist, or you are just starting out, you might try to arrange stable competitions with other clubs around you as often as possible, and these competitions should be defined in the invitation of the promoter to suit your vaulters' needs. Depending on the organization of the sports in your country, your provincial vaulting association will be able to help you in this, as they will have examples on file. In any case, you should submit your format to your local association and get it sanctioned by them (you may otherwise not be covered by your insurance for the event).

In these local events, you can show compulsories as well as all kurs in walk or trot or canter, just make up categories for it to find a fair level to judge them on. We usually don't let vaulters enter the same event (single kur or compulsories) in two different categories (in walk and canter), because then the better vaulters would forever win in all categories and the juniors don't have a chance to ever place. Refer to the example included in Appendix B to see such an invitation, which tries to provide a fair chance for everyone.

- *A team kur for competition*: Writing a team kur for a competition is similar to writing a show, with the difference that you are dealing with a set time limit. This is internationally set at five minutes maximum for canter, but in walk you might be allowed more time, as set out in the invitation. You still only pick the exercises which really work in a bombproof way. Flow of the kur is the same as for a show, the horse never goes empty, and all the other things mentioned above. But this time, don't keep your best highlights to the very end! In case of a fall and necessary remount, you might be slightly short of time at the end — and when the judge rings the bell, the vaulters must finish, or whatever is shown after three more canter strides does not count for scores any more. So you don't want to risk your best exercises — those that score highest for the technical merit mark — in case you're running out of time!

- *Writing a pas-de-deux kur*: So far it was not even stated in the international rules that a *pas-de-deux* routine *must* be performed by a male and a female vaulter, although that was always the intent. Internationally, this will change now. But for stable competitions we should definitely allow vaulters of the same gender together, because so many clubs don't have *any* male vaulters! Internationally, the age limit for individual and *pas-de-deux* routines is set at sixteen years and up, but this also does not have to apply to stable competitions. You will see that your children will really enjoy doing a *pas-de-deux* kur with a close friend; it is a very different way to work together from team work!

In a *pas-de-deux* kur (which hereafter I will call double) the two vaulters only mount *once*, although ground jumps in between exercises are permitted, as long as the vaulter stays in contact with the grips. These ground jumps should be touchdowns — a quick down and up sequence — which does not involve any running alongside the horse.

As the same rules for an 'optimal kur' apply as mentioned earlier, you will see right away that transitions can now not be avoided! They rather take on a great importance and have to be executed fluidly and without bumping into each other — which is not as easy as it sounds! A good double takes on a dance–like quality at least part of the time. Many symmetrical exercises can be included, but also changes in direction and highlights such as lifts.

In an international competition the double kur consists of two rounds. The first round has a time limit of a minute, and will emphasize, but not be limited to, synchronized and mirror-image exercises. In the second round there are no restrictions, but the time limit is two minutes maximum. Each static exercise must be held for at least three canter strides. Synchronized exercises are the ones where the two vaulters do moves at the exact same time and in the same rhythm, which creates this dance-like quality. Mirror-image exercises are the likes of a double flag (on neck and back of the horse) but with difference in direction. Another example would be a double sideways shoulderhang, performed on the inside and outside of the horse. There are also mirror image dynamic exercises, swings and transitions, as well as dismounts (for example a double roll dismount, one vaulter to the inside, the other out).

I am including an example of a little double trot kur in Appendix B, which was written for a two-minute competition for two small eight-year-olds. They performed this almost flawlessly and with smooth transitions (after vaulting for about a year). Since it is difficult to describe all the transitions on paper, try out a kur like this on the barrel with two of your vaulters, and you will quickly understand, which transitions are necessary. Watching videos and writing down the exercises (there is your homework as a trainer!) is a good way to learn, especially in double routines, where it is easy to copy on the barrel. (In a team kur it is much harder, since your vaulters may not be able to do the same things as the vaulters on the video in terms of 'bunching up' the exercises, but trying to copy is an excellent way to learn about actual levels of difficulty.)

● *Writing an individual kur*: You should include individual routines in your training sessions frequently, because the children very much like to shine alone in between team sessions. Teach your vaulters early to write their own individual kurs. It teaches them a lot about necessary transitions — and you will never have time enough to write all the single kurs for all your club members... When singles are performed in canter, ground jumps can make them interesting, inside and outside the horse preferably. Have a healthy mix of static and dynamic exercises! Nothing is more boring in a kur than a vaulter who basically does nothing but sitting exercises, and the only dynamic feature (which does not qualify as such) is the waving of arms. Use the neck, the back, the stirrups. Use all directions. Include some mounts, fast transitions, high (shoulderstand) and low (hangs) exercises.

The included example in Appendix B shows a little routine written for a Walk Single, for an eight-year-old, who had vaulting experience for a year and a half. Let someone copy it on the barrel and work out the transitions. Then let the vaulter write down for next time, what she remembers... That is the way to start.

Although a lot of work, writing good kurs is a lot of fun. Whether show or competition, offer your vaulters something new every time. It is true that kurs can only be perfected to world championship polish after having been trained the same way for quite a long time. But for a beginning team it is much more interesting to do new things frequently, and to pass the exercises around. If a vaulter has the feeling that 'this is *my* exercise, and nobody else should get it', she has been performing it too long exclusively. To build a good team, which can also function, if one or two vaulters fall sick before a competition, you need a broad base. This means that no vaulter will be irreplaceable, that you have two or three performers for each exercise.

In most cases, you will first show to a public mainly made up of riders, and if you show a lot in the same general area, you will have the same spectators over and over again. It will be the greatest credit to you if these people notice that each and every show is different, and *better* than the last. And that you have changed the music again. And people *do* notice. (The judges in competition even more so! You don't want them to start yawning the second your music comes on because they already know which kur will follow!) The parents (those valuable supporters of your efforts) will certainly notice if their child is doing different exercises in each show, or if they are stuck in the same routines over and over again, so that it isn't worth the trouble to bring their camera to the event any more.

After the first five shows you write, you'll become an expert and the progress needs much less time. So don't despair over the work load too early! This is the most creative part of your job: show your sense of choreography!

26   *How to train for your kur*

The run-in

To simplify things, let's start with a show. Plan for ten minutes, plus two minutes for run-in and run-out. Don't underestimate the time you will need to practise those, either! With an indisciplined bunch of 'babies' this can be an exasperating task! Running in, every vaulter should be in step. They can either line up next to the horse, or line up on two sides of him, or fan out. We have done shows where all the vaulters do a cartwheel to end up in line, or fan out and curtsey — it's up to your imagination and the discipline of the team. They then all bow together, facing the audience, or bow and turn and bow again, if the spectators are sitting on two sides of the arena.

In competition you can choose how you want to present your team; curtseys (if you have an all female team) are permitted, but fancier than that you should not get. Cartwheels and handstand-walkovers are felt to be too circus-like. In competition the team *must* face the main judge for the salute, and *only* he will be saluted. (Judge A will be defined by his position. If there are several judges you'll you have to find out before the run-in which table he is at.)

Pick some really upbeat music for the run-in, because you want to get those spectators enthused straight away. The run-in is always done in trot. Let your vaulters run and time it with a stop watch as soon as you have determined the way. Leave the length of the piece of music flexible (don't make it too short) if you don't know the lie of the land of the facility where you'll be showing, because your approach may be a little longer than anticipated. It makes a bad impression if the music runs out — whereas if you have a bit too much you can always use that for the first canter round to warm up the horse. Then practise the run-in and salute on music before every training session.

For competition, tape the run-in music onto a different tape from the main show, so there is no danger of the time lap in between not being accurate. When the judge gives the signal to start, the first vaulter *must* be on the horse within a minute — music or not. When you have put a lot of effort into timing your show onto music, you don't want to risk having it begin too early or too late. So simply instruct the person at the sound table to switch tapes after the run-in and have both tapes stopped at the correct spot, so all he has to do is start them.

Inexperienced vaulters will not perform their *show* precisely in time with the music, but the run-in should fit. Your tallest vaulter will be at the head of the run-in line if you are leading the horse; if not, the second tallest will run first and the biggest takes the horse. The first person in line will carry the lunge whip in his hand and give the horse a little tap with it, if he is unwilling to enter the ring. Discuss the run-in path with her or him, as soon as you arrive at the show facility, so there is no confusion about where to line up and which way to face. You may choose to run in with your team, if you are lunging, or join them from the side once they have lined up. In competition, the lunger always runs in with the team, as he is considered an integral part of it, and therefore *must* salute with them.

After the salute, the team will leave the circle on a predetermined way, in a neat line and in step, running to the point outside the circle, where you want them to line up. Teach them right from the beginning that while in line for a show, all arms must be held in the same fashion (behind the back works best for beginners) and scratching, bending and wiggling around is not making a good impression. Somebody nowadays always makes a video — show them how evident bad behaviour in the back line is to the audience!

While the team is lining up somewhere in the back (showing their fronts to the spectators) you let the horse out in the circle and direct him to canter. The vaulters in the first planned exercise will join you in the circle right away, and as soon as you 'open the gate' at the correct spot in the music, they will approach and start the show.

The music

As mentioned before, the run-in music will be very upbeat and befitting the trot speed of your horse and team. You will start to train the canter—walk—trot—canter phases (or whatever they will be) of your show, first separately, and time them with the stop watch, as soon as they work more or less. Keep in mind that over a six-week period the vaulters will improve and get slightly faster. Then in the show they have a tendency to get faster again, because they are nervous. If you teach them consistently to count the four or five beats (or three in competition) for which they have to hold their static exercises, you can get a fairly accurate estimate of the necessary time quite early in the game.

For an inexperienced team you may of course choose some kind of background music so that the different phases of the show do not matter. In that case, tape something that will be long enough for sure, and put some reliable person next to the stereo to turn it down slowly, then off, when the show is finished. But as your team gets better and more accurate, it is fun to try to 'stay on the music'. The vaulters will learn to recognize when they get close to the end of the canter piece and whether they therefore have to hurry a bit or slow down, because they are performing too fast — and the trot piece will be very different in speed and mood. This of course harbours the risk that you might really miss your music. Often our last training sessions were dead on and we were all smiles — and then in the show the kids got so fast that we had miles of music left over!

But it is worth trying for, because they have to learn sooner or later — and the audience does not seem to notice the mistakes in most cases. Vaulting judges later on however will, so the sooner the vaulters learn to keep their ears with them when vaulting, the better.

In competitions it is prescribed that you perform with instrumental music only. This makes sense, as you don't want to distract the judges, rather just paint a fitting background to your performance. The same is true for shows, but since it is sometimes very difficult to find interesting music of the right mood which is wholly instrumental, you can use songs as well. Or you might *want* the audience to sing along. I think that Country Western Songs are quite all right when showing at a rodeo. Many good teams perform on classical music, but get the input of your vaulters before you choose. They must like to perform to the chosen piece — and who knows what will be 'cool' by the time you read this book. My troop wanted to vault on rap — and they gave it up after three songs by their own decision.

If you work with a metronome (you can get quite sophisticated) canter speed lies at around 100 to 110, and most of these pieces fit for walk too. Tempo 85 to 95 is very collected canter. Most classical marches are around tempo 100, and many of those were composed for horse shows. Trot music is around tempo 150, and if you have a very regular horse, you'll be able to fit something exactly onto his step.

The sequence of turns

Very young teams *will* sometimes forget their turns, so have an adult behind the line to prompt if necessary. Don't let your team get used to this service for too long though; it is unprofessional, and every six-year-old is able to learn four to five turns by heart! In competitions prompting is out of the question. You are there to show the level of performance your team is capable of — if this means writing a simple kur, because they are too young to remember anything else — so be it! You are presenting their brainpower as well as their muscles, and I have *never* experienced that a young vaulter was not able to learn his sequence of turns, if *not* knowing them meant exclusion from the competition.

There are different ways to learn the sequence: they can write numbers next to each block, that is, learn that they are 'second, then fifth in the first canter block, fourth and fifth in the walk, no turns in trot, and third/fourth/fifth in the second canter block'. This is a good method for very young juniors — the easiest way to memorize. But not the best! Obviously, if someone else messes up their turn (simply forgets it and does not run in) everything else will be out of phase and chaos ensues. It is better to learn that 'I'm doing this, after A, B and C are doing that, then I stay on the horse for exercise X and dismount over the front after Y has mounted.' The best way to learn is of course to know the complete routine, and be able to skip an exercise without losing control of the whole show. Some of my teams have done incredible feats of improvisation, once turns were forgotten. Their sequence of exercises looked so fluid and worked out, it could have been written by myself...

The lunger must concentrate on the horse, while staying aware of what is going on up top, in order to know when to bring the horse into walk after canter promptly and without making a 'hole' in the show. S/he must help to keep an ear for the music, tell the kids to slow down or speed up — and if the horse is jumpy, to anticipate each exercise with a stand to try and prevent irregularities. So you'll have your hands full! Tell your older vaulters to prompt *you*, if they realize you have been too busy to notice that the trot piece should start here...not just to stand behind your gate, waiting! Remind them that you are also a part of the team, everybody takes on responsibility for everyone else.

Of course it helps the vaulters in training if they get the written show into their hands early and few (if any) changes are made to it. Don't throw the sequence at them a half hour before the show. And don't confuse them by re-writing your show five times. The last changes should be made two weeks before the show, as this is the point where all the exercises should be excluded which somehow don't work until then. While training for a show, tell the team to bring their sheet with the written show *every* practice session, so they can mark these changes when they occur. Otherwise they might mistake you for their secretary and you can spend your time re-typing, re-copying and passing the rewritten sequences out again and again.

The canter pieces

With a bit of experience you can begin timing the length of your canter pieces even in walk. Let someone push during the mounts, as these happen of course faster when in canter, then count for your vaulters holding the exercise with the speed you remember from your horse. Time differences later will actually not occur in the static exercises, but mostly in the mounts and transitions. If two vaulters are mounting one after the other, the second one must run next to the horse, just far enough away not to disturb the mount of his partner, so he is there immediately when the first one is up. Beginners will waste enormous time during the mounts − encourage them to discipline themselves early. Advanced vaulters will grab the hand of a partner and mount directly without running for several steps. Juniors should be allowed to count the familiar '1, 2, 3, hop' for the mount, but not more! Running for over half a round should never be per-mitted, it is a sign of indecision, wastes the horse's energy and bores the audience. The horse may of course never run empty. Part of this rule is also consideration of the horse; you want to keep his work time really efficient. As soon as some vaulters start out for the horse, the participants in the *next* exercise run into the centre of the circle, but stay well behind your whip. Never let the lunger stand 'empty' in the middle either. Personally it makes me very nervous, when the next vaulters don't run in promptly, because while lunging for a show, I am concentrating on the horse so much that I do not have time to look at the team to figure out whether they are asleep, or have forgotten their turns, or whatever else may be happening in the rank and file!

The walk phase

As you know, mounting in walk without the use of the horse's momentum is quite difficult, so arrange for a 'pusher' in case your beginners can't make it up. Instruct the pusher to *be* there, when needed (it will usually be a vaulter waiting to mount for the same exercise, or one of the next ones waiting in the circle) and give the push as quickly and inconspicuously as possible. It is a nightmare in a show to have the surcingle turn on you. Although you want to show off how well everyone can do by himself, don't risk having one of your inexperienced vaulters hang on the side of the horse, without help, while the grips are slowly sinking... You would have to stop the horse, take the surcingle off and refit — while your music is running out and the audience gets bored, not to mention the howling child, who ended up under the horse...

The trot part

Not much else has to be mentioned for the trot phase which does not also apply to the others, except that trot, depending on the horse, can be a lot bouncier than the previous ones. Do not put vaulters into undermen lifting positions, if they don't have the subtle hip movement to 'sit' the stride. They then have a tendency to bounce out of balance, slip right and left and feel very insecure. Trot is a good gait to show off the stand, and even a simple double stand, performed by two little ones will get a good round of applause. Transitions from the back to the neck can also present quite a problem to the junior in trot; don't use any which don't really work.

The salute and run-out

When the last vaulter dismounts, you collect the horse (which should stop for you on the track of the circle, instead of coming in) while he runs back into the line-up. The tallest vaulter starts running with the line to join you at the horse, as soon as he sees that you have managed to bring him into salute position — with thundering applause and waving flags this can be quite a job. Hopefully your helper at the stereo is awake and turns down the music a bit, if you have not used it up as you had planned. Your team then assumes their salute position. This will be a line or fan configuration in a competition, followed by a simultaneous bow from the members, including the lunger, basically the same as after the run-in. (If the horse acts up, the lunger can get away with a nod of his head.) In a show however, you should make a bit more of it — this is the time when most pictures are taken, and when the children finally hold still long enough, so the average photographer will get something into focus. Refer to the previous chapter for the ways to design this configuration, and train for it often enough that the vaulters can assume their position quickly and without hesitation. Stay away from intricate build-ups if the time to practise them was not sufficient. Nothing looks worse than an attempted line up, where kids run from the left to the right because they can't remember where their place should be...in that case, a simple line is preferable. However professional your team looks at the very end, this is the impression which every spectator will take home with him. And we want them back for more vaulting demonstrations.

If you arranged with the promoters that the children would receive a little gift, the person at the stereo must be aware of this and stop or turn down the music while it is happening. The children will drop back into line after dismantling their pyramid position, and give a visible sign of 'thank you' when handed the gift. Even this must be practised beforehand. You can of course use the same music for the run-out as in the beginning. Make sure the whip was passed to the right person in time. You can also tape artificial applause over the last music — I have done this in shows, where I know in advance that the audience will be rather stingy with their signs of appreciation, but I needed the applause on the video for the next promotion...

Refer to the next chapter for the team's behaviour after the show. Tell them in advance before every show what you expect of them.

27 *Working for a show*

Your team (and their parents) should realize how much work is involved to get a good show on the road, and they should know what is expected from them in terms of help. These related chores are not necessarily the job of the trainer! And they can be very time consuming. . .

First the show has to be booked: this should preferably be done at the beginning of the year or at least of the season. You should have the show confirmed six weeks in advance in order for there to be time for proper training. You may have to inspect the facility. You have to ask what kind of footing the ground offers (whether your horse needs shoes or not), whether you show indoors or out.

One week before the show you must confirm and make sure that you will be able to put on your music: do they offer a sound system or do you have to bring a cassette player — how can you wire up?

Someone has to arrange for the sponsoring for the transport, unless your club is willing to show at their own expense. Arrange when the cheque will be handed over, made out to whom. Someone has to arrange for the transport and reconfirm before the show. Especially in the summer, when all the riders are driving to shows, it can be very difficult to find transport, unless you have your own trailer.

It will be your job to arrange for the farrier, if the horse has to be shod, to design the preliminary show, pick exercises, time, etc., train for the show, time again, make changes if necessary, search for and compile fitting music (here the vaulters can help).

The team's job will be to spend one hour together cleaning

bridle, surcingle, and side reins thoroughly. Someone must take the show wraps, the lunge and the pad home for washing — with enough time to let it dry before the show.

The day or the morning before the show the horse should be prepared: that is, the tail must be washed, mane plaited, etc. The older team members should help to get the horse ready for travelling and help loading him. It may take quite some time to assemble the equipment — if you have to go 'Canadian distances' for a show, make sure you carry a second surcingle and bridle. (Borrow from another club...). Find out in time, if you have to take your own feed, and even if feed is offered, make sure it is up to your standards. We usually carry our own hay in any case. Don't forget the fly-spray, if showing in mosquito areas — if your horse is not used to the flies, it can really kill your show! Carry a fly-mask for the rest periods. Take coolers or blankets if needed. For your vaulters bring some 'sticky spray' for the croup for your standing exercises if the horse tends to get wet and slippery.

Transport

It is a good idea to have someone follow the horse-box or trailer in a different car, depending on the remoteness of the area. If you get a flat tyre, you may need someone to get help and carry messages. (If your trailer has a flat tyre, never try to unload your horse on a busy freeway. Wait for help with a jack to lift trailer and horse, or help to stop traffic.) For long trips, philosophies greatly differ: make sure the horse gets enough stops to drink; all else depends largely on the horse and what he is used to.

Arrival

Don't let the horse stand in the trailer any longer than absolutely necessary: unload promptly and walk him. Especially after long trips (and we have travelled up to ten hours to shows) it is very important that the horse can move and stretch his limbs. You can't vault on him if he is stiff from a long trip. Let him sniff at his new surroundings and if at all possible let him check out the ring before the show.

Assemble the team, find a good meeting point and assemble your equipment (at the stall, or whatever place you have been assigned). Now tell your team members their respective jobs: who will take care of the horse until when (and what this means: grooming, walking, lunging etc.) who will babysit the smaller team members (and how). If you want to involve the parents as well, be very specific. Make sure your team understands that, once arrived, the main concern is not beautifying themselves, but getting the horse and the team into shape in a disciplined and calm manner. Because now you'll have other things to do...

Before the show

You'll have to check the run-in path (if you haven't seen the facility before) and speak to your tallest vaulter (first in line) about the line-up. Get the music to the sound booth and see who is responsible for putting the tape in: if nobody, assign one of the parents and give him or her very clear instructions. Find the announcer and find out what and how much he intends to say: jot down a brief outline (this is your chance to promote the sport) so the correct things will be mentioned. Don't forget to note the sponsors, if you had any! Thank the organizer of the show (make sure this goes over the speakers) for inviting you (and paying for the travelling, if they did...)

Check who the 'whipper-in' is at the show and arrange for a runner (of your team or somebody else, preferably) to let you know, ten minutes and again five minutes before the show, when your turn comes. Because directly before the show you should lunge your horse for the warm-up, and you should be able to do so in a relaxed manner, being sure that ample notice will be given. Your nervousness will transfer directly to the horse! So try to avoid unnecessary troubles.

Introduce yourself also to the chief steward or the host of the show, if you have not met them personally. It is very nice to establish a personal relationship before you are showing (you want to be invited back), and at a horse show it can easily take half an hour to track such a person down...

You must be back in time to tack up the horse (with your team's help, of course), say ten minutes in total. To warm him up (I always prefer to do that personally), ten to fifteen minutes, if you want to be able to calm him down. Don't lunge him till he is tired because you're afraid of the horse acting up. A tired vaulting horse will not make for a good show. (And won't promote the sport either...) The warm-up should be walk and trot as usual − to take the 'beans' out of him, he mainly needs a chance to check out the strange new surroundings. (If your vaulters have taken him for a good long walk to sniff at everything beforehand most of the calming down will have been done for you. So make sure that the team and horse arrive well in advance of the show at the premises − an hour is not too long!) The team should do their usual warm-up routine: assign somebody to supervise that this is done properly. (Make sure the team is at the meeting point at the prescribed time, rather than running all over the place showing off.) You may hand the horse to an experienced (and calm) helper ten minutes before run-in and briefly talk to the team. Check their uniforms. Check the tightness of the surcingle again personally. Line up for the run-in, when you get the five-minute warning from the runner.

Now the show should be a success!

After the show

After the run-out see to it that the team stays disciplined until their jobs are done. The horse must be taken care of first. The team must immediately take off the side reins, loosen the surcingle and then reward the horse with a treat. Then take the blanket off, offer him water, and walk him until he is cool. Cool his legs with water and rub them with a water-camphor-mix (sixty/forty per cent) or similar substance. Don't let the vaulters run off before the equipment is re-assembled, cleaned and packed. The trainer's presence should not be necessary during this time: you will retrieve the music from the sound booth and do some more thanking and promoting. See if the local newspaper is present: hand the reporter your name and address, and tell him that you could provide him with pictures if his did not turn out. Or ask him for a copy of his, if they did — because you can use them for more promotion. Straight after the show is the best time to hand out your card with the phone number where you can be reached for further bookings (promoters of other shows are most likely present), as well as for contacts with interested prospective vaulters. So you must find the time to be approachable — rather than being left stranded with the horse while the vaulters are basking in their glory!

But they deserve the glory too, so try to relieve them as soon as possible after they have prepared the horse for travelling, if this happens straight away. The trainer should be present for the loading of the horse — hopefully somebody else might do the driving if the horse has to go home promptly, so you can do some more socializing with the promoters and your team, before everyone goes their own way. A show should be more than just a job to the team, and should always end on a nice and festive note, with good memories to prepare for the next one.

After a strenuous day at a show or competition the horse should *not* remain standing the next day. He should be walked or taken into the countryside in walk to reduce lactic acid and avoid muscle soreness — just as you would treat any other athlete. If your horse did the full fifteen minutes canter at a competition or show, he has covered a distance of approximately seven kilometres (almost four and a half miles), which corresponds to an eventing performance. The same applies if he has been on a long trip in the horse-box, as mentioned on the trip to the show.

28 *How to organize your first stable competition*

This chapter is meant to help you to organize your first stable competition, if you are too remotely situated to get help from a vaulting association, and if your (and the other clubs) are so young that international rules can not yet be made applicable to your vaulting situation. Where national guidelines for vaulting are in existence, there will also be guidance as to how you may modify those rules. Until then you might have to improvise.

Use of the horse

It is stated in the International Rules how often a horse may be used per competition day — and you should stick to that, taking into account that your stable competitions will not be all canter performance. Keep in mind that you'll do great damage to this sport if the spectators see that you are overworking your animal. I know that the temptation may be great: if there are only one or two competitions per year, and of course all vaulters of the clubs want to enter as many events as possible — but each club only has one horse. There is only *one* solution: limit the entries. Don't make the horse suffer. And take hot summer temperatures into account.

Other rules

For all other rules, which you may state in your invitation (which should be approved by your provincial association, if there is one) keep in mind that they should help us to get this sport going, rather than making it difficult. We want as many people involved as possible, as many young vaulters encouraged to participate. Speak to the other invited clubs and write the rules to suit your needs.

Judging

Try to look as professional as possible to build up good credibility. Don't invite judges who might favour your own club. If your association has a list of certified judges, contact them first. In the international rules such judges must be paid for their services — this is often impossible for us in small stable competitions. Ask them if they'd volunteer — then make their day as agreeable as possible (coffee service and nice social contacts!) so they'll come back for you! If you have to improvise with older vaulters or trainers of the respective clubs, let them judge together, always two from different clubs, to ensure impartiality.

Entry fees

In international competitions no entry fees may be charged, and the same should apply for provincial or national competitions. But for the time being, with no sponsors in sight for this 'new' sport in our country, we often can't get around charging some fee for our stable competitions. We have to pay for the extra day for the use of the horse, we have to pay ring time, rent the decoration for the ring, pay for the ribbons, and the list goes on. We feel that it is important to keep the costs as low as possible, to guarantee high participation. Get your vaulters and helpers to volunteer, make it a work-party event.

Helpers

- Before the event you need a show secretary or a group of people, who collect the entrance fees, write the time table, get the whole thing into a sequence which works for the vaulters as well as the horses in terms of breaks between events. You must order ribbons and organize prizes.

The helpers you will need during the competition are the following:

- You need the judges, as mentioned above. The main judge needs a bell, with which s/he gives the signal to start or to stop (in case of unforeseen circumstances). Have scrap paper and pens ready for the judges, and offer them the score sheets in the correct order. Especially when the judges do not know the vaulters, it can be total chaos if the sequence of the forms gets shuffled.

- The judges need writing assistants, as they never take their eyes off the vaulters. Those assistants (one per judging table) must be familiar with the format of the forms, so the filling in may happen fast and efficiently. The assistants do *not* watch the vaulters. They only listen and write − so *do* give them a break by making this job two shifts.

- You need a timer: this person must have a back-up stop watch in case of problems, and he must be aware of the rules. When to start timing, how to stop and restart the time in case of falls. Refer to the rule book for all this.

- Very important helpers are one or two score calculators (so they can cross check or take turns) − their fingers should be nimble and their figures must be correct. It is a very embarrassing situation to collect your prizes and ribbons back, because the average marks on the score sheets were computed wrongly... There should be backup batteries for the calculator machine, which should be the type that prints out the results, so the paper can be tacked onto the score sheets. The people for this job should be awake enough to spot obvious mistakes without the use of a computer − such as an average coming out lower than all the numbers, which were averaged! The more often you present ribbons in between classes, the more the calculators must be on their toes. Seat the calculators in a quiet back room, so they can concentrate, and let nobody but the runners enter.

- You need runners, at least as many as you have judges' tables. Each runner stands next to the table (but far enough away not to overhear the judges) and receives the score sheet, as soon as the judges have filled in the marks. The runner then carries it to the calculators, while the next runner takes up his position next to the table. During the competition nobody except the runners may approach the judges.

- You need a whipper-in: this person is positioned at the entrance of the ring and keeps the records of who is in the ring and who gets ready to go next. The children vaulting on the same horse will run in groups (you specified this on the time table you worked out), and the whipper-in keeps track of vaulters dropping out or groupings being changed for any reasons. Vaulters or teams who are more than three minutes late should not be allowed to start, because they play havoc with your scheduling. If the competition runs significantly faster or slower than predicted, the whipper-in should change the time table, which is tacked up to the wall at the entrance of the ring. This way the trainers of the teams and the vaulters can keep track themselves as well.

- Announcing and presentation of the ribbons: give the announcer a microphone if the announcement is not made from an announcer's booth. If you have an announcer for the whole event, also call out the name of the team entering the ring, the horse's name, the lunger and the vaulters. You have the choice of presenting the ribbons in between the individual classes or all at the very end. If you do it in between, the little people can go home early – which is very good in cold weather conditions! But keep in mind that the presentation depends on the way you spread the classes. In 'real' competitions all vaulters do the compulsories first, then the freestyle after an adequate break for the horses. But in those competitions you will see up to twenty horses march in at the end of the competition. If you are dealing with three clubs with one horse each, you must of course break up the canter classes and intersperse them well with walk events to make the competition possible at all. Plan a generous lunch break for the horses and fill the time with a social event or a barrel competition for the vaulters.

- You need somebody at the sound table: this could be the announcer as well. If all vaulters hand in their individual tapes, this person must check as the tapes come in that they are clearly marked and stopped at the correct spot. Give the sound person a copy of the time table, so s/he can check off the names, and remind the whipper-in to inform this person in case of changes.

For our first stables competitions we have changed some of the rules to suit our own needs as well.

Age and performance grouping

In fledgling vaulting clubs age groupings do not always make sense, as they assume that somebody who is fifteen years old has vaulted for several years. So if you have several older vaulters, who are nevertheless beginners, you might also group the events by 'beginner and advanced'. This might allow the beginners some advantages: state if you'll allow boosting of vaulters, and define the conditions clearly in the invitation. We have broken the walk and canter classes sometimes into 'beginner' and 'advanced' as well, which was simply a way to be able to hand out twice as many prizes. The judges should be aware of how you have planned to place, and this should be cleared with your Vaulting Association.

You may have beginning vaulters, who are able to to do some exercises in canter, and would like to show this off. Introduce a 'transitional class' to your compulsories if this helps your purposes, that is, let the vaulters show the first block of compulsories (mount, seat, flag – with or without free hand – and mill) in canter, but the second block in walk. Keeping the entries for compulsories separate from the freestyle gives the vaulters an additional flexibility of performance. As stated in our very early stable competitions, they can then choose to be in a canter class in compulsories, but still in walk for their individual freestyle.

We have left the size of the competing teams flexible as well. At the time our first competition was held, some clubs could simply not muster a team with eight vaulters plus an extra. Therefore we also left the maximum allowable time open: the clubs were expected to use the time according to the number of vaulters competing on one team. This worked very well.

In Appendix C I have included the forms we used for our first stable competitions. To simplify matters for the organizers, we combined the entry form with the score sheet, which is usually not done in 'real' competitions! But this served our needs very well, and saved a lot of paper work and photocopying. By now we are using internationally accepted rules, scores and score sheets, and you can find copies of those in the back of the international rule book. They should be used as soon as you can.

The time table is included, so you can compare how much certain groups and performances (whether in walk, trot or canter) will take – and this competition was right on the button and finished at exactly 4:00 pm. The pauses were adequate and both horses (there were only two clubs) had enough rest and walk periods in between performances.

Try to keep a record of the score sheets for your club and the association. In later competitions you will start to carry the scores forward, find out the best average vaulter of the year, or set up some tailor-made kind of medal award system. In the medal awards we have tried to adhere to commonly accepted rules straight away, so we can compare our rules with the rules in Europe and the United States.

Appendix A Insurance

Most sports carry certain risks and if an athlete chooses to participate, s/he must take on board those risks.

Parents should sign a consent form before they let their children join your vaulting team, and for each show or competition (be it only to prove that the child *did* ask for permission), and a waiver slip, which indicates that the parent or legal guardian of the vaulter agrees that they waive the right to hold the trainer responsible for injuries suffered during the execution of this sport's activity. However you should be aware that these slips do not carry much weight before a court in case of a law suit. They *do* help to make the parents more aware of inherent dangers and the reality that a coach can only really be sued if proven negligent.

Negligence is defined as: the omission to do something which a reasonable man would do, or the doing of something which a reasonable man would not do. This reasonable man (or woman) is assumed to possess normal mental capacities and intelligence, average perception, memory and information.

Even once you are certified as a trainer by your provincial association, this does not imply perfection. But it implies 'state of the art' awareness and knowledge of your 'trade', including safety precautions. It means such a coach must acquire the expertise for the level of training s/he is certified for.

Negligence exists only if all four of the following points are met:

if there is existence of a legal duty on the part of the coach to exercise proper care in protecting the athlete

if there is failure to perform that duty, the degree of which is
in relation to the circumstances involved

if an injury is suffered by the athlete (his person, property,
legal rights or reputation)

if there is a reasonably close *causal* relationship between the
breach of duty and the athlete's injury

I am not in the position to give any legal advice, so please
speak to your insurance agent or lawyer. But possible causes for
negligence in vaulting could in my opinion be something like
this:

if a vaulter is forced by the trainer to perform an exercise
when injured, and this makes the injury worse

if a vaulter is supplied with drugs or forced to use drugs

if the exercises imposed are unsuitable to the age or condition
of the child or youth

if a vaulter is forced to perform under unsafe conditions

if unsafe equipment or horses are used

if improper supervision can be proven

if inadequate safety precautions were taken

if improper or inadequate instructions were given

if a vaulter is put under strong pressure to perform an exercise
that s/he is really afraid of and not ready for.

A coach must have basic First Aid knowledge (and this will be
part of any certification program). A coach is obliged, by his/her
relationship to the athletes in loco parentis, to do the best s/he
can and give immediate first aid where this is necessary. 'Failure
to act, as well as acting in an improper manner may lead to a
claim for negligence.'

Possible precautions you can take against claims of negligence:

do not permit participants to attempt exercises which are
potentially hazardous, until they have received the proper
instruction and had adequate practice (for example on the
stationary horse)

never allow vaulters to train unsupervised

don't allow riders to use the same part of the ring in which you are training. Provide adequate space for falls (no hard objects in the way, such as jumps)

procure medical approval (in written form) to participate again in the sport after an injury

provide adequate spotting where indicated

administer first aid *only* when necessary. That means when no doctor or nurse or ambulance are to be reached, or to save a life

never treat serious injuries

use a public carrier or properly insured people for driving to and from events

Consult an insurance agent as to which insurance would cover your needs best. Your insurance should cover:

The premises where the activity takes place. This means training facility as well as all other locations where your shows and competitions take place.

There are possible blanket insurance policies that cover *all* premises. They must cover bodily injury as well as property damage

If the coach has assumed a contract, he should be covered by the employer's insurance. A blanket contractual liability insurance could be printed on all contracts

A personal injury liability endorsement can be added

Insurance against catastrophic loss can be taken out or an umbrella liability program

Your insurance may only cover you, if the events are sanctioned by the appropriate association, so enquire beforehand.

Appendix B   Samples of kur routines

The numbering of the exercises in the following examples refer to the numbers given in the Catalogue of vaulting exercises in this book. Abbreviations and names of exercises are explained at the beginning of the catalogue and in the Glossary. Where an 's' or 'c' is given after a number, it means 'similar to' or 'compare to' the exercise of that number.

Example   *3-minute single in walk* (intermediate beginner vaulter)

mount and hang	Numbers 147
tailor's seat (crossed legs)	120
FW candle (come down on neck)	
kick-up on neck (upside-down bench) (stick-through leg transition and turn)	190
BW stand	221
bridge (slide down on croup)	197
roll-up into flag on neck	97
flag on neck (free?) and swing around	176 and 87
FW arabesque on horse's back	249
FW shoulderstand (down with scissor turn)	
BW flag on croup (free)	175
INS SW sign post	156
belly lie (free?)	127
parallel skyways	136
outside pistol (sitting hang)	143 2 hands,
swing onto neck	leg high!
BW arabesque on neck	250
'Lean-to' (support on two arms, legs extended downward)	194

curtsey from prince's seat twice	89
stand on one foot	226
walk to croup and high jump off	55

Example *trot double for intermediate* 8-year-olds

		Numbers
mount A first, B stand over bench		167
wheelbarrow (B on croup)		200
sw flag (A) and FW arabesque	s	185
hang (A) and prince's seat (B)	c	147 and 161
2 × pistol (sitting hang) (B inside) A swing around		143 s
2 × flag FW and BW on neck (A)		179
A stick-through leg transition, B half mill		
2 × kick-up FW and BW,		192
B into BW seat, A turn		
BW supported wheelbarrow on croup (B down with scissor turn)		201
2 × parallel skyways	s	136
2 × hunter stand (knee stand) in stirrup (B stick through leg transition to front)	s	215
supported shoulderstand with tilt-off		266
A straddle jump off		54

Example   *Long show* with 11 vaulters

			Numbers
Canter	v2	mount into flag, OUTS lady seat, swing into BW arabesque	250
		handstand transition into FW seat	103 s
	v2/v6	2 × hang	147
	v6/v4	'discord'	222
	v4/v8/v1	'rocket angel'	299
	v9/v3	(assisted diep mount onto neck)	26
		roll-up into shoulder lie	112
		(v9 dismounts down in back)	

	v3/v5	2 × prince's seat (v5 turn)		161
	v5	roll-up		97
	v5/v8	bw flag on neck & arabesque (v5 swing around)	s	253
	v5/v4/v10	(assisted mount) sit on high bench		163
Walk	v7/v6/v11	supported arabesque on flag		259
	v6/v11	candle on bench		166
	v1/v8/v4	high wheelbarrow		203
	v7/v1	(ass. mount to bw seat on neck)		
		bw arabesque on supine w/roll-off over the supine position		254 and 72
	v1/v2	(v1 scissor transition onto neck, v2 scissor mount behind)		95 6
		slide down and roll-up into ass. shoulderstand (down w/twist)		100
	v2/v11	ass. mount in front, bridge from seat on shoulder and off over hand-stand on croup		comp. 149
	v2/v9/v3	sw lifted split		296
Trot	v9/v10/v4	dbl wheelbarrow (tilt off v9)		211
	v4/v5/v10	hungarian post		171
	v11/v5/v7	'family round' (v5 swing around)		219
	v5/v3	'tango'		227
	v9/v3	(assisted mount to front) wheelbarrow (v9 over belt)		200
Canter	(v9/v1)	(roll over v1 shoulder transition)		112
	v1/v9/v4	Draped lift		302
	v9/v2	supp. handstand (1 hand, tilt off)		277

v8/v2	(supp. mount) BW flying angel	140
v8/v4	(1/2 'flea' transition from neck	108
	to back) dbl decker flag	184
	(try simultaneous dismount)	
v1/v10	free stand on shoulder	233
v10/v1	skater's lift	199
	(down to handstand on croup & flip off)	
v1/v9/v3	'carried angel' (flying angel)	298
v3/v10/v4	high handstand	283
(v3/v10)	1/2 'flea' transition)	108
v3/v10/v9	2 × jump (over head of sitting)	111

Example   *5-minute competition kur* with six vaulters only

M and D in the first column are the given degree of difficulty, with '?' it depends on the more or less difficult variation the vaulters choose to execute under the given circumstances (how nervous the horse is!). The vaulters in this example were intermediate. The whole kur is performed in canter.

			Numbers
M	v2	mount into flag and swing onto neck	14 and 87
		(v6 mount into crouch)	15
D	v2/v6/v1	'high cross arab' (all hands joined)	260
D?	v1/v6	'skater's lift'	199
D?	v1/v6	tip v6 into BW handstand, tilt off	280
M/M	v4/v1	ass. diep mount, roll-up and shoulder lie	26 and 112
M		jump over with twist, land standing	111
M	v4/v1	BW flying angel (down front, slide off)	140
	v1/v5/v3	(v5 mounts into crouch, shoulder sit,	125
D		v3 mounts) 'draped lift'	302
		(v5 down middle into stand, v1 swing onto neck)	
D	v1/v5/v3	'spider' tilt into:	300

M		sw assisted handstand (v5 tilt-off, vi off w/twist)	281
M	v3/v4	(assisted diep mount onto neck)	26
		bridge over v3's back from shoulder sit	125
M		double decker flag (v4 stand while vi mounts)	184
D	v3/v4/vi	'rocket angel' (flyer) (with tilt off, v3 off neck)	299
D	v6/vi	assisted mount onto feet on neck and jump over bw	111
D		free stand on shoulder (v6 down in front and dismount direct, v2 mount front lady seat, transition over surcingle, vi flank off, v5 mount behind into stand)	233
D	v2/v5	supported handstand on one hand (with tilt off, v3 mounts)	277
M	v2/v3/v6	sit on high bench (transition into)	163
D	v2/v6/v3	high handstand (v6 into outs lady seat, v2 dismounts, v5 mounts assisted into ins stirrup)	283
M	v6/v5/v3	2 × sidesplit in stirrups and prince's seat	214s
D	v6/v5/v3	double wheelbarrow	211
M	v3	handstand transition into lean-to	194
		'squat-through' dismount	49

Appendix C   Sample copies of forms for simple stable competitions

. . . . STABLES
VAULTING COMPETITION date/year

SINGLE COMPETITOR   £   per entry

name of competitor   start no.

birthdate   age

name of horse

name of trainer

COMPULSORIES	RS	FLG	ML	SC	ST	FLK	TOTAL
LEVEL C walk							
LEVEL B trot							
LEVEL A canter							

comments

JUDGE   ASSISTANT

Signature

NOTE   entries must be received by (date)

. . . . STABLES
VAULTING COMPETITION date/year

SINGLE COMPETITOR £ per entry
----

name of competitor start no.

birthdate age

name of horse

name of trainer

FREESTYLE		min. dur.★	no. of exer.	added points	tech. merit	art. imp.	TOTAL
LEVEL C	walk	3	( )				
LEVEL B	trot	2	( )				
LEVEL A	canter	I	( )				

$5 - 9 = 1.0 / 10 - 14 = 2.0 / 15 - 19 = 3.0 / 20$ & over $= 4.0$

comments _____

_____

_____

JUDGE ASSISTANT

Signature _____

NOTE entries must be received by (date)
★ min. dur. = max. duration of kur in minutes. We counted no. of exercises
performed and gave added bonus points. Tech. mer. means technical merit. Art.
imp. is artistic impression, i.e. performance

. . . . STABLES
VAULTING COMPETITION date/year

PAS DE DEUX   £   per entry
----
name of competitor 1   start no.
----
birthdate   age

name of competitor 2   start no.
----
birthdate   age

name of horse
----
name of trainer

FREESTYLE		min. dur.	no. of exer.	added points	tech. merit	art. imp.	TOTAL
LEVEL C	walk	3	(	)			
LEVEL B	trot	2	(	)			
LEVEL A	canter	1	(	)			

$5 - 9 = 1.0 / 10 - 14 = 2.0 / 15 - 19 = 3.0 / 20$ and over $= 4.0$

comments _____

_____

_____

JUDGE   ASSISTANT

Signature _____

NOTE   entries must be received by (date)

. . . . STABLES
VAULTING COMPETITION date/year

TEAM KUR   £   per entry

name of team

name of horse

name of trainer

FREESTYLE		min. dur.	no. of exer.	added points	tech. merit	art. imp.	TOTAL
LEVEL C	walk	5–8	(	)			
LEVEL B	trot	5	(	)			
LEVEL A	canter	5	(	)			

$5 - 9 = 1.0 / 10 - 14 = 2.0 / 15 - 19 = 3.0 / 20$ and over $= 4.0$

comments

JUDGE   ASSISTANT

Signature

NOTE   entries must be received by (date)
please advise us of entry by (date). Thank you!

★ min. dur. = max. duration of kur in minutes. We counted no. of exercises performed and gave added bonus points. Tech. mer. means technical merit. Art. imp. is artistic impression, i.e. performance

NOTE
For official competitions, team compulsories are part of the team entry. The sheet would then look like the one on the next page.

SCORE SHEET FOR VAULTING GROUPS

On _____ At _____
Group _____ Lunger _____
Class A/B/C/CN _____ Horse _____

Time allowed for Compulsory and
Freestyle = 15 minutes
Compulsory section   Max. time for Freestyle: 5 minutes

Vaulter number	Surname, Christian name	Age	Basic Seat	Flag	Mill	Scissors	Standing	Flank	Total
1									
2									
3									
4									
5									
6									
7									
8									
Reserve									
Total									Compulsory

Comments	Total Compulsory		÷ 8 =	
	Freestyle			
	Difficulty		× 2 =	
	Composition		× 1	
	Freestyle Execution		× 2 =	
Penalties	General Impression		× 1	
	Total Compulsory + Freestyle:			
Judge A/B/C	÷ 12 = Final Mark			
Signature	Place			

Abbreviations:
T = rhythm fault
C = canter stride missed
K = failed to kneel
R = repetition
G = touched ground
F = fell

Marks:
10 = excellent
9 = very good
8 = good
7 = fairly good
6 = satisfactory
5 = sufficient

4 = insufficient
3 = fairly bad
2 = bad
1 = very bad
0 = not performed

SCORE SHEET FOR PAS DE DEUX VAULTING

Judge at _____

Date _____

Event _____

Competition _____

Vaulter _____

Vaulter _____

Lunger _____

Horse _____

Free Style 1st round	Artistic	Performance			
			Total		
				:2	

Free Style 2nd round	Artistic	Performance			
			Total		
				:2	

Record			
	Total		
	:2/	Final Score	

Judges A _____
        B _____
        C _____

SCORE SHEET FOR INDIVIDUAL VAULTING

Judge at _____

Date _____   Vaulter _____
Event _____   Lunger _____
Competition _____   Horse _____

Compulsories

Basic seat	Flag	Mill	Scissors	Stand	Flank	Total		Compulsories
							:6	

Free Style

Content		Performance			
Degree of difficulty	Composition				
X1	X1	X2			
			Total	:4	Free Test

Record		
	Total	
	:2/ Final Score	

Judges   A _____
      B _____
      C _____

SCORE SHEET to be submitted to E.V.A.   Competition Name and Date

SINGLE COMPULSORIES   *W A L K*

placing	*name* of competitor	*age*	*av. mark*
first place			
second place			
third place			
fourth place			
fifth place			

SINGLE COMPULSORIES   *T R O T*

placing	*name* of competitor	*age*	*av. mark*
first place			
second place			
third place			
fourth place			
fifth place			

SINGLE COMPULSORIES   *C A N T E R*

placing	*name* of competitor	*age*	*av. mark*
first place			
second place			
third place			
fourth place			
fifth place			

(and a similar form for individual, *pas-de-deux* and team vaulting)

.... STABLES VAULTING COMPETITION   (date)

(promoter)   (phone number)   (please call for exact time later)

INVITATION

As we have to limit the number of entries for time constraint reasons there will be no barrel competition at this event.

We invite you to compete in the three classes A, B and C in the following categories:

CLASS C   beginners, age 4 to max. 10 years
           all exercises in WALK only
           vaulters may be assisted in mounting
           compulsories – single   (all 6 basic exercises)
           freestyle – single   2 min.
           freestyle *pas-de-deux*   3 min.
           team kur (6 to 8 people) min. 5 to max. 8 minutes

CLASS B   intermediate level, age 6 to max. 16
           all exercises in TROT only
           children up to age 8 may mount in walk unassisted
           compulsories – single   (all 6 exercises, no dismount after the mill)
           freestyle single   2 min.
           freestyle *pas de deux*   3 min.
           team kur (6 to 8 people) min. 5 to max. 8 minutes

CLASS A   advanced vaulters
           all exercises in CANTER only
           all mounts unassisted★
           compulsories – single   (dismount after mill with immediate mount – one
                                     touchdown only – into scissors)
           freestyle – single   1 min.
           freestyle *pas de deux*   2 min.
           team kur (6 to 8 people) min. 5 to max. 8 minutes
      ★ the judges may consent to allow the smaller children starting in this category
        to mount in trot unassisted.
        PLEASE LET US KNOW two weeks ahead of time, if you plan to enter a team kur
        in this competition. Thank you.
        The promoter may cancel a category if less than two persons register for it.
        We may suggest shifting these competitors into a different category.

NOTE   please bring your own tape if you wish to perform to music.

NOTE ALL ENTRY FORMS MUST BE RECEIVED BY US AT THE LATEST 4 DAYS PRIOR TO THE COMPETITION TO ENSURE PROPER ORGANIZATION BY THE PROMOTER. Later entries will NOT be considered.

Starting rules

Vaulters may NOT start in the same category (e.g. single kur) in two different starting classes (e.g. class A and B). Vaulters are expected to decide within a category, if they consider themselves intermediate or advanced. They may however, for example, be advanced in compulsories, yet intermediate in freestyle.

Vaulters may *not* start in the category or in a lower category (i.e. class B compulsory trot) if they have been placed 1st to 3rd place in this category in an earlier competition. It is considered that by placing thus they have been proven to be ready to advance into the next higher category or class. These rules are made to be fair to the less advanced vaulters, to give them a chance to be placed in the category they are starting in.

Judging rules

No person may act as a judge in any competition in the same *class* (e.g. class B) in which s/he is competing him/herself. Normally no judge may compete at the same time at all. We are only modifying these rules, because of the lack of trained judges in BC.

(We now have the rule in British Columbia that nobody may be invited to act as a judge if s/he has not completed the judging workshop, which the EVA is offering to interested people. As soon as we are in the position to certify judges, only those may be invited. If your province does not have certified judges, and if it is prohibitive in terms of cost to invite qualified judges, contact the next association for help in improvising! As soon as we have national guidelines, those will provide for the difficulties we have with the great distances within Canada.)

There will be a minimum of two judges per event (single vaulter or *pas-de-deux* or team) at separate tables. Marks shall *not* be compared before the final calculation and therefore distribution of placings.

Because of the lack of trained judges for our competitions we invite you and/or some of your senior vaulters to serve as judge. Please let us know one week before the competition how many volunteers you can offer and send us their names for proper organization of this event. Later applications for 'judge' will not be considered.

Marking sheets are handed out to competitors after the competition by request. Trainers are encouraged to take them home for teaching purposes.

Entry sheets and registration form for judges will be sent to the respective trainers in September.

Judging procedures
Compulsories will be judged according to:

the MOUNT (mount in class A after the mill will count into the mark for the scissors) Mounts with help of the stirrup are *not* permissible

minimum time wasted between the exercises
(after more than 4 beats 1/2 point shall be deducted for each 4 beats wasted)

number of beats the exercise is held steadily
(4 beats is minimum for a perfect mark in compulsories)
If the first 4 beats are wobbly, a maximum of another 4 beats may be added)
Points will be deducted for less than 4 beats held per exercise
Points shall be deducted for 2nd and 3rd tries

the elegance of the dismount or transition back to sitting position

the fluidity and artistic impression of the whole sequence

Freestyle (Kur) performances will be judged according to
the number of exercises shown within the set time limit (inclusion into the mark as follows:
     for 5 to 9 exercises add 1.0 point
     for 10 to 14 exercises add 2.0 points
     for 15 to 19 exercises add 3.0 points
     for 20 and more exercises add 4.0 points
NOTE   simple transfers between exercises do *not* count in this number! Simple mounts into the sitting position do *not* count as an exercise.)

technical merit:
i.e. the degree of difficulty of the content of the kur (see the international rule book for guidelines)

artistic impression:
i.e. how fluid and harmonious the composition of the kur is and how well it was executed by the vaulter.

Entry fees will be

Example for a

date/year

Please note   All times are approximate. Please be ready prior to your turn, in case proceedings move faster. Check this list for corrections. Entries are void if more than three minutes late. Thank you for your cooperation!

11:00   Greeting of the judges and participants

Level C compulsories

11:15	Group 1	Vaulter 1	horse A
		Vaulter 2	horse A
11:20	Group 2	Vaulter a	horse B
		Vaulter b	horse B
		Vaulter c	horse B
11:25	Group 3	Vaulter 3	horse A
		Vaulter 4	horse A
		Vaulter 5	horse A

Level C pas-de-deux

11:40	Group 1	Vaulter a & vaulter c	horse B
		Vaulter b & vaulter d	horse B
11:50	Group 2	Vaulter 4 & vaulter 5	horse A
12:00	*Distribution of ribbons*		

HALF HOUR BREAK

and so on. As a rule of thumb, a group of three individuals will take about ten to max. fifteen minutes with run-in and salute, a group of two *pas-de-deux* will last about ten minutes. After each hour of performance there should be a ten minute break (for the judges). Make sure your 'calculator' can keep up with the work, so the distribution of ribbons can happen on time.

Appendix D How to build a simple barrel horse

There are many different kinds of stationary horses around, most of them 'home designed'. The main thing is that your barrel be stable, and it depends on your talents as handy-man (or woman!) what kind you will choose. If someone of your club has access to a welder, you can use a steel barrel and weld legs and handles (similar in shape to the handles on your surcingle) right onto it. Pad the barrel and wrap the handles generously and you're set! If you have to build out of wood, the simplest way to achieve a more or less realistic form is to cut oval shapes out of plywood (double them up and laminate for stability), one for the rear, one for the front, and at least one for under the surcingle. Screw strapping overtop, as shown in the cut-away, then pad with thick foam.

The body's circumference should be 2.00 metres maximum, as otherwise your surcingle will not fit. If you will strap your surcingle onto the 'dummy', you need to build up some withers on the barrel. Otherwise the surcingle will turn. You could also bolt some kind of handles onto the wooden support, but with the lateral forces being applied, they have the tendency to come loose or break very soon. Using the real surcingle also has the advantage that the vaulters use the same kind of handles, and experience the height (the 'step') of the surcingle, which comes into play in many exercises (such as the backward scissors!)

A neck is not absolutely necessary, but it is nice for practising team exercises. Two rings at the front to affix the side reins is useful to practise keeping your feet away from them in transitions and jumps (nothing is more painful to the horse than a vaulter jumping directly onto the side reins). A cover of plastic works well if your have to park it outside, carpet samples work as well, but the vaulters need long pants — or else, carpet burn! Best cover would be something you can take off and wash occasionally. The height the legs should be is debatable. If you spot high exercises (like handstands) you want the dummy low; when you practice mounts, not too low. A good average height is about 1.30 metres or just above 4 feet, which allows you to practise both reasonably well. Lucky vaulters, like ours, use stationary horses with adjustable (and removable) legs. This also has great advantages for transport, if you drive your barrel around to clinics all the time, as we do. The main thing is that the legs be well secured (bolted in several places) and braced, and far enough apart so the barrel does not tip during exercises. Don't underestimate the motion in a good swing, or the pull of a vaulter who flips over in a handstand.

Please don't succumb too much to making your barrel horse 'cute': tails are fine...but I have seen pointed wooden ears on some — an absolute nonsense, because your vaulters can seriously injure themselves, if they come down hard on them.

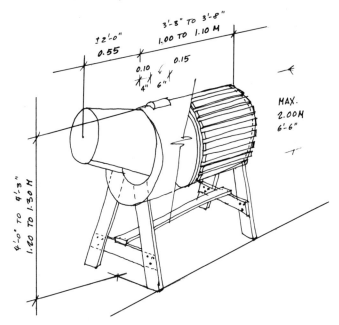

Illustrated catalogue of vaulting exercises

Grouping of the vaulting exercises

Catalogue of common vaulting exercises

This catalogue of vaulting exercises shows the most common combinations — to be performed singly or with partner(s) — grouped into mounts, dismounts, transitions and dynamic exercises and static exercises.

The possibility for combinations is virtually endless, as anybody foolish enough to try to draw them all will tell you! All exercises may be varied in terms of direction and height, with differing arm movements. Make full use of directional variations to add to the harmonious flow of your kur! Static exercises may be combined into dynamic ones by moving partners — for example by rotating a flyer. Mounts may be turned into dynamic exercises by repeating them; for example doing an assisted roll mount with touch-down and remount. Complex transitions between exercises will count as exercises themselves. Partners may be tilted, twisted, rotated, dropped or lifted into the next position. Exercises shown as triples can sometimes be performed as doubles and vice versa (for example an sw supported handstand can be done as double).

When combining exercises, keep in mind that for good choreography the arm movements, as well as the sequence and the choice of transitions, should make sense. It never looks good to do a transition onto the neck, if then no logical exercise follows using that achieved position. Arm movements seem all too often like mere fidgeting if they do not harmoniously lead to another grip, or express some theme (as given, for example, by the music). Arm movements in the Flamenco Style don't make sense to 'The little night music' by Mozart! A basic riding seat does not turn into an interesting exercise, just because the vaulter waves the arms about...

The degree of difficulty will depend on the height and added or decreased security, as well as on variations in the complexity of move or combination. The degree of difficulty indicated in this catalogue mostly follows the rules of the 1993 FEI rule book. Exercises which were not listed in that book are assigned an appropriate degree by me, this being marked in brackets. Where two degrees are given, the one in brackets is assigned by me; often it depends on the variation of complexity. So please use them only as a guideline!

There are three degrees of difficulty: s superior
                                         M medium
                                         E easy
and a fourth one, added by me: (x) most difficult.

This is meant to point out a level of performance, which will be rewarded by a judge under 'composition' for performance, which exceeds the common S-category.

The choice of exercises and/or given variations for your vaulters will depend on their experience and strength, as well as the proportion of the of the size and weight of flyer and undermen.

The names given to the exercises are either commonly accepted ones, or, when given in inverted commas, are the ones we use in our club. Invent your own! Let me know if they are good ones! Short names are really useful for writing down shows.

For abbreviations used in the following pages, see Glossary.

In the dynamic exercises the sequence of the phasing will be indicated as follows:

 first phase   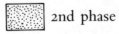 2nd phase    end phase

Single mounts

| 1(a) | 'Flank-in mount | mount from INS into inward side seat | E |
| (b) | 'Flank-over MT' (illustrated) | mount from INS into outward side seat | M |

2(a)	OUTside Mounts:	into seat astride	E
(b)		OUT side seat	M
(c)		INS side seat	S
(not illustrated)			

| 3 | Free flank into | OUT side seat (depends on height) | (M) S |

4(a)	Turning mount to NK	via INS seat from INS	M
(b)		same from OUT	S
(c)		via flank-over into OUT sideseat w/immediate swing onto NK	(M)
(d)	'Special' (illustrated a)	like (c), direct (no fleeting seat)	(S)

5   Direct turning MT to Neck   S

6(a)   Scissor MT to BK   w/left turn from INS   M
  (b)   w/right turn from INS   S
  (c)   from OUT   S
(illustrated a and b)

7   Diep mount   from INS   S

8(a)   Mount to belly lie   FW or SW from INS   E
  (b)   FW or SW from OUT   M

9(a)	Mount into back lie	with legs together	S
(b)		with legs in straddle	M
(illustrated a)			

10(a)	Mount to 'lean-to'	from INS to INS lean	M
(b)		from INS to OUT lean	S
(illustrated a)			

11(a)	Mount to 'push-up'	from INS to FW support	M
(b)		from OUT to FW support	S
(c)		from INS w/immediate squat-through	S
(illustrated a)			

12(a)	Mount into FW kneel	from INS	E
(b)		from OUT	M
(not illustrated)			

13(a)	Mount into SW kneel	facing IN	E
(b)	Same, facing	OUT	M
(c)	From OUT		S
(not illustrated)			

| 14(a) | Mount into flag | from INS | M |
| (b) | | from OUT | S |

15(a)	Mount into crouch	from INS	M
(b)		from OUT	S
(not illustrated)			

| 16(a) | Mount direct into stand (slight time lag) | | S |
| (b) | w/immediate stand | | (X) |

| 17 | Mount direct into arabesque (leg above horizontal) | S |

18   Mount into shoulderstand   S

19   Mount into shoulderhang FW/BW/SW   S

20(a)	Roll mount into	belly lie on NK or BK	S
(b)		back lie on NK or BK	S
(illustrated a)			

21   Roll mount to   riding seat   S

22   'Cartwheel mount'   to BW seat on NK   S

23   'Rollmops'   roll-down from shoulderstand with
                            touch–down and immediate roll mount   (s)

Partner mounts

24(a)   Double mount   from INS   M
  (b)   from OUT   S
  (illustrated a)

25   Mount under flank   to sitting   M

26   ass Diep mount   from sitting   M

27   'Skip' mount under free jump
  (a)   to seat astride   E
  (b)   to outside seat   M
  (illustrated a)

28(a)   ass MT by standing   into sitting   E
  (b)   into kneeling/standing   M

29   ass MT from BW stand into kneel/standing   (s)

30   Mount under swing into high handstand (depends on height M/s)

31   Mount into supp handstand   s

32(a)   Mount onto bench/flag, assisted   (M)
  (b)   not assisted   M

33   Mount into 'Hanging spider'   (s)
          (not illustrated, compare drawing no. 150)

34   Mount into wheelbarrow over supine   s

35   Mount into wheelbarrow over supine w/immediate tilt-up into
          handstand   s

36   Mount into rocket angel (flyer)
    (a)   over reclining partner   s
    (b)   direct   (x)

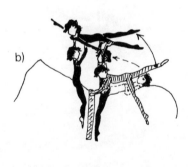

37   ass sim Scissor mount from INS and OUT   (s)

38   Direct mount into 'Zigzag'   (s)

39   'Peak mount' with suspension in the air   (s)

40   ass Roll mount by standing FW/BW/SW   S

41   ass Roll MT into sw belly lie under sw stand   (x)

Single dismounts _____

42   FW 'push-away' w/suspension in air (also assisted)

43   BW 'push-away'   E

44   Vault-off w/½ turn flank from CP or NK   M

45   Vault-off w/½ turn flank over BK/over NK   S

46   Flank-off from cross lie to INS/OUT (not illustrated)   M

47   High ½ flank off to INS or OUT
  (a)   from flag (depends on height M or)   E
  (b)   from kneeling   M
  (c)   w/landing behind horse   S
  (not illustrated)

48(a)   Flank-off over CP   from sitting   M
  (b)   from flag   M
  (illustrated a)

49   Squat-through from 'lean-to'
  (a)   as dismount   M
  (b)   to sustained support   S

50(a)   Leap frog over CP   from kneeling   E
  (b)   from sitting/standing   M

51   Leap frog over the NK   S

52(a)   Tuck/Straddle or straight jump to INS or OUT   E
  (b)   to the rear   M
  (illustrated tuck jump)

53   Straight jump w/full turn on vertical axis   S

54(a)   Straddle jump w/legs at right angle to body INS/OUT/rear   M
  (b)   over the NK (depends on height X or)   S
(illustrated a)

55   'Clip dismount'   (M)

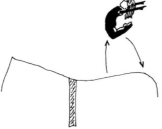

56(a)   FW Roll dismount   down shoulder to OUT   M
  (b)   over the CP   M
  (c)   across horse to INS/OUT   S
(illustrated a)

57(a)   BW roll dismount   across the horse to INS/OUT   M
  (b)   on the shoulder of the horse M

58   BW Roll dismount   over the croup   S

59(a)   'Handstand-off'   from arabesque   E
  (b)   from sitting   M
(illustrated a)

60   Handstand walk-overs in all directions   s

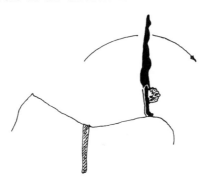

61(a)   Shoulderstand flip-off   (s)
  (b)   Handstand flip-off   (s)

a)

b)

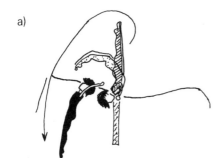

62(a)   Cartwheel off   with hands   s
  (b)   without hands   (x)

a)

b)

63   Flic–Flac off   (x)

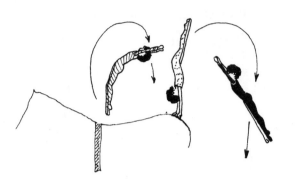

64   Salto off, straight or tucked FW/BW   (x) s

Partner dismounts _____

65   Double flank-off   M

66   'High handstand off' (over shoulders of sitting)   M

67(a)   Jump-through off   FW over 1 or 2 sitting partners   M
   (b)   BW over 1 or 2 sitting partners   S
   (c)   FW/BW over kneeling partners   S
(illustrated a)

68   supp straddle jump off   M

69(a)   Squat vault jump over sw stir arabesque   M
  (b)   Squat through or straddle over sw stir arabesque   S
(illustrated b)

70   ass Cartwheel off   (M)

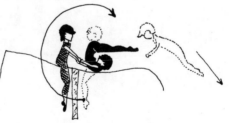

71   ass Roll-off dismount (with high push off)   (M)

72   Back roll-off over supine partner (high push off)   (M)

73(a)   Vault off   from cross lie on bench   M
   (b)   from cross lie on high bench   S
   (illustrated b)

74   Underswing from high bench over BK   M

75   Roll-off from high bench   (M)

76   Straight arm roll from shoulders   M

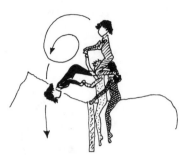

77   'Star DMT': Tucked/piked straight arm flip-through   S

78   sim Salto off FW and BW   (S)

Single transitions

79   'Touch-down'   vault-off w/immediate re-mount   M

80   Balanced leg-swing NK to BK or BK to NK   E

81   Squat-through to FW seat from 'push-up' support, direct   (M)

82   Swing-around w/½ turn from seat to seat   M
      (not illustrated)

83   Swing-around w/1¼ turn from FW seat to FW seat on NK   S

84   'swinger' TR (FW roll from BW seat on neck to FW seat on BK)   (M)

a)   b)

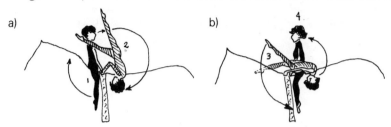

85   'Eggbeater' TR (scissor turn over supine position)   (M)

86   'Pancake flip' (swing from belly lie to back lie)   (M)

87   Flag TR from flag on NK, supported on arms:

    (a)   into FW seat   E
    (b)   into FW kneel   M
    (c)   into FW/sw flag w/leg change   M
                             into FW/sw flag no leg change   S

(illustrated a)

88   Flag TR from flag on BK to flag on Neck
   (a)   w/leg change   E
   (b)   without change of supporting leg   S
   (c)   full 360 degree swing   (x)
   (illustrated b)

89   'Curtsey' (TR prince seat to stand)
   (a)   FW alone (or 2 vaulters) two times   M
   (b)   once FW w/three vaulters   M
   (c)   BW or SW minimum once   S

90   'Knee jump'   (Kneel to stand)
   (a)   FW alone twice   M
   (b)   FW pair twice, BW alone twice   S
   (c)   knees to feet opposite sequence   M
   (d)   knees to feet opp sequence BW   S
   (illustrated a)

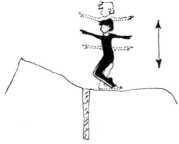

91   'Knee jump' w/½ turn during flight phase   S

92   'Jump-around' (from FW stand to BW stand) w/½ turn   M

93   Scissor transition REV from FW seat on NK, supp on arms   M

94   Scissor TR FW from BW seat on NK to FW seat on BK   S

95   Scissor TR REV, supported on CP   S

96(a)   BW-Roll DN from NK to cross lie on horse   M
   (b)   to FW seat on BK   S
   (illustrated b)

97   BW-Roll UP from BW seat on BK, or lay-out on BK
   (a)   into flag on NK   M
   (b)   into arabesque on NK   S
   (c)   into shoulderstand   M
   (illustrated a)

98   BW-Roll UP from BW seat on BK, or lay-out on BK
                                 w/½ scissors into FW seat on NK   M

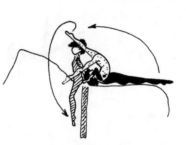

99   FW-Roll DN from BW seat on NK into lay-out
   (a)   from sitting   S
   (b)   from flag or arabesque   S
   (illustrated a)

100   FW-Roll DN from or up into shoulderstand to lay-out
   (a)   landing legs straddled   E
   (b)   landing legs together   M
   (illustrated b)

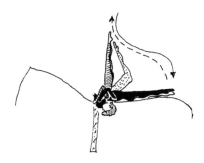

101   FW-Roll DN from arab. on NK to lay-out, legs together   S

102   Flying leg changes (over handstand) from flag/arabesque   M

103   Swing-up into shoulderstand or handstand from seat/arab.   M

104   High flank-around from FW seat on BK to BW seat on NK
or vice versa   S

105   Handstand roll-under TR to belly lie   (X)

106   'Kick-over' from bridge to BW seat on NK   (s)

Partner transitions _____

107   'Musical chairs'
   (a) sitting turns   ½ turn   E
   (b)   ¾ turn   M
   (c)   full turn   S
   (illustrated b)

108   The 'flea'   (swing around partner) from FW seat
                            behind partner to BW seat on NK and
                            vice versa   E

a)

            b)

109(a) ½ scissors to BW seat on bench   M
   (b)   on high bench   S
   (c)   from flag on bench   M

110   'Jack knife'   from high handstand onto high bench   S

111   Jump-through to standing/sitting
   (a)   FW over 1 or 2 sitting partners   M
   (b)   BW over 1 or 2 sitting partners   (M) S
   (c)   straddle jump FW over sitting   M
   (d)   jump over kneeling   S
   (e)   jump over standing partner   (X)

112   Roll from or to shoulder lie

    (a)   supporting partner sits   M

    (b)   support kneels or stands   S

113   'Rock 'n Roll'   (x) S

           a)   b)

114   Double mill   S

115   Double scissors   (if also BW: x)   S

116   Turn flyer FW/SW   (without coming down)   S
                               (from standing)   (X)

117   'Flying pancake flip'   (rotating flyer UP and DN)   S
                               (from standing)   (X)

118   'The dump'   (roll down from flyer and suspend)   (S)

119   'Flying cartwheel'   (suspended and turned by partners)   (S)
                                  (depends on scope)   (X)

Seats single and combined

120   'Taylor' seat
   (a)   FW/BW holding   E
   (b)   FW free   M
   (c)   BW free   S
   (illustrated b)

121   'Ballerina seat'   (straddle seat one leg extended)
   (a)   FW holding   E
   (b)   FW free and BW holding   M
   (c)   BW free   (M)
   (illustrated a)

122   'Lorelei'   all dir (sit on heel, one leg extended)
  (a)   holding   (E)
  (b)   free   M
  (c)   'the thinker'   (S)

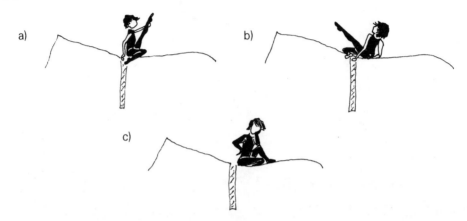

123   Full splits, all directions
  (a) holding w/both hands   (M)
  (b) holding w/one hand   S

124   Basic seat combinations FW/BW/SW, double, triple   E

125(a) Shoulder sit   on sitting partner   E
   (b) bridge from shoulder sit   (M)

Lying exercises ─────────────────────────

126   'Siesta'   (reclining on arm)   (M)

127   'Cross lie' on BK   (sw lie on belly or back)
   (a)   holding w/one hand   M
   (b)   free   S
   (illustrated b)

128(a) Cross lie on NK   holding w/both hands   M
   (b)   holding w/one hand   S
   (illustrated b)

129	'Swan'	(belly lie FW on BK extended arms)	(E)

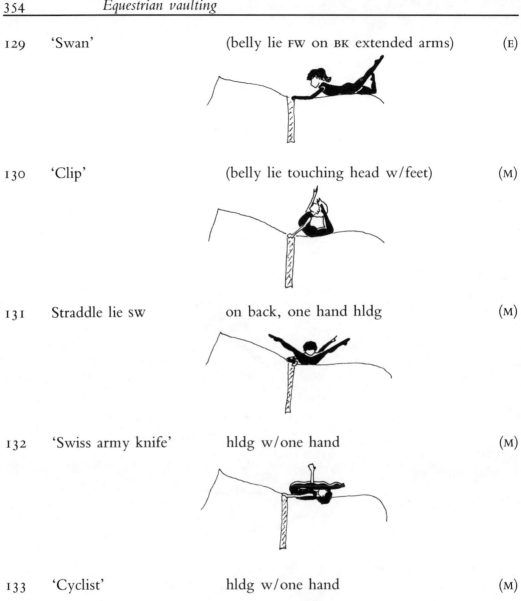

130	'Clip'	(belly lie touching head w/feet)	(M)

131	Straddle lie sw	on back, one hand hldg	(M)

132	'Swiss army knife'	hldg w/one hand	(M)

133	'Cyclist'	hldg w/one hand	(M)

| 134 | 'Cracker Jack up' | support on shoulder, one hand | (M) |

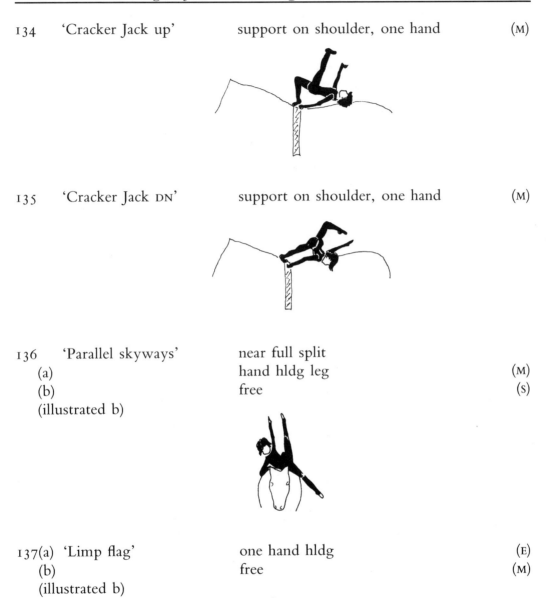

| 135 | 'Cracker Jack DN' | support on shoulder, one hand | (M) |

136	'Parallel skyways'	near full split	
	(a)	hand hldg leg	(M)
	(b)	free	(S)
	(illustrated b)		

137(a)	'Limp flag'	one hand hldg	(E)
	(b)	free	(M)
	(illustrated b)		

138   'High limp flag'   on sitting partner, free   (M)

139   'Spanking'   cross lie on stir hunter stand   (M)

140(a) 'BW flying angel'   from sitting   M
    (b)   supported from kneeling/standing   S
    (illustrated a)

141(a) Shoulder lie   supported from sitting   E
    (b)   supported from kneel   (M)
    (c)   supp. from standing   (s)
    (illustrated a)

142	'Cross lie'	on interlocked arms	
(a)		holding w/one arm	E
(b)		free	M
(illustrated b)			

Hanging exercises

143(a)	Sitting hang	one leg horiz, other in stir, 2 hands	E
(b)		one leg horiz, one in stir, one hand	M
		both legs horizontal	S
(illustrated b)			

144	'Hammock'	leg hooked over grip, one hand	(E)

145	Horizontal lying hang		S

146(a) 'draped hang'   without use of stir, hldg   (M)
   (b)   free   (S)
   (illustrated b)

147   Cossack hang   single or double   E

148   'Cliff hanger'   one hand hldg, extended leg @ 90 (S)

149   'High cossack hang'   BW/SW from high bench   (S)

150   'Hanging spider'   free   (S)

151   'Hangman'   (s)

152   'High hangman'   free on interlocked arms   (x)

Kneeling exercises ——————————————————

153(a) Pair kneel   FW free   E
   (b)   BW free   M

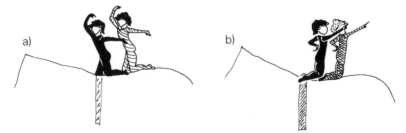

154   'Look-out'   free   (s)

155   'sw Sady'   INS/OUT, foot on NK or BK, free   S

156(a) 'FW sign post'   bench FW w/leg & arm extended sw   M
    (b)   same BW   S
    (illustrated a)

157   'sw sign post'   holding w/one hand   S

158(a) 'High sign post'   on bench, also ass   S
    (b)   one hand, on high bench   (x)
    (illustrated a)

159 'Hunter kneel'   knee stand, all directions

(a)   standing leg in stir   E

(b)   standing leg not in stir   M

160   'Cha-Cha-Cha'   interlocked hunter kneel   (M)

161(a) Prince seat   FW, also double   E

(b)   BW, free with lean   M

(c)   dbl sw princes   S

a)   b)

162   Shouldersit on kneel (w/sitting)   M

Benches

163(a)   Sitting on bench (or flag) FW/BW   E
   (b)   on high bench   M

a)

b)

164(a)   'Lorelei' on bench   FW   M
   (b)   BW   S
   (illustrated a)

165   Crosslie on bench,   all directions
   (a)   holding w/one hand   M
   (b)   free   S
   (illustrated b)

166   Candle on bench   M

167(a) Stand over bench FW   E
  (b) FW stand over flag or BW over bench   M
  (c)   BW   S
  (illustrated a)

168(a) Kneeling on bench FW   M
  (b)   BW   M
  (illustrated b)

169(a) Flag FW/BW on bench holding (BW or opp: M) E
  (b)   free
  (illustrated a)   M

170 Stand on bench   S

171   Hungarian Post   S

172   'Limp flag' on high bench, free   (M)

173(a) Sitting FW/BW and high bench, flag hldg   M
  (b) Kneel and other variations on high bench   S
  (c) all exercises free on high bench   S
  (illustrated c)

174   Stands on high bench   S
       (Shoulder hang on high bench see exercise no. 275)

Flags

175(a) BW flag on croup   holding   E
   (b)   free   M
   (illustrated b)

176(a) BW flag on neck   holding   E
   (b)   free   M
   (illustrated b)

177(a) Cross flag   1 hand on grip, other on BK   E
   (b)   free   M
   (illustrated b)

178(a) Doubled-up flag   both holding   E
   (b)   both free   M
   (illustrated b)

179(a) '2 × flag'   holding   M
  (b)   on NK free, both free   S
  (illustrated a)

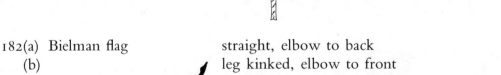

180(a) Crossed flags   holding   M
  (b)   both free   S
  (illustrated a)

181(a) BW double flag   holding   M
  (b)   on NK free, both free   S
  (illustrated b)

182(a) Bielman flag   straight, elbow to back   S
  (b)   leg kinked, elbow to front   S

183   BW stand over BW bench or flag   S

184(a) 'Dbl Decker flag'   both holding   M
   (b)   one/both free   S
   (c)   BW, holding   S
   (d)   facing opposite ways S
   (illustrated b)

185   Triple flag   flag and arabesque, all directions
   (a)   holding   M
   (b)   all one arm   S
   (illustrated b)

186(a) Shoulder flag   FW/BW on two partners, hldg   (E)
   (b) Same free   M
   (c)   on one partner, hldg   M
   (d)   on one partner, free   S
   (illustrated b and c)

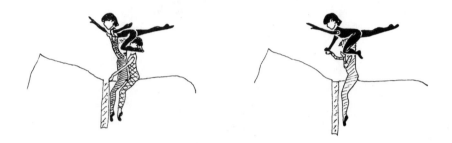

187   'Babysitter flag'   (s)

188   Lifted flag   (s)

Kick-ups

189(a)	BW 'Kick-up'	on BK, hldg	(E)
(b)		one arm free	M
(illustrated b)		

190	FW 'Kick-up'	on neck, holding	M

191	FW 'Kick-up'	on the croup, holding	S

192	'2 × Kick-up'		(s)

Supports

| 193 | 'Push–up' | on one leg | (M) |

| 194 | 'Lean-to' | INS or OUT | M |

| 195 | 'The killer' | supported free | (S) |

196(a)	'The prop'	with two feet	(E)
(b)		on one foot	(M)
(illustrated b)			

| 197 | Bridge | on one/two feet | (S) |

198   'Propped split'   held in suspension   (s)

199(a) 'Skater's lift'   held   (M)
  (b)   free   (s)
  (illustrated a)

Wheelbarrows

200(a) Wheelbarrow   held   E
  (b)   free   M
  (illustrated b)

201(a) BW wheelbarrow on croup   E
  (b)   BW wheelbarrow on bench   (M)

202   'High wheelbarrow'   from standing
  (a)   held   M
  (b)   free   S
  (illustrated a)

203   'High wheelbarrow'   from sitting, pushed up   E

204   'High wheelbarrow'   from standing, on shoulders
  (a)   holding   M
  (b)   free   S
  (illustrated b)

205   'High wheelbarrow' on kneeling variations   S

206 'Superhigh wheelbarrow' from standing   s

207 Wheelbarrow on two standing   s

208 Wheelbarrow on lie (supine)   (M)

209 'Babysitter lift'   (S)

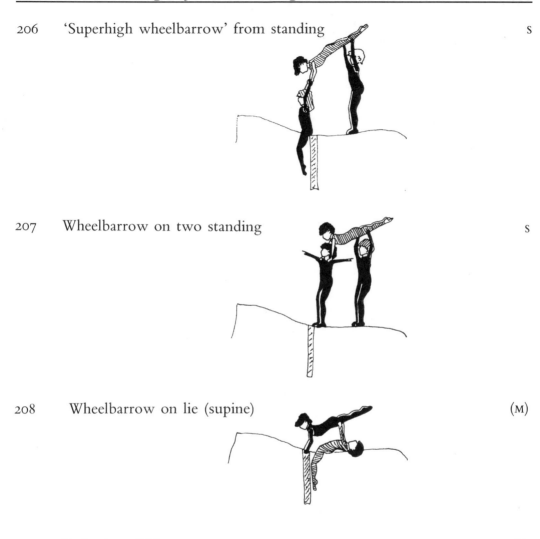

210 'High babysitter lift' (s)

211 Double wheelbarrow M

212 'Double decker' wheelbarrow S

Standing exercises

213 Stirrup stand FW/BW E

214   'Side split' FW/BW   S

215   Stir hunter stand FW/BW/SW
  (a)   hldg w/one hand   (E)
  (b)   free   (M)
  (illustrated b)

216   'Coat hanger'   FW/BW/SW
  (a)   two hands hldg   (M)
  (b)   one hand free   (S)
  (illustrated b)

217   'Contortion'   hldg or free   (S)

218   Multiple stands
　　(a)   double stand FW   E
　　(b)   triple stand   M
　　(c)   all BW/SW   (S)
　　(illustrated b)

219(a) 'Family round'   FW   E
　　(b)   BW   S
　　(illustrated a)

220   Shouldersit and stand   E

221   BW stand   NK, BK, or CP   S

222   'Discord'   (M)

223(a) sw stand   s
    (b) 'Speed skater'   (s)

224   Crouched stands   back horizontal, all directions   (s)

225   'Discus thrower'   all stands w/crossed legs   (s)

226   Stand on one foot   all variations   (s)

227   'Tango'   (s)

228   Prince seat and hunter stand, free   (s)

229   Ass 'Can Can'   (standing with one leg extd & raised)   (M)

230   'Can Can' free   (s)

231   Galleon   at least 45 degree lean   s

232(a) Star   (with knee support and arms extd)   s
   (b)   as stir hunter stand hldg at hips   (s)
   (c)   with crossed arms, extd   (s)

a)

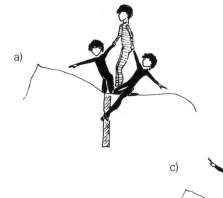

b)

c)

233   'Free stand on shoulder'
    (a) on two partners, hldg   E
    (b) on two partners, free   M
    (c) on one partner, free   (s)

234   ass 'Can Can' on shoulder   (s)

235   'Stepping stone'   (s)

236   sw stand on partners, all variations   (s)

237   'Superhigh hunter stand'   (s)

238   'Superhigh free stand on shoulders'   (s)

239(a) 'Figure head'   (s)
   (b) 'Statue of Liberty'   (s)

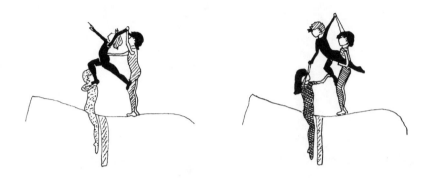

240   'Hip Shot'   fully lifted in front   (s)

241   'Lifted needle'   (s)

242   'Reclining figure head'   (s)

243   'Totem pole'   free   (s)

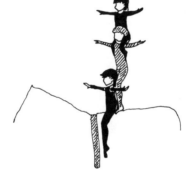

244   'Superhigh flying flag'   (s)

Arabesques

245(a) Stir arab   FW/BW/SW hldg   E
   (b)   all dir one hand   M
   (c)   free   S
   (illustrated c)

246(a) '2 × stir arab'   hldg   E
   (b)   one hand each   M
   (c)   free   S
   (illustrated a)

247(a) Triple arab   all directions, hldg   M
   (b)   all one hand   S
   (illustrated b)

248   Stir needle   full 180 degrees   M

249(a) Arab on BK   hldg   E

    (b)   one hand   M

    (c)   free   S

    (illustrated a)

250(a) BW arab   on NK or surcingle, hldg   M

    (b)   on NK or surcingle, one hand   S

251(a) ass BW arab   on NK, supp from sitting, hldg   E

    (b)   same w/one arm   M

    (c)   same free   S

    (illustrated a)

252(a) '2 × arab'   on BK and NK, hldg   M
  (b)   on BK and NK, one hand each   S
  (illustrated b)

253   Flag and arab on BK or NK
  (a)   both hldg   E
  (b)   FW one free one arm   M
  (c)   both FW, free one arm each   M
  (d)   both BW or opp, one or both free one arm   S
  (illustrated d)

254(a) 'Dbl coathanger' and arab   (s)
  (b) arab on supine   (s)

255   Free arab on BK   S

256   ass free arab on BK from stand   (s)

257   Straddle shoulderstand and arab, hldg or free   s

258(a) Shoulder arab   on two sitting, hldg   M
  (b)   on one, or free   s

259(a) ass arab   on bench, FW/BW   M
  (b)   on flag, FW/BW   s
  (illustrated b)

260(a) 'High cross arab'   on interlocked arms, both hldg   (M)
(b)   same one hand   (s)
(illustrated a)

261   'High FW arab' on arms   (s)

262   'Dbl decker arab'   (s)

263   Stir Bielman arab   kinked leg, elbow to front   s

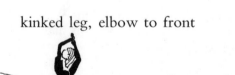

264   Double Bielman   (s)

265   'Superhigh Bielman' on high bench   (s)

Shoulderstands/hangs

266   Ass shoulderstand   from sitting   E

267(a)   Shoulderstand   FW/BW, both hands   (M)
   (b)   all dir one hand   S
   (illustrated a)

268   Double shoulderstand   S

269   'High candle'   facing away from horse,
                                     both or one hand   (s)

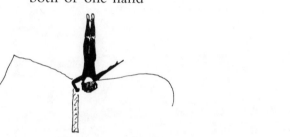

270   Shoulderhang   FW/BW   M

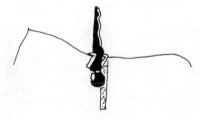

271(a)   'The Jester'   SW   M
   (b)   Double sw sh.hang   (also direct mount into!)   (s)

a)   b)

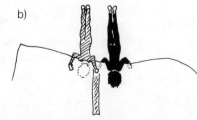

272   'Extrovert'   sw and 1/o   (s)

273   'The flame'   shoulderhang on sitting person   s

274   'Doubled flame'   (parallel bar stand)
       (a)   flyer holding grips   M
       (b)   flyer hldg arms of partners   s
       (illustrated b)

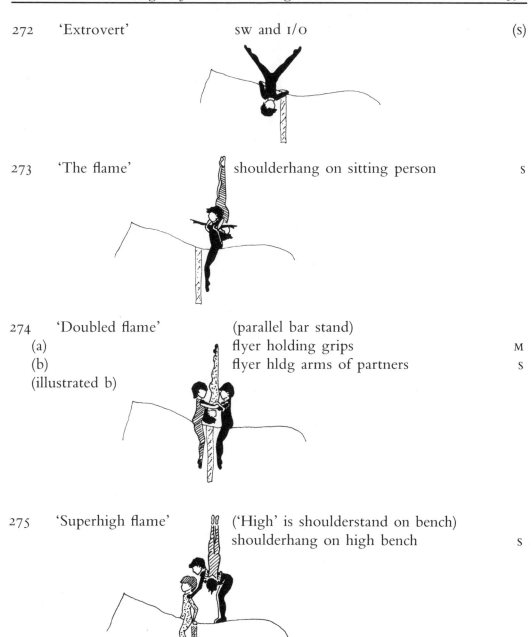

275   'Superhigh flame'   ('High' is shoulderstand on bench)
                              shoulderhang on high bench   s

Handstands

276   'Elbow stand'   (s)

277   Ass handstand   Supp from FW seat
      FW/BW

  (a)   supp with both hands, on both hands   M
  (b)   supp w/one hand, or on one hand   S
(illustrated b)

278   Free handstand   FW/BW/SW   S

279   BW handstand   supp from BW seat
  (a)   on BK or grips   M
  (b)   held w/one hand/or on one hand   S
(illustrated a)

280   BW handstand on   supp from FW seat   S
      CP

281   'VW'   SW handstand supp by one partner
                    or by two partners w/one hand each   (S)

282   Handstand supp from standing
   (a)   FW on grips from FW stand   M
   (b)   FW supp w/one hand, or on one hand   S
   (c)   BW handstand, from FW stand   S
   (illustrated c)

283   'High handstand'   on shoulders of sitting, from stand   S

284   Handstand on parallel bars, all directions   (s)

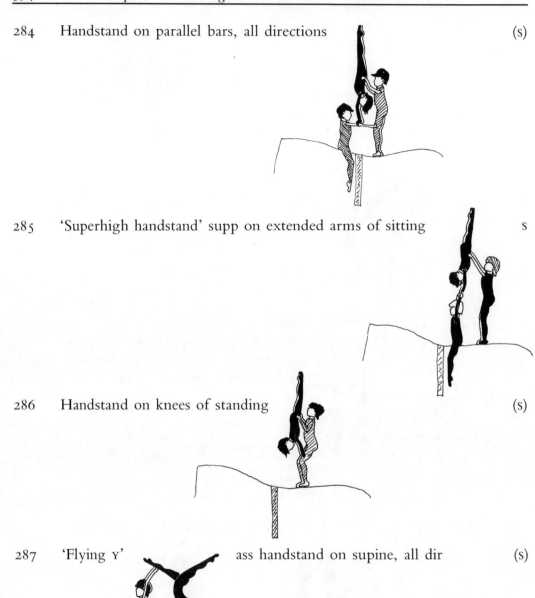

285   'Superhigh handstand' supp on extended arms of sitting   s

286   Handstand on knees of standing   (s)

287   'Flying Y'   ass handstand on supine, all dir   (s)

288 'Rocket launch' handstand on knees of stir hunter (s)

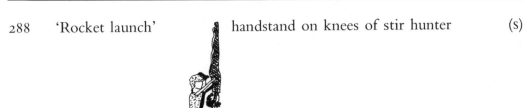

289 'Harlekin' ass BW handstand on FW flag M

Lifts

290 'Flying handstand' lifted by shoulders on extended arms from sitting, supp by standing S

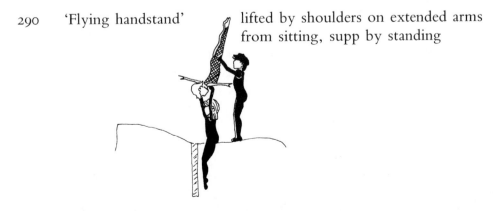

291   'Eiffel Tower'   flying handstand lifted by arms only   (s)

292   'Highchair'   sitting flyer   s

293   'Exhibit'   lifted at armpits, free split 180
    (a)   from sitting   (M)
    (b)   same from standing   (s)
    (illustrated a)

294   FW 'shoulder split'   supp by two sitting partners
    (a)   held by body or arms   M
    (b)   held by legs only   s
    (illustrated b)

295   FW shoulder split   on one sitting, one supine partner   (S)

296(a) 'Lifted split'   FW/BW/SW lifted by two sitting or
                                 one sitting/one standing partner   (S)

297   'Carried angel'   w/legs 'locked' supp from kneeling   M

298(a) 'Carried angel'   with legs locked and sitting partner in
                                 front (as triple exercise)   M
    (b)   with legs extended (resting on hips)   S
    (c)   crosswise to the horse   S
(illustrated b)

299(a) 'Rocket angel'   flyer lifted on extended arms, all
                                 directions   (M) s
   (b) 'High rocket'   supp. from kneeling   s
   (c) 'Super high rocket'   supp. from standing   (X)

300   'Spider'   lifted from BW and FW seat, SW   (M)

301   'The diver'   free balanced lift   (S)

302   'Draped lift'   ups flyer, bent back, all dir   (M)

303   'High draped lift'   from sitting and standing   (S)

304   'Keyhole'   from sitting and supine   (S)

Glossary

abbreviations TR = transition; MT = mount; DMT = dismount; arab = arabesque

CP = croup; BK = back; NK = neck (the horse's); SH = shoulder (a partner's); stir = stirrup

BW = backward; FW = forward; SW = sideways; INS = inside; OUT = outside (referring to the centre of the vaulting circle regardless of direction); DN = down; UPS = upside down; I/O = inside out; REV = reverse; OPP = opposite; DIR = direction

hldg = holding; fr = free; ass = assisted; supp = supported; extd = extended; hi = high; sp hi = superhigh; crd = carried (held at mid point of body); w/ = with; dbl = double; 2 × = same exercise mirror image; dbl decker = stacked exercise; sim = simultaneous

alignment parallelism of the limbs to the plane appropriate to the exercise

'angel' by 'angel' exercises we generally mean an element where the flyer is fully supported in a horizontal position by his partners and without direct contact with the horse. These exercises are technically described as flyers

arabesque 'standing flag': vaulter stands on one foot, other leg is held free away from the horse

blanket dimensions of a vaulting blanket: extending 10 to 15 cm max. in front of the surcingle, max. 70 cm behind. No wider than 90 cm measured from side to side

bridge exercise where vaulter pushes up to support on both arms and legs from supine position, back rounded. Support on one leg is possible

bridle allowable snaffles are: single-jointed loose-ring snaffle with round mouth piece; simple egg-butt snaffle with round, single-jointed mouth piece; simple D-ring snaffle with single jointed round mouth piece; straight-bar/ mullen mouth snaffle with round mouth piece. All mouthpieces to be 14 mm minimum thickness at corners

bench	position where the upper body is horizontal and the lower legs or feet (in high bench) lie or stand on the contact surface
candle	exercise where the vaulter lies on his back with both legs extended into the air, hip at right angle
cavesson	lunging cavesson: strong noseband with a jointed metal nose piece, well padded all around with a metal ring in the centre and two side rings. Some cavessons have nosebands with two joints and no padding at the back; these fit under the bit as a drop noseband. Only cavessons with a padded back-strap to the noseband should be worn above the bit as a cavesson noseband. The lunge line is fitted to the cavesson rather than the bit of the bridle
chambon	kind of running rein from the bit via 'earrings', so the horse feels pressure on top of the head when in the wrong position. See drawings on page 41
composition	arrangement of elements in artistic form
compulsories	the six basic exercises (seat, flag, mill – scissors, stand, flank) which are precisely defined and prescribed for competition
continuity	smooth connection or uninterrupted flow in the entire composition
difficulty of execution	the relative difficulty of an exercise increased or decreased by the mechanics or degree of scope in the execution
'double decker'	all exercises where two partners perform the same move on top of each other. Can be a double exercise (see no. 184) or triple (see no. 212) depending on the nature of the exercise
dynamic exercise	an exercise which consists of movement, such as swings, rolls, jumps etc.
elevation	height of the legs off the horse
essence	intent or purpose of exercise (what are we trying to prove? what is the value of this exercise?). The most important aspect of an exercise
extension	straightness of the arms during flight exercises
flag	element where one leg is held free while in a (low) bench position. Sometimes also called 'flare'
flight	dynamic passage through the air as the result of a vigorous swing or kick. Flight is an essential element in the achievement of extension
flyer	a vaulter supported fully by his partners, the 'undermen'. Standing flag positions, are also sometimes called flyer (as a translation from the German 'Flieger'), although this position is technically an arabesque

form   posture and stretch of the body, stretch and straightness of the limbs and extremities, correct position of the hands, feet, head

hangs   exercises in which the shoulders are below the point of support

height   usually means height off the horse

kneel   elements where one or both lower legs lie on a contact surface, with the hip joints straight

kur   a freestyle exercise or composition thereof. May be performed, invented, combined at the vaulter's discretion

lunging   the skill of controlling and directing the performance of the horse via a lunge rein with the aid of a lunge whip

lunging whip   with thong long enough to reach the hock of the horse

lunge rein   or lunge line, affixed to the bridle and held by the lunger in the centre of the circle. Should be at least 7 metres long to allow for a prescribed lunging circle of 13 m diameter

lying exercises   elements in which the body is stretched out in an almost horizontal position

mechanics   correct position and arrangement of body parts to fulfil the criteria of an exercise as defined and described. Note: height and straightness of arm and leg and duration of exercise are *not* mechanics. Sufficient deviation from outline *is* a matter of mechanics

needle   standing position on one foot with upper body extended down onto one leg and legs in full split position

off centre   placement of vaulter's body weight other than centred over the horse's spine (usually to the outside)

originality   use of unusual or new exercises or combinations

pas-de-deux   exercises performed by two vaulters together as a pair

polish   extra smoothness and style

rolls   exercises which contain a rotation around the side axis of the body, with the body bent and rounded

scope   height, width and stretch of extremities

shoulderhang   vertical up-side-down hanging exercise supported by arms and with hip joints straight

shoulderstand	vertical up-side-down element with support of arms and on one or two shoulders, hip joints straight
side reins	with rubber ring inserts for give, fixed to the surcingle and the ring of the bridle (see illustration page 39). All types of running reins are prohibited in competition, but can be very useful for training, see chapter 7
splits	exercises with legs stretched out to sides or front and back at an angle of 180 degrees
static exercise	an exercise during which a pose is held without change for a prescribed number of canter strides (4 in compulsories, 3 in kur)
stirrups	for vaulters means the foot loops on the surcingle for hangs
support exercises	also press-up or push-up exercises: elements in which the shoulder axis is above the hands, with the weight transferred through the arms onto the support area (like in a wheelbarrow)
surcingle	the 'belt' around the horse, equipped with two solid handles and two foot loops for hangs (sometimes called 'stirrups')
swings	swinging exercises starting from the hip or shoulder. The side axes of the body are parallel to the axis of revolution
transitions	the linking movement between two exercises. May be counted as an exercise in itself in competition, if complex and difficult enough
twists	or turns: elements containing a rotation of the body around the vertical axis
underpad	'fuzzy', the long padding in the shape of the surcingle and long enough to extend to under the buckles on both sides of the girth
use of space	optimum utilization of all three dimensions in the space on and around the horse
variety	diversity in choice of exercises and/or composition
vaulting	the performance of gymnastic exercises on horseback

References

Erfolg mit Longe, Hilfszugel und Gebiss, Rolf Becher, Erich Hoffmann Verlag, 1973

FEI *Rules for Vaulting Events*, effective 1 January 1993, 3rd edn, printed in Switzerland, and FEI *Guidelines for Judges*

Voltigieren, Andrea Martin, Paul Parey Verlag, 1988

Gruppenkur, A. Henatsch/M. Muller-Kaler, Munsterschwarzacher Beitrage zur Theorie und Praxis des Voltigierens, 1988

The manual of horsemanship, British Horse Society and Pony Club, 9th Edition, 1989

Richtig Voltigieren, Ulrike Rieder, BLV Sportpraxis, 1991